D1319549

Preacher

Preacher

David H. C. Read's Sermons at Madison Avenue
Presbyterian Church

EDITED BY JOHN MCTAVISH

WIPF & STOCK · Eugene, Oregon

PREACHER
David H. C. Read's Sermons at Madison Avenue Presbyterian Church

Wipf & Stock
An Imprint of Wipf and Stock Publishers
199 W. 8th Ave., Suite 3
Eugene, OR 97401

www.wipfandstock.com

PAPERBACK ISBN: 978-1-5326-0574-1
HARDCOVER ISBN: 978-1-5326-0576-5
EBOOK ISBN: 978-1-5326-0575-8

Manufactured in the U.S.A.   APRIL 19, 2017

In Memory of David H. C. Read

" . . . he being dead yet speaketh . . . "

HEBREWS 11:4

Contents

Introduction

PREACHER

I HAVE STOOD TOE to toe with cheering Spaniards and Italians as Pope Paul was carried into St. Peter's on a throne for a Sunday Mass. I have gazed with wonder at the lofty Gothic architecture of New York's Riverside Church and Dr. Coffin at his eloquent preacherly best. I have seen Jimmy Swaggart cry on television.

Striking experiences all. But the preacher who has most nourished my soul and stimulated my mind over the years has been a Scottish import by the name of David H. C. Read. From 1956 to 1989 Dr. Read was the pastor of New York's Madison Avenue Presbyterian Church. For twenty-five of those years he was also a regular preacher on NBC's National Radio Pulpit. He had his own weekly Sunday program on WOT-AM radio entitled "Thinking It Over" and he published over thirty books, which included some of the only collections of sermons that major publishing firms such as Eerdmans and Harper and Row have ever dared to cast into print. All in all, a modern day prince of the pulpit, if there ever was one.

Yet search the internet for the names of great modern day preachers and Read's name is not likely to appear. Instead we get names like Billy Graham, John Stott, and Joel Osteen representing the evangelical side, and Fred Craddock, William Sloane Coffin, and Barbara Brown Taylor carrying the torch for the liberals. Inspiring preachers all, but no mention of David Read.

Why?

Perhaps the minister from Madison Avenue Presbyterian Church was too much of a theological centrist to enjoy what passes in ecclesiastical

1

circles as a fan club. The crowds tend to gravitate to simplistic extremes if only because the extremes give the impression of radicalism and rigor. Yet surely the true radical is the person who gets to the *radix*, or "root," of things. This in any event is what Read's preaching does, displaying a combination of theological discernment and literary charm that puts this preacher pretty much in a homiletical class by himself. Who was this man, what made him tick, and what can we learn from his powerful proclamation of the Gospel?

David H. C. Read was born in 1910 and grew up in Edinburgh, where he attended the Church of Scotland with his family. He flirted briefly with agnosticism, but then one day a high school friend invited him to attend a popular evangelical summer camp. There, in the magnificent countryside of the Scottish Highlands, Read enjoyed games, expeditions, concerts, songs, and a spiritual awakening. The camp teemed with university students and young professionals who spoke of Christ as a real person whom one could get to know in a deep and intimate way. David Read accepted the message and became, as he tells us in his autobiography *This Grace Given*, "if not a dyed-in-the-wool fundamentalist, at least a fervid evangelical ready to do battle for the faith."

Even so, the young convert couldn't help noticing that the camp leaders often applied psychological pressure on the campers to make decisions for Christ. They condemned the worldliness of smoking and dancing while spending lavish sums on sports cars and fancy clothes, and railed against issues of personal immorality while saying nothing about the crushing economic issues that many were facing in those early years of the Depression. Worst of all, they blithely ignored the fire-breathing madman who had recently emerged in Germany. Still, these were the people who had given David Read the pearl of great price, the incomparable gift of the Gospel, and for that he remained thankful.

After graduating from high school, Read enrolled in an Honors English course at the University of Edinburgh. He now began juggling the world of Shakespeare and Milton with soccer on Saturdays and worship services on Sundays. He continued attending the local parish of the Church of Scotland with his family, but on Sunday evenings he often made the round of churches, imbibing the pulpit eloquence of such Edinburgh greats as James Black, James Stewart, and George Macleod.

Read also enjoyed listening occasionally to Graham Scroggie, a Baptist minister who delivered expository sermons in a rather dry but straightforward and no-nonsense way. One Sunday evening he went to hear this fellow Scroggie preach, only to learn that the minister had been called away for the weekend and a substitute stood in his place. Read considered leaving, but at the last minute he decided to stay and hear what the substitute had to say. The experience proved life-changing. As he recalls in his memoirs: "I remember neither the preacher's name nor anything he said. What I do remember, with luminous clarity, was that in the middle of the sermon I was suddenly and totally convinced that God wanted me to be a minister." Never before or after did David Read experience such an overpowering sense of the divine summons. Make of this moment what one will, but that night the bright young university student went home and quietly resolved to become a minister.

After gaining his degree in English, graduating *summa cum laude,* Read began making plans to study theology at New College, the Edinburgh-based seminary of the Church of Scotland. (He had come to realize that, for all his concern that a theological liberalism might amount to "little more than agnosticism with a halo," the Church of Scotland was still basically his spiritual home.) But then the budding young theologian learned that New College was offering a scholarship which would allow him to study theology at the three seminaries—Montpellier, Strasbourg, and Paris—of the French Protestant Church. This was even better. Read immediately contacted the donor of the scholarship, and gained the coveted opportunity to begin his theological studies in Montpellier, France.

A transforming learning experience soon occurred when Pierre Maury came to the Montpellier seminary to conduct a retreat. The dynamic Maury, on his way to becoming one of France's greatest preachers, was known to be a disciple of Karl Barth, and in fact was coming from Bonn where he had been studying under the great Reformed theologian. The impact that Maury had upon Read was both profound and lasting. Read had been clinging to the theology of the evangelicals as a refuge from the theological wasteland of a liberalism that seemed to reduce the gospel to little more than what Matthew Arnold once called "morality tinged with emotion." But now here was Maury and behind him, as Read notes in *This Grace Given:*

> " . . . the magnetic figure of Barth—two men who spoke of God in all his glory with a far greater power than the fundamentalists (whose God tended to be as narrow as the range of their own imaginations); who spoke of God's Word in language so dynamic that it shattered my previous concept of the Bible as a code-book of doctrines and morals plus a few stories and passages of dramatic power; who lifted up Christ in his incarnation, death, and resurrection as the unique Savior and Lord of a fallen world; and who obviously were able to accept the critical view of the Scriptures not grudgingly but joyfully, as a sign of the true humanity through which God speaks." (p. 56)

This did not mean that David Read now became a slavish Barthian. On the contrary, as he tells us in his memoirs, he gratefully appropriated insights over the years from Catholic theologians such as Karl Rahner and Hans Kung, from philosophically-oriented theologians such as John Baillie and Reinhold Niebuhr, and even from Paul Tillich, "not to mention Dietrich Bonhoeffer." Still, as far as the young man from Edinburgh was concerned, Karl Barth remained "*the* theologian of the twentieth century."

Barth's name calls to mind an amusing incident that I witnessed during one of Read's post-Christmas preaching seminars at Princeton Theological Seminary. A number of us in the class had joined him for supper one evening at the college cafeteria. In turn we were joined by a talkative young seminarian who, upon discovering that we were all ministers, volunteered for our edification Paul Tillich's comment according to which preachers should stand in the pulpit with the Bible in one hand and the daily newspaper in the other. There was a brief pause, and then Read gently corrected the student: "I think it was Barth who gave us that choice *bon mot.*" "Oh no," said the student full of confidence, "it was Tillich all right." At which point Read smiled mischievously and said, "No, no . . . *Tillich* was the theologian who encouraged preachers to stand in the pulpit with the Bible in one hand . . . and a copy of *Playboy* in the other."

But to return to our story: Before David Read completed his formal theological education in Scotland, he went on to study in Paris and Strasburg. He also enjoyed a semester along the way in Marburg, Germany, studying with Rudolf Bultmann. Read had actually wanted to study under Barth in Bonn, but the Principal of New College, "a strong liberal," ordered him to go to Marburg so that he could imbibe the wisdom of the New Testament scholar and subsequent advocate of demythologization. The young Scot's theological horizons were consequentially widened under Bultmann's challenging interpretations, but not at the expense of diluting the Christological heart of the gospel.

In the spring of 1936, David Read was ordained. That same year he married Pat Gilbert and began his ministry with the Presbyterian Church in a small, quiet town on the Scottish border. All of this might well have been idyllic except for the storm clouds that were gathering in Germany. Many in Britain ignored these clouds if only because they couldn't bear the thought of another war with the memories of the last one still so painfully fresh. But Read took the signals to heart, remembering perhaps the rising militant fanaticism that he had witnessed during his semester in Marburg. He had actually been arrested that year and hauled off to the commandant's office by an S. A. guard for taking pictures of Nazi officials. In his defence he claimed that he thought that the Stormtroopers were a perfectly harmless group like the Boy Scouts. However, it was probably only on account of his British passport, and the fact that the Nazis had been instructed to be polite to British and American visitors, that Read escaped imprisonment. Returning to his residence he couldn't help reflecting, he tells us in his memoirs, on how different things might have been had he been a German, let alone a Jew.

When Britain declared war with Germany on September 3, 1939, David Read volunteered as a military chaplain and was soon working at a hospital in Le Havre where he experienced the period of the so-called "Phony War." Western France in fact was so quiet that fall and winter that Read finally requested a transfer to another division on the Belgian border. Again, things were very quiet for several more weeks. But then, in the spring of 1940, Germany struck and suddenly all hell broke loose.

The fledgling British troops quickly found themselves pushed back to the sea. Some of their units attempted to escape back to England, but Read's division was trapped in a town near the sea. General Rommel now decided to concentrate on killing the British soldiers who were making for the boats and trying to escape by water. This decision probably saved the lives of the soldiers in Read's battalion. Instead of being shot, they were taken prisoner and marched 250 miles to Germany where they spent the next five years behind barbed-wire fences.

This was the war, then, for David Read: one hair-raising, life-threatening moment after another spent almost entirely behind barbed wire. Even so, the young chaplain survived, and when the guns finally fell silent in the spring of 1945, Read was able to return to Scotland and take up his ministry afresh in a suburban church in Edinburgh. This was Greenbank Presbyterian Church which he served for the next four years (the ex-chaplain requiring the first six months, he wryly notes in his memoirs, to re-learn the accepted language of respectable society). Five years as a chaplain at the University of Edinburgh followed the suburban pastorate. Then, in 1955, Read was offered the opportunity of a lifetime—a teaching chair at St. Andrew's University, following in the ranks of Donald Baillie and other world-famous Scottish scholars. But while he was mulling over this golden opportunity, an invitation came to leave Scotland altogether and move to America where a whole new adventure awaited him.

Here's how it happened.

During the summer of 1955, free from his chaplaincy duties, David Read had accepted an invitation to spell off two ministers in North America on their holidays. The month of July was spent preaching at Deer Park United Church in Toronto, and catching up with a number of Canadian cousins. Then in August, Read went to New York to occupy the pulpit at

Fifth Avenue Presbyterian Church where, even on sweltering summer Sundays, over a thousand worshippers normally formed the congregation.

That first weekend in the Big Apple proved especially dramatic. It began with Read and his wife Pat arriving in Manhattan on the first Saturday of August and settling into a small apartment that a friend had loaned them for the month. Their first night in New York was spent enjoying a Broadway play. Alas, when the young couple got back to their residence they discovered that they had left their only key inside the apartment. Every trick in the book now failed to gain them entrance into the flat, and they ended up going to a hotel for the evening.

But no sooner had they settled down to sleep than Read realized that the flat held not only his luggage and church robes, but a copy of the sermon that he planned to preach the next morning. The distraught preacher simply had to get back to the flat even if it was well past midnight. He accordingly called the police who came around and tried to find an extra key by waking up the neighbours in the apartment building. When this strategy proved fruitless (not to say, in some cases, offensive), Pat Read came up with the bright idea of calling the chauffeur of the woman who had lent them the apartment. Success! The key at last was retrieved and the Reads were finally able to get into their flat.

Only now it was almost morning. There was barely time for a couple hours of sleep before the exhausted couple had to get up and dash off to the service at Fifth Avenue. So it was that, with croaky voice and bleary eyes, David Read preached what was surely the most consequential sermon in his lifetime. For though he didn't know it at the time, a number of key people from Madison Avenue Presbyterian Church were sitting in the pews at Fifth Avenue that day. In the wake of George Buttrick's recently announced retirement they were looking for a new minister, and this was the unsuspecting preacher's opportunity to win their hearts. Their hearts, needless to say, were captured. And before the month was out Read had accepted their invitation to leave his homeland and the promise of academia, and embark upon a whole new adventure in his life and work.

Madison Avenue Presbyterian Church proved a marvellous fit for this gifted but unassuming Scot. The sanctuary itself was modest in size, at least by Manhattan standards, and designed, as Read gratefully notes in *Grace Thus Far*, not as an auditorium dominated by a pulpit, but as a place to worship. The congregation's community-oriented philosophy and egalitarian working relationship amongst the staff also appealed to Read's interest in serving the various needs of a fully rounded congregation and not playing the role of a pulpit star. In 1956, then, the Scottish implant became the minister of Madison Avenue Presbyterian Church, and ended up serving the congregation for thirty-three years, retiring in 1989, at a still vigorous eighty years of age.

Throughout his career, David Read never comported himself as a pulpit star or ministerial big shot. He liked in fact to tell the story of the inflated preacher who says to the secretary, "Tell that nuisance to go to hell—I'm composing a masterpiece on Christian love." That Read never screamed at people is something to which I can personally attest. I once drove him to the airport in Toronto after a preaching seminar in nearby Hamilton. Plying him with questions, I shot right past the exit for the airport. For a few tense moments it looked like my pulpit hero might miss his flight back to New York. Read's voice, as I recall, grew a bit testy, but he didn't scream. Fortunately, he didn't miss his flight either.

In the preaching seminar that I mentioned earlier, Read encouraged us to play a tape of one of our recent sermons. The group then discussed each sermon in turn. Our comments were largely appreciative, especially at first. But as the seminar wore on, we became more and more critical of each other's efforts. In fact at one point, I suddenly realized to my chagrin that Read's voice was the only unreservedly positive one in the room. The rest of us had forgotten, it seemed, his introductory remarks in which he had stressed that preaching is not a competition but a response to Christ's call: "Go and proclaim the kingdom of God." It doesn't matter, Read said, whether we respond to the call with one talent, two talents, or ten. The important thing is to respond, and thus share the good news with whatever talents the Lord has given us.

On the final day of the seminar Read played a tape of the Christmas fantasy sermon that he had delivered on Christmas Sunday a few days earlier in his church. I well remember the hush that fell over the room at the conclusion of the recording of this sermon. No one said a word. No one murmured polite little compliments. And certainly no one offered a critique! We all just sat there kind of stunned and thinking: Ah, that's what it means to be a ten talent preacher.

The bulk of this book features forty-one sermons by this super-talented preacher. All but one of the sermons is published for the first time beyond the in-house press of Madison Avenue Presbyterian Church. The sermons have been arranged according to the pattern of the church year, and brief introductions have been added by way of elucidating Read's theme and style.

A list of David Read's books that remain available today through *www. abebooks.com* has also been included along with some brief reviews that I have written, highlighting the contents of some of these works. Finally, David Read's sermon *Virginia Woolf Meets Charlie Brown* is reprinted at the end of the book, giving the reader a taste of the kind of homiletical material that remains available through *www.abebooks.com*.

MINISTRY AFTER DAVID READ

After David Read retired in 1989, an interim period followed, and then Madison Avenue Presbyterian Church called the Rev. Dr. Fred Anderson to replace Dr. Read. I am sure I wasn't the only person in the ecclesiastical world who wondered how Fred Anderson, how *any minister*, was going to replace a pulpit giant like Read. Recently I contacted Anderson and asked him how, in fact, he managed this feat. What Dr. Anderson told me was so moving and instructive that, with his permission, I am relaying exactly what he said:

> "When the Presbytery's Committee on Ministry approved me for membership, allowing my name to be announced to the congregation, I asked if my wife Questa and I could visit David and Pat in their new apartment the church had provided them for retirement. There were some things I needed to talk over with him. The following morning, we went to see them for coffee. We sat in their sunny dining alcove having coffee and biscuits, and exchanging pleasantries. Before long, David began to fidget. Wanting to smoke his beloved pipe, he said, 'Fred, let's go to my study,' and so we did [it was the only place in the new apartment Pat would let him smoke!]. Once we were settled in the privacy of his study I said, 'David, there are three things I need to say to you. First, few people have the opportunity to follow who they think is the very best at what they do, and that is what is happening here—you have been a preaching role model for me since I first read your sermons in Seminary. Second, you are still a Pastor at MAPC, and I expect to see you in worship on Sundays when you are in the city. It will be intimidating for a while, but I will get over it. But you need to be in worship and the people need to see you, for you are still their pastor—we can share them! Third, when they ask you to do a wedding, funeral or baptism, please direct them to me so I can invite you. You are welcome to do as many as you like, or not, but better yet, we can do them together.' David broke into a broad grin, saying, 'I can see we are going to get on together very well.'
>
> "And we did. For the next several years we shared all sorts of liturgical events, he always taking one of the six lessons-sermons for the three-hour Good Friday services, vesting and reading scripture in festival services, sometimes calling on parishioners with me—he always casting his mantle over me, telling folks I had

given him back his church. We even toured Scotland together one spring after Easter. It was a momentous trip. I met him in London (Pat stayed behind in London to visit her brother, Jimmy, and then went on to their new home in Majorca). We took the train north to Glasgow, rented a car and drove the countryside, retreating for three days at Iona, visiting all of his old friends from war days ranging from the captains of various industries (Forres) to Dukes and Duchesses (Argyle and Aberdeen), St. Andrews, his brother in Edinburgh, where we returned the car, and from there back to London, again by train. We rounded it out, with a wonderful few days, joining Pat and her older brother, John, at the Read's retirement home in Majorca.

"In the first few years of retirement David was a bit lost—as first years of retirement often seem to go for pastors. After re-reading all of his P.G. Woodhouse books, he fell into a bit of a depression, and I encouraged him to write another book. He agreed and began making a few notes. But as was his practice with sermons, he really couldn't get into the swing of things with his writing until he had crafted a title. Then one day, a year or so later, he called me on the phone and said, 'Fred, I've got it. What do you think of *God Was in the Laughter?*' 'It is perfect,' I told him. He began to write, and I began looking for someone to help with the type-script and then finding someone to publish it, as most of his older publishing connections were gone. The book includes David's reflections on his own impending death, and it is classic David Read! Shortly after finishing the book, he fell into physical decline, becoming homebound. We celebrated his 91st birthday, January 2, 2001, with a few close friends from the church. Five days later, I celebrated communion with him and Pat and two elders in their apartment at his bedside. He died peacefully, later that night."

N.B. God Was in the Laughter *is published in conjunction with David Read's earlier autobiographical works:* This Grace Given *and* Grace Thus Far *(cf. p. 273).*

Please also note: A CD recording of David Read preaching on three memorable occasions is available. Contact John McTavish for information (jmctav@vianet.ca).

DAVID H. C. READ'S SERMONS AT
MADISON AVENUE PRESBYTERIAN CHURCH

All of the sermons in this book were preached by David Read at New York's Madison Avenue Presbyterian Church with the exception of "The Smug and the Saintly," which was preached by Dr. Read at St. James' Episcopal Church on Thanksgiving Day, November 22, 1984.

The Season of Creation

Jesus, the Killer of Hate

EDITOR'S INTRODUCTION

HATE CRIMES WERE ON the rise when David Read preached this sermon in 1973. Sadly, such crimes are on the rise again today. What sick passion prompts the human heart to turn with hatred towards Blacks, Jews, Muslims, gays and others? All this hatred makes about as much sense as the old Punch cartoon that shows a couple of urchins spotting a man in the village walking by:

"Who's 'im, Bill?"

"A stranger!"

"'Eave 'arf a brick at 'im."

Is it the strangeness in us, then, that triggers hate? The mere fact that some of us are white and others Black? Or some Christian and others Jewish or Muslim? Or some straight and others gay? In this sermon, David Read tries to get at the sad, sick secret of prejudice while pointing to Jesus as the one in whom God kills the hatred in our hearts by submitting himself on the cross to the worst that it can do.

JESUS, THE KILLER OF HATE

A Sermon preached by David H. C. Read at Madison Avenue Presbyterian Church on September 9, 1973

> *"For he is himself our peace. Gentiles and Jews, he has made the two one, and in his own body of flesh and blood has broken down the enmity which stood like a dividing wall between them; for he annulled the law with its rules and regulations, so as to create out of the two a single new humanity in himself, thereby making peace. This was his purpose, to reconcile the two in a single body to God through the cross, on which he killed the enmity."* Ephesians 2:14–18 (NEB)

A COUPLE OF WEEKS ago, many miles from here, I found myself sitting reading this passage in the French of the Jerusalem Bible. At my feet lay the newspaper that I had just finished. I don't know exactly what had been in it that morning, but it had left me with the usual feeling of depression at the amount of violence, corruption, and terror that fills our world. In Marseilles an Algerian worker had run amok in a bus, killed the driver, and wounded several passengers. In the following few days four Algerians had been found murdered in the same city. In London a secretary had her hand blown off by a bomb planted in a letter she was opening. In Stockholm four bank employees were being held day after day at the mercy of a couple of desperadoes. From the Middle East came tales of murderous threats and sabre-rattling speeches. From the United States, apart from the usual stories of violence, one learned that corruption had now reached the level of the soapbox derby. Strife, conflict, hate, murder—of course, one knows that such things make news, but somehow it all seemed just a little bit worse than usual this summer.

I didn't pick up the Bible to forget it. For that I turned to the adventures of Inspector Maigret or the amiable lunacies of Bertram Wooster. Having been through Genesis in the French Bible, I had discovered enough murder, war, crime, corruption, and violence to satisfy any reader of the tabloids. But here I was in Ephesians reading about Jesus. And from this striking passage one sentence leaped out at me as it never had in our English versions. "Il a tue la haine," I read. "He has killed hatred."

"He has killed hatred." Here is this writer summing up the story of Jesus who, to the secular historian, was simply one more among millions of victims of human cruelty and hate, as a victory over hatred itself. In the New English Bible we read of the "cross, on which he killed the enmity."

This is either nonsense, or else it contains the ultimate secret of hope and confidence for a despairing world.

The newspapers at my feet seemed to say that it was nonsense. If Jesus killed hate, they seemed to say, how do you account for this mess we are living in two thousand years later? If Jesus killed hate why have these so-called "years of our Lord" been filled with wars, persecution, and vicious animosities even among his own followers? This is a hard question for the Christian to answer in any age, and perhaps harder than ever in this age of disillusionment when so many hopes of sixty years ago have been shattered in the fires of war and persecution.

"Jesus killed hate." We are here this morning because we believe that, in spite of all that has happened, of all that is still poisoning our world, and of the evidence of our own hearts, these words have meaning. In them is the secret of a faith that can nerve us to face the hate-filled world in which we live, to overcome the hostilities that smoulder in our own lives, and to be instruments of peace in the place where God has set us. We are not prepared to write off the Gospel as an illusion or the testimony of the saints as pious fraud. And so we are ready to listen again to what the Bible means when it speaks of the victory of Jesus over the powers of hate.

It doesn't take long to realize that the writers of the New Testament were as aware as we are that the brief life and early death of Jesus did not immediately and miraculously banish hatred from the earth. These men, a generation after the crucifixion, were surrounded by the forces of hate, and exposed to its cruelties every day of their lives. They were hated by every section of the community, except perhaps the poor. The world around them seethed with hatred just as if Jesus had never lived and died. So what did they mean when they pointed to that Cross and said: "He has killed hate?"

I believe they were talking about the very center of the Gospel—the good news that "God was in Christ reconciling the world unto himself." They were saying that God had released into the world a power greater than all the legions of hatred and division, a power that would never be extinguished before mankind had found its ultimate unity and harmony and "the kingdoms of this world are become the kingdoms of our Lord, and of his Christ." In the very teeth of their own experience of violence and hatred they proclaimed Christ's victory of love. Like their Lord they looked beyond the battlefield to the place of ultimate decision and saw "Satan as lightening fall from heaven." Since faith, according to the New Testament, is "the substance of things hoped for, the evidence of things not seen," they lived in this conviction that "Jesus has killed hate," that love is the final victor, and that all who truly live in Christ share in his reconciling power. After all these years we have still the same choice to make: either this is a chaotic and meaningless world where hate runs rampant until human beings blow one another to pieces, or there is a God who has injected into the human family a redeeming and reconciling force that works in everything for good with those who love him.

We can understand how Jesus has killed hate only from the Biblical perspective where hate is seen as a consequence of human rebellion against God. This is illuminated for us dramatically by the myth of the Tower of Babel. As an attempt to explain the origin of the multiplicity of human languages this tale can be read as a picturesque piece of folklore. What it is really saying, as the Word of God to us, throws a light on our human situation as brilliantly today as when the Book of Genesis was compiled. The confusion of languages is a perfect symbol of the breakdown in communication, the suspicions and misunderstandings, the barriers of race and culture, which breed the hatreds and the wars that afflict the human race. This summer the old farmer who was next door to our summer home in the south of France was watching our little boy one day as he tried to communicate with his grandchildren. As he saw the frustration and vexation of children who couldn't understand each other's language he shrugged his shoulders, grinned, and said to me: "La Tour de Babel." What this story does is to link this confusion and division to the arrogance of humanity in seeking the place of God. "Go to, let us build us a city and a tower, whose top may reach into heaven." The rivalries of mankind stem from the ultimate rivalry, the desire to play God and the rejection of his rule. The chasm between groups of human beings is a measure of the chasm between them and their God. They begin to hate another because, in their pretension, they hate the Lord who made them.

Another way of describing this predicament is the picture of humanity as designed to form a great circle facing inward to the light of God. When they turn round and face outwards, not only has each one lost the central Light but can no longer see his neighbor's face. The answer, then, to the hatreds that burn in the human race lies in a turning back towards the face of God. Reconciliation between human beings depends on a common reconciliation with our God.

It is in this light that we are asked to look again at the mission of Jesus. The Gospel is nothing less than a summons to accept the reconciliation that he brings. Every word and act of Jesus has to do with his reconciling power, and for him the breaking of the barriers between human beings and human groups has always to do with the breaking of the barriers between them and their God. "Forgive us our debts as we forgive our debtors." He plainly said that it was useless to express our desire for reconciliation with God if we are unwilling to be reconciled with our neighbor. "If, when you are bringing your gift to the altar, you suddenly remember that your brother has a grievance against you, leave your gift where it is before the altar. First go and make peace with your brother, and only then come back and offer your gift." It was because he walked with an unclouded communion with his heavenly Father that he ignored completely the divisions and hatreds that rent the community in which he lived. Roman soldiers, Samaritans, tax collectors—all objects of the most intense hatred—he treated exactly the same as Jewish patriots and the devout of the synagogue. It was as if hatred itself had been killed within him. He loathed the cruelties and hypocrites he saw around him but seemed incapable of hating anyone at all. So when he said that he had come "to seek and to save those who were lost" he was really offering to restore to any who would accept him the communion with God and one's fellows which human hate had broken.

But there was something more in this story than merely the picture of one who rejected hate and taught his followers to eliminate it from their hearts. The Gospel is not simply a tale of a good teacher whose advice on the whole has been rejected. It is about the cosmic struggle between love and hate. It is about the reconciliation of mankind with our God. It is about the recreation of the world, the creation, as our text says, of "a new humanity."

Therefore, it is the story of the Son of God who comes to bind up the wounds, to absorb the hatreds, to eliminate the barriers, and to move mankind towards the ultimate harmony of God's design.

Therefore, Jesus did not kill hate with words, nor even with spectacular deeds. He killed it by submitting himself to the worst it could do. This is why the Cross hangs over every celebration of Christian worship and is never far away from true Christian preaching. For this was the divine answer to the rebellion of men and women against their God and to their hatreds and their fears. When Jesus died, the victim of the very forces that threaten us so terribly today, the power of hate was broken. There was nothing more fearful that it could do—to torture and kill the Son of God himself. And so when his disciples met him on Easter morning and knew that he had come back from the hell through which he had passed for us, they could look back on that Cross as a sign, not of defeat, but of victory. "He has killed hate," they said. "He is himself our peace."

The man who wrote these words was no secluded mystic. He knew the hatreds that still raged. Paul himself was the victim of one of the most virulent hatreds that has ever stained the pages of history—the mutual hating between Jew and Gentile. And so he takes this bitter division as an illustration of the killing of hate. Writing as a Jew to Gentiles he says: "Gentiles and Jews, he has made the two one, and in his own body of flesh and blood has broken down the enmity which stood like a dividing wall between them . . . so as to create a single new humanity." "This was his purpose," he wrote, "to reconcile the two in a single body to God through the cross on which he killed the enmity."

"He killed the enmity." Have we yet learned that we cannot find in the Cross the symbol of our reconciliation to God, the pledge that our sins are forgiven, and that we are accepted in spite of our rebellions, unless we at the same time find there the symbol of our union with every human being, no matter what label they bear? Have we yet learned that the fostering of resentments, prejudices, and petty hates in our heart draws down the shutters on the grace of God that is waiting for us in the Gospel? And do we really believe that there is still no more powerful instrument for dealing with the fearful hostilities that rampage in our world, and in our city, than the Spirit of Christ, the Killer of hate?

A letter arrived in our Church House just as I was finishing this sermon. It was addressed to no particular minister—just to the church. And it contained one sentence: "Dear Sir, What must I do to save my soul from hell?" I've no idea what lies behind that cry and have to guess as I answer. But it was like a call from the world of today, from the millions who are not perhaps so worried about the fate of their individual soul, but are being driven to despair by a world that seems hell-bent on the path of hatred, violence, and lunatic destruction. It is still the joyful task of the Church to point to Jesus, the Killer of hate, to insist that there is no technique for saving the world that ignores the grace of God (no matter what our humanist friends may say), and to invite all our contemporaries, no matter what their racial, social, or religious background may be, to discover in Jesus their Savior and their Lord.

We Belong to God

EDITOR'S INTRODUCTION

THIS BACK-TO-CHURCH-AFTER-THE-SUMMER SERMON FINDS David Read raising a fundamental question with the congregation. Why are we here? Why return to church when we could be at home in our pajamas reading the Sunday Times? And why *remain* in church when the culture today is so contentedly and even vibrantly secular?

Belonging to the church, Read suggests, is linked with our sense of belonging to God, and not just any God but the God who made us and redeems us and has fixed a point beyond which we cannot fall—"the solid rock of an eternal love."

The text for this sermon is taken from the Prologue of John's Gospel: "He came unto his own . . . " Read hears these words telling us that we don't belong to ourselves. We belong to the God who claims us in Christ *as his own*. Here is the underlying reason for belonging to the church. And when we realize that we belong to God, we are moved to share this discovery with our neighbors. For "his own" includes, Read reminds us, "the entire human family, but there are millions in our world who don't know it. Shouldn't we tell them, by what we say, what we do and what we are?"

WE BELONG TO GOD

A Sermon preached by David H. C. Read at Madison Avenue Presbyterian Church on September 21, 1986

Text: *"He came unto his own . . . "* John 1:11

Readings: Genesis 1:27–31; 1 Corinthians 6:12–20; Luke 12:13–21

WHY ARE WE HERE? What brings together this mixed group of people at this time and in this place? There are so many things each of us could be doing, strolling in the park, pottering about at home, sampling the offerings on the TV screen, or just lying in bed smothered by the New York Times. So what brings us here? In this city and in this generation we can discount the cynical answers that used to be given—it's a sign of being a respectable citizen, your neighbours will look sideways at you if you're not a church-goer. Today in New York there are other circles to move in if it's prestige and reputation you're after, and your neighbours (if you know who they are) don't give a damn whether you go to church or not.

For the most part, I believe, we are here because we belong, or want to belong, to a community that believes in God and tries to act on that belief. A living church stands for a *working* belief in God. After all, the polls tell us that just being an American citizen means belonging to a community that believes in God. About 95 percent say they do. That can mean almost anything, or nothing, and is hard to square with the almost totally secularized society in which we live. A working belief in God means, in the Christian and Jewish tradition, that God is a real factor in all we think and do, that we seek a relationship with him that is as close and personal as that we have with our dearest friend. It means that in the great circle of belonging—belonging to this nation, belonging to a home, a circle of friends, a club or a community—we find, as the lodestar of this mysterious voyage through life, that the most powerful truth is that we belong to God. Such a conviction will inevitably alter the way we confront all the great choices that come our way in life, and the ultimate question mark in death.

Psychologists have said that the two most powerful instincts in human beings are religion and sex. That may account for the fact that when religion loses its grip on society, sex is apt to take over as the reigning god. Some days ago when I was pondering this sermon, I turned on the TV at random. A bad habit, you may say, but this time I was rewarded. There was John Updike, the novelist, being interviewed about his latest book. When I came in he was being asked how he reconciled the strong, religious theme in his novel with the candid treatment of sex. His answer revealed that he saw no discrepancy, and that for him, as a confessed Christian and church-goer, the two great instincts are not necessarily at war but that everything profoundly human is related to our deep sense of belonging to God. On the spur of the moment he put the case flippantly: "People go to church," he said, "because they want to live forever. They go to bed because they want to feel what it's like." As I let that remark sink in I felt I'd like to hear a sermon by Mr. Updike enlarging on my theme this morning! It's that working, all-inclusive sense of belonging to God, that should be the real reason for allying oneself with a community that seeks above all else to love the Lord our God with heart and mind and all we have, and our neighbor as ourselves.

"He came unto his own." These words are familiar to church-goers. They come from that perpetually stimulating, illuminating, and puzzling poem we know as the Prologue to the Gospel of St. John. I expect that if I asked one familiar with this phrase what was intended by the words: "He came unto his own," the answer might be: "It means that Jesus was born a Jew," or that his message was directed to the Jewish people, or perhaps, as some modern versions actually translate, "He came to his own country." But the context of these words reveals that the author was not speaking about the historic Jesus: the climactic words—"The Word was made flesh and dwelt among us" occur some verses later. He is speaking about the *Word*—which means God revealing himself to the human race, God communicating with his human family. He is speaking about God's call to the great human family that had wandered away from the Father's home. For him the Incarnation was the supreme act of God's parental love, but from the dawn of history to this very moment, God comes unto his own. Everyone—American, French, German, Russian, African, Chinese, prosperous or starving, cultivated or uncivilized, healthy or disabled, believer or unbeliever, belongs to him.

This is one basic belief of a Christian church. It is a belief that marks live church members off from all who, consciously or unconsciously, reject his claim, that marks off a church as a community that proposes another aim in life, another conviction about life's meaning (or lack of meaning) from those that seem to dominate the society in which we live. It is our business now to ponder the implications of such a working belief. "He came unto his own"—if you are now hearing the claim of the living God, if you are now among those who, in the words of the Prologue "receive him," then we are ready to explore "belonging to God" as a working belief.

The men and women of the Bible, characters who have left their mark on history as believers, and those who impress and influence us today as examples of faith in action, draw one tremendous conclusion from the fact that we belong to God. For them it's not a theory lurking in the back of the mind—"Yes; of course, in the end he's the boss." For them it is a daily working belief, and what it says is this: since I belong to God then *nothing*, not my worries, my pains, my fears, my sense of loneliness or depression, not the worst catastrophe that can happen to me, not death itself, can separate me from his love. The great images of the Bible come to life: He is our Rock, our Refuge and Strength, our mighty Fortress, our sure Foundation. He is the ultimate Lord of all being and underneath us are his everlasting arms. Jesus descended into this hell of alienation from man and God that is our deepest fear in the working belief that nothing could break the tie that bound him to that everlasting love. "Father, into thy hands I commend my spirit," were his last earthly words, and when he appeared again his disciples were given for all time their share in this assurance. They knew what he had meant when he said: "I give unto them eternal life; and they shall never perish, neither shall any man pluck them out of my hand. My Father who gave them to me, is greater than all, and no one is able to pluck them out of my Father's hand."

This working belief can be expressed very simply: to accept that we belong to God means that there is a point beyond which we cannot fall—the solid rock of an eternal love.

Belonging to God is then a belief that is lodged in the depth of the soul and begins to shape the direction of our lives. But there is more to ponder. We're not just talking of that mysterious self that we call the soul. We are not invisible angel-spirits but human beings clothed, like the animals, with bodies, solid, complicated, bodies, from which we cannot escape, although we may rise beyond them in dreams and prayers. Yet it has become so difficult to persuade people that religion, this business of belonging to God, has to do with these bodies as well as our souls. The Bible has much more to say about the body than the soul. A worshipping congregation is a marvelous assembly of bodies which cannot be transformed into some nebulous flotilla of invisible spirits. So when I realize deep down that I belong to God, I should realize that this goes for my body too. It's a gift from God which I hold in trust for him. And that has practical consequences as a working belief.

In the passage we heard from Paul's letter to the Corinthian Church, he dealt with one aspect of our treatment of the body. Corinth was known for its total sexual license. It was one big 42 Street. And Paul had discovered that some of his young Christians there were interpreting his Gospel of the grace of God and freedom from the law to mean that, so long as their soul had been saved, they could do what they liked with their bodies. Hence his thunderous denunciation of the licentious bed-hoppers of Corinth, "What? Know ye not that your body is the temple of the Holy Ghost, which is in you, which ye have of God, *and ye are not your own*?"

Your body, he is saying, is not your own. It belongs to God, and you are responsible for it as a steward of God's gift. This has implications far beyond the point that Paul was making here. If we, including our bodies, belong to God, then we have a duty to respect them. Without giving in to the prevailing hypochondria of the moment, we owe these bodies of ours at least enough care to keep them in repair, as good stewards of this gift of God.

So when we talk about the Christian doctrine of stewardship we mean much more than the use of money. When people come to recognize that word as an ecclesiastical code word for fund raising, they are tempted to switch off. Money and possessions do come into the picture, but only because they are such an integral part of the lives that belong to God. The basic belief is what Paul meant when he simply said: "You are not your own." The power and glory of the Gospel—and the joy—lie not only in the assurance that since we belong to God, we have a safety net through which we cannot fall: but in the discovery that all we have—bodies, homes, talents, ambitions, bank accounts—we hold in trust for the God to whom they belong. When that becomes real belief, a new and satisfying power is at work in our lives.

"He came unto his own." What we really are: *his own.* This is the crucial decision in anyone's life: recognizing that we are "his own" and not "our own" to do what we like. That is what's meant by receiving him, this living, giving, loving God. To as many as receive him, the One who became one of us in Jesus Christ, he gives the power to become the sons and daughters of God. To receive him means just saying: "Yes, Lord, I'm not my own. I belong to you. Take the *whole* of me."

Then it must become as clear as daylight that a community of Christians with this working belief will want to share this discovery with all our neighbors. Evangelism is for us not an attempt to brainwash others into becoming Presbyterians. It's the joyful invitation to all who are feeling lost or alone to share what Christ has given us. Rejoice with me! "He came unto his own" and "his own" are not the members of a holy club. "His own" includes the entire human family, but there are millions in our world who don't know it. Shouldn't we tell them—by what we say, what we do, and what we are?

Prayer: Lord, we are thine, help us to know it, to know it in the depth of our heart and to act accordingly, through Christ our Lord. Amen.

God's Love—
A New Pope and an Old Text

EDITOR'S INTRODUCTION

DAVID READ HAD A standard routine for preparing sermons. He would begin thinking about the upcoming sermon on the weekend before it was preached. On Tuesday morning he chose the topic, text, readings, and hymns. On Wednesday morning he did his ruminating and researching. On Thursday morning he composed the first half of the sermon, and on Friday morning he completed the task.

However, when this sermon was prepared, Read wasn't typing in his study on Friday morning. As we learn from the sermon itself, he was standing in a gale-like storm in Battery Park. Pope John Paul had recently been installed in office and was visiting New York. Along with thousands of others, David Read was braving the elements in the hope of getting a glimpse of the new leader.

The sermon that resulted should warm the hearts of Catholics and Protestants alike as it throws bright and engaging light on a beloved text that speaks to almost every churchgoer regardless of their ecclesiastical background. Indeed, I am confident that the Pope himself would have found this sermon on John 3:16 deeply moving.

GOD'S LOVE—A NEW POPE AND AN OLD TEXT

A Sermon preached by David H. C. Read at Madison Avenue Presbyterian Church on Worldwide Communion Sunday, October 7, 1979

> Text: *"For God so loved the world, that he gave his only begotten Son, that whosoever believeth in him should not perish, but have everlasting life."* John 3:16
>
> Readings: 1 Corinthians 13; John 3:14–21

WHAT HAPPENED TO OUR city last week? We had a visitor—a distinguished visitor. But we have had many before. We have saluted heads of state, war heroes, astronauts, athletes; and, for a few hours, the city has seethed with excitement. This time it seemed to me that there was a unique quality about the reception given to our visitor. It was not only that he came with the nimbus of a holy office, one of the most ancient and celebrated throughout the world. (It is a little surprising in 1979 to see ticket-tape raining on the head of one who bears the title of His Holiness.) But it was not the office that electrified this city. It was the man. This was a new Pope, and we didn't really know him till he was right here with us. We are told in the Gospels that when Jesus came into Jerusalem on Palm Sunday "all the city was moved, saying, Who is this?" Like everyone else, I wanted to know. I am willing to pay my respects to any leader of a venerable, worldwide religious community, but it was not mere ecclesiastical politesse that made me stand for two hours and be literally drenched to the skin, in order to be near him last Friday morning in the gales of Battery Park.

Of course our Roman Catholic brethren turned out in thousands to cheer their Pontiff. Of course, there was curiosity that made many want to get a glimpse of the new Pope—"Who is this? What is he really like?" But what emanated from beneath that sea of umbrellas was something far more than the enthusiasm of one Christian community, or the desire to catch sight of one who has been much in the world's news in the few months of his tenure. I can describe it only as a yearning for something different from the passing excitements of our secular city, a longing for someone who expresses another dimension of our human condition, for a living symbol—not of political power or material success, or the affluent society—but of the missing element in our restless, consuming, and undirected world—faith and hope and love.

Let me put it simply. This man exuded Christian love. And by that I don't just mean that he seemed to be a genial, kindly man with an encouraging word for everybody. I'm speaking of that formidable and revolutionary Agape that is at the heart of the Christian Gospel. It proclaims, against all evidence to the contrary, that God loves us—and not only us but every single human being on this planet. It soars towards God with an answering love for him, and it finds expression in a warm compassionate caring and concern for every man, woman, or child who crosses our path. The Pope was among us as a man of high intelligence and profound experience of the tragedies of our age who openly declares in every word and gesture: "God loves us." And without qualification he summons our generation to express again our love to God in worship, prayer, and a holy obedience. It is this divine love for which so many hearts are aching. But what brought it down from the clouds where so many Popes and prelates, and Protestant preachers have hidden it, was the sight and the voice of a real human being with a twinkle in his eyes, a man who obviously preferred the gift of a t-shirt from a teenager to listening to official orations. So with all the Scottish covenanting and Ulster Protestant blood in my veins, I salute him as a man for *this* season, a very human symbol of the divine love from which our generation longs, and as a loyal servant of Jesus Christ our common Lord.

With gratitude for this irruption of the holy and the human into the drab procession of the sordid, the violent, the self-centred, and the callous that seems to fill the headlines and the TV screens, let me turn to the most familiar and best-loved text in the entire New Testament. Perhaps it's not as familiar now as it used to be. Perhaps, even to those for whom it is familiar, it no longer speaks with life-changing power. Can we hear it again, as if we had never heard it before? For here is the answer to the question we are sometimes asked: What *is* this Gospel that churches talk about? What *is* the Good News that all who call themselves Christians are supposed to believe and to live by? Is it just that God is love, and we are supposed to love him and our neighbor in return? That is true—but it is not the Gospel. We don't need the New Testament to tell us this: it's all there in the Old. Is it, as some would put it, that we ought to be more like Jesus? That's true, too, but I don't call that Good News. In fact for me to be told that God expects me to be like Jesus and will judge me accordingly could at times be very *bad* news. No; the Gospel isn't a message about what God is like, or what you and I ought to be like. It's about what God has done, and what he keeps on doing. It's not a formula to give us a guilty conscience. It's a way to get that conscience clean. It's not another demand upon us but a word of hope and liberation. It's the news of God's rescuing love. Listen: "For God so loved the world, that he gave his only begotten Son, that whosoever believeth in him should not perish, but have everlasting life."

Something happened. In this Gospel God's love is not idea but action. When we say "God is love" that can be just an idea. And we often accept it as such—just as we accept the idea that the sun is always shining out there even though we may be fogged in or passing through the hours of darkness. But the moment someone constructs a house that is warmed by solar heat, the rays of sunshine are trapped and concentrated on one specific place and become the energy we need. So the Gospel gives us far more than a vaguely comforting thought that the whole of creation is being sustained by the love of God. It tells us that this love is a divine energy that came to a burning focus in Jesus Christ. "God *so* loved that he gave his Son." The Lord of the universe cared enough about his human family to give us his human Self. At one particular time and place Christ came. The love of God was translated into flesh and blood and visited our planet as one of us. And he came without security guard, one of the poor and powerless with no weapon but that love. And we know what happened. For a few short years this concentrated energy of love blazed warm and then it seemed as if the switch was pulled, and Jesus died. But Easter morning broke the news that he was alive again and that love was released into the whole world by the little company that believed in him. And this morning there is hardly a tiny corner of the world where his Church is not celebrating the feast that commemorates his victory.

We may often wonder why God tolerates the antics of the human race with all its cruelties and horrors. This summer a French friend of mine who has nothing to do with any church but loves to grow crops, tend animals or float in his little yacht under the Mediterranean stars, said to me with sudden vehemence: "I consider the human race the dirtiest and most villainous species that ever soiled God's world." The trouble with such judgments is that we are always tempted to exclude ourselves. Let God obliterate Ninevah, we say with Jonah, but keep my little Jerusalem safe. But God, you remember, did not destroy Ninevah—and God has not yet wiped out his human family. For God is love, and obliteration is not the way of love. And God *so* loved that he let Jesus come and die—why? Just to show us up in our selfishness, our hatreds, and our indifference? No. He tells us why he sent his Son—"so that everyone that believeth should not perish but have everlasting life. For God sent not his Son into the world to condemn the world, but that the world through him might be saved."

This energy of love that was concentrated in Christ is the Good News for all the world to hear. It was lived out in a real Jesus in a real place among real people at a particular point in time. But, after the Resurrection, his energy of love was passed to those who believed to be spread by his Church across the centuries and across the world. "You shall receive power," said the Risen Lord, "after the Holy Spirit is come upon you; and you shall be witnesses unto me both in Jerusalem, and in all Judaea and in Samaria, *and unto the uttermost part of the earth.*"

Yes; "God so loved *the world.*" This rescuing love was meant for the entire human family. How often it has been translated: "God so loved the good people; God so loved the people to whom Jesus came; God so loved the western world in which his Church took root." But we cannot throttle the universality of this glorious text. He didn't give his Son in order to add another religion to the repertory of the human race. His love was not directed exclusively to the kind of people we might find congenial. It was the world for whom Christ came to live and die and rise again, the Cosmos with its kaleidoscope of races, colors, languages, affluence, poverty, ideologies, and clashing hopes and fears. It is this universal appeal of God's love in Christ that this Pope is symbolizing in his travels and his pronouncements, and that we today experience as we share in a Worldwide Communion with Christians from every continent and island.

The world. Every time that word comes up on my typewriter I pause. For it seems to appear too often. And I hear a voice whispering: "Beware of abstractions. Beware of generalities." It is so easy to talk glibly about the world that God loves, and neglect to fill it with real people—your next door neighbor, the kid playing in a garbage-ridden street just a few hundred yards away, the beggar on the steps of a European cathedral, the refugee child on the frontier of Cambodia, the boat people. So let me turn to this other word in our text. "God so loved the world that he gave his only Son that *whoever* believes in him should not perish but have everlasting life." That "whoever" focusses the love of God on one single human being, as if for the moment there is no one else. That whoever is *you.*

There's divinity in this famous text—but there is also an intense humanity that embraces each one of us just as we are, just as John Paul II broke away from the crowd and the speeches to hoist a little girl into his arms. Have you noticed how often the Gospels tell of Jesus singling out one man, woman, or child, as if he had come to heal them alone? As we receive the symbols of God's universal love in Christ today, surrounded as we are with the whole worldwide family of his Church, and by the company of the saints in heaven, can we also hear the voice that says: "God loves you. He has given his Son so that when you respond, you will not perish but have everlasting life"? "Whoever believes in him"—this isn't a question of twisting our minds into some theological affirmation. It's the kind of response made by a lover to the beloved—"I believe in you."

We are a vast multitude at this Table today, visible and invisible, and we share a communion with one another. But there is also the moment when there is no one else—just you and the Lord whom you receive with the bread and wine, and your intimate, personal communion with him. "God so loved me" is the word as we take and eat this nourishment of eternal life.

Then we go out—not to revel in a private possession of this energy of love, but to reflect it wherever we go and whatever we may be doing, and to whomever we meet. One day last week I caught these words from the Pope and with them I close: "Keep Christ in your heart, and then you will see his reflection in everyone you meet."

The Gospel in the Galaxies:
What Message for Mars?

EDITOR'S INTRODUCTION

OVER FORTY YEARS HAVE slipped by since David Read preached this sermon in the wake of the launching of Voyager II. The reference to Mars in the sermon's title would seem to have been intended figuratively. In any event, the space craft, according to Wikipedia, is currently beyond the limit of the solar system. Long past Mars, it is flying at the speed of 19.4 kilometres per second.

Voyager II includes recorded information about our mathematics, chemistry, geology, and biology, as well as samples of our music. Nothing, however, is said about the faith convictions of the human family. This is what prompted Read to frame his own "Message for Mars."

David Read doesn't presume to speak here on anyone's behalf but his own. Indeed, he encourages us to compose our own letter for Mars, or for anyone out there in space beyond our tiny family here on earth. What he offers in this sermon is simply one person's attempt to communicate with anyone living beyond our planet in our unimaginably vast universe. And the message Read offers is unapologetically informed by "the one who fills the whole wide universe" with the presence and love of God.

THE GOSPEL IN THE GALAXIES: WHAT MESSAGE FOR MARS?

A Sermon preached by David H. C. Read at Madison Avenue Presbyterian Church on October 23, 1977

> Text: *"God has placed everything under the power of Christ and has set him up as head of everything for the Church. For the Church is his body, and in that body lives fully the one who fills the whole wide universe."* Ephesians 1:22, 23 (Phillips)
>
> Readings: Psalm 139; Ephesians 1:15–23 (Phillips); John 1:1–9

"THE WHOLE WIDE UNIVERSE." Even as we worship here this morning in this corner of the city, a spacecraft is humming on its way to the planets and beyond. At the end of August "Voyager" was successfully launched—"a bottle cast into the cosmic ocean" someone said, because, for the first time, a message was sent to the galaxies to be read by any conceivable sentient, intelligent beings who might pick it up.

Such things are taken so casually nowadays that I don't remember hearing a single comment on this unique event, far less a debate about what should be included in such a message. Perhaps most people feel that the odds are so long against the possibility of there being any astral civilization within our reach and of anyone finding and being able to interpret the message that the incident should be shrugged off as a romantic gesture designed to tickle the imagination. I may indeed be the only one to worry at all about what we are conveying to these hypothetical neighbors in outer space, but I confess that the contents of that capsule set off a train of thought which I want to share with you this morning in the light of our Christian convictions. I'm really asking what you feel is important to tell whoever is listening in the "whole wide universe" about our experience as temporary residents on spaceship Earth. Suppose the message is picked up and deciphered by some super-sophisticated being engaged in happy research in a civilization superior to ours—or perhaps caught up in some planet-shattering "Star Wars"—what would you like him to know about us, our aspirations, discoveries, hopes, and fears?

I checked again on the content of this capsule and confirmed my impression that there is a curiously missing factor. There is nothing whatever to indicate that human beings on this planet have any kind of religion, any belief in a God who is responsible for the existence of "the whole wide universe," or conviction that we have a destiny that is located in another dimension than that which can be explored by the instruments of science. The capsule, I am told, contains information about our mathematics, chemistry, geology, and biology, but there is no mention of theology. Some magnificent music is included, but none, apparently, that relates to the great statements of our faith. It looks as if the American principle of separation of Church and State has now spawned a new one—the total separation of Church and Space. It may well be that the authorities who determined what this message should be were terrified to include something that might turn out to be too Catholic, too Jewish, too Presbyterian, too Episcopalian, or too Baptist for popular consumption, and so decided to eliminate religion altogether. But surely the end-result is to convey to these Martians (or whoever) a seriously truncated view of the deepest concerns of our human race. The major religions of the world are estimated to claim the adherence of more than two and a half billion human beings at the present time. Whatever the views of the composers of this message may be it seems hardly scientific to exclude all reference to the religious convictions that have to a large extent shaped the course of our history and still command the assent of the majority of the human race.

The actual message that is on its way is stimulating and thought-provoking. "We cast this message into the cosmos" it begins. Then comes a reference to the staggering dimensions of the universe. "Of the two hundred billion stars in the Milky Way Galaxy," we read, "some, perhaps, many—may have inhabited planets and space-faring civilizations. If one such civilization intercepts Voyager and can understand these recorded contents, here is our message."

It is short enough to be quoted in full. Here is what we are going to tell any who may chance to pick it up. "This is a present from a small, distant world, a token of our sounds, our science, our music, our thoughts, and our feelings. We are attempting to survive our time so that we may live into yours. We hope someday, having solved the problems we face, to join a community of galactic civilizations. This record represents our hope and our determination and our goodwill in a vast and awesome universe."

This is a brief, comprehensive, and moving statement. Some might say that it does well to exclude any religious speculations and confine itself to simple, observable fact. But, of course, it doesn't. In some ways these words are as much a statement of faith as the Apostles' Creed. When I queried the omission of theology from the disciplines mentioned in the capsule some may have thought: "Well, that's no loss: why bother these people with God-talk when we can stick to the objective sciences?" But this is no objective statement (even if there is such a thing—which is doubtful). There is a philosophy here—even a theology. Listen: "We are attempting to survive our time so we may live into yours." That is a new theological answer to the first question of the Catechism: "What is the chief end of man?" It is also a statement of secular eschatology, eschatology being the department of theology that deals with the ultimate destiny of us all. It is spelled out in greater detail than most theologians would care to risk. "We hope someday, having solved the problems we face, to join a community of galactic civilizations." Is that really your great hope, the working hope of the bulk of human beings on our planet? I find this a fascinating, mind-stimulating speculation and have no inclination at all to rub it out in the name of my religion. But it in no way corresponds to the final hope that billions find in the Bible—the hope of the triumph of the Kingdom of God. And I am sure that our President, in whose name this message went, would be the first to declare that his ultimate hope lies elsewhere.

Hope is not a word from the lexicon of science. It is a theological virtue—one on which I intend to concentrate this year during the Sundays of Advent. I find this statement stimulating, and thought-provoking, but theologically defective. What it does do, however, is to force us to relate what we profess to believe as Christians to this dazzling picture of the universe presented by modern science, and our first attempts to voyage into its mysteries. We cannot shut ourselves into our sanctuaries and express our faith in the words and images of another era in human understanding of the universe, and then emerge into a space-age which seems to demand different ways of thinking and believing. In other words, there should be no wall of separation between Church and Space. I have said here more than once that the God revealed in the Bible is not one whose glory is in the least diminished by any discoveries about the vastness of the universe, and that the values for which Christ stands—love, truth, peace, humility, hope—are as valid for the first colonizers of the planets as they were for the Galileans who heard the Sermon on the Mount. But it would be wrong to pretend that there are no questions raised for an orthodox Christian by the new picture of the universe with which we are now living.

Most of these questions will relate to the figure of Jesus Christ himself. I once sat at a table with a very distinguished astro-physicist and a Christian evangelist, the late D. T. Niles. Niles was about to conduct a Christian mission at Edinburgh University and the other was in agreement that the students should have the opportunity to be confronted with the claims of the Gospel. Then he opened up his own doubts and reservations. "What I find hard to believe," he said, "is that one who lived two thousand years ago in a little corner of this planet could possibly have the supreme importance you attach to him in this immense universe." Niles thought for a moment and then said: "That's a big question—but, first of all, you have to make up your own mind about Jesus Christ. Who is he?"

This is why I have set before you in apposition to the message to the planets this extraordinary statement of the apostle Paul. "God has placed everything under the power of Christ and has set him up as head of everything for the Church. For the Church is his body, and in that body lives fully the one who fills the whole wide universe." If the apostle were to have lived on into our new understanding of "the whole wide universe" I don't believe he would have altered one word of what he says here about Jesus Christ and his Church. It is commonly thought today that the first Christians were those who had actually met, or heard about Jesus and were so impressed that later they began to spin greater and greater myths about him until he ceased to be an historical character but became a kind of heavenly King. In fact, it was the living Christ, risen and ascended, who first awoke their faith, and it was only later that they began to collect the material about his earthly life. What they were saying was not that there was once a Jewish teacher whose life was so amazing, and whose death was so tragic, that he must be thought of as reigning somewhere in heaven but that they had been gripped by a living Lord in whom God himself had come to share their human adventures and rescue them from evil. They knew that they had been called into a company so closely united to this Lord that it could be called his body on earth. "For the Church is his body" as Paul reminded them, and then added the tremendous words: "and in that body lives fully the one who fills the whole wide universe." The Gospel tells us of a man who lived our life, shared our sufferings, died our death, in one particular place on this tiny planet at one particular time ("under Pontius Pilate," says the creed) and at the same time announces that he is the disclosure of the eternal God, the rescuer of the whole human family, and the final Lord of the entire universe. We have lived for about a hundred years with a vivid picture of the historical Jesus. Perhaps now the Bible is speaking to us again of this cosmic Christ.

Having said that, let me confess that I have trouble relating this cosmic Christ to the possible existence of other beings, other civilizations elsewhere in the "whole wide universe." I have no answer to such questions as: "Did they also experience an incarnation? Was Jesus born more than once elsewhere? Did other races need to be redeemed? Or did God have some other way to communicate with them?" I feel no urge to deny that any such creatures ever existed in order to preserve my belief in the uniqueness of Christ. I am content to believe that the God revealed to me by Jesus is the Creator and Governor of the whole wide universe, and therefore have no hesitation in singing: "Crown him with many crowns, the Lamb upon his throne," or praying with the apostle that I "may be able to comprehend with all saints what is the breadth, and length, and depth, and height; and to know the love of Christ, which passeth knowledge, that (I) may be filled with all the fullness of God." That Jesus is the one who "fills the whole universe" I can joyfully affirm without having all my questions about how or when or where satisfactorily answered.

So let me now try to compose a little message for Mars (or anybody else who might be out there). I am not implying that this is what should have been enclosed in that capsule that was tossed into the cosmic ocean since I am speaking specifically as a Christian. But there are some things that I am sure millions of other faiths would also have liked expressed. I would want to add to some of the good things that were said and enclosed in that packet something like this:

Dear Martian, this scientific information, these records of music, these expressions of our hopes and aspirations are the product of a long story (as we count time), and in that story by far the most powerful influence has been the belief, held in every section of our planet from earliest times, that our lives—and everything that exists, including your planet—are not accidental happenings with no meaning but the result of the activity of a supreme Mind and Will that we call God. This God has been pictured in many ways and some of these pictures have led us badly astray. But over the centuries there has been a growing consensus that he is a Being who demands of us a life of honesty, kindness, peace, and love; and he promises us a destiny that will fulfill all the highest aspirations of our race. That destiny lies beyond this physical universe which we share. It is in another dimension altogether.

The most powerful religious impulse in our civilization is one that springs from a revelation of this God that we have now bound up in a book called the Bible. It tells us not only that God is the Creator of all that is, and that he made the human race to live in communion with him and to share a life of love and peace and joy, but frankly shows that something went wrong. At the heart of this revelation is the story of God's rescuing action, what we call his "grace" offered to forgive what we have done wrong, and keep us on the right path. Roughly a billion of us recognize one called Jesus Christ as the Savior of the world, one who by living and dying for us has reconciled us to the living God. We believe that he is the true Lord of all of us and that as the perfect reflection of God he will reign over the whole universe. We believe that he is the one in whom all things will find their ultimate meaning and coherence. These beliefs have, in one way or another, been the driving-power behind the story of our civilization.

Dear Martian, you may know this already. You may have a far deeper knowledge of this God than we have. You may not have fallen into what we know as sin and therefore didn't need to be redeemed. You may have a far closer communion with the Eternal than we have ever known. I just wanted you to know that billions of us would not express our hopes and aspirations entirely with the words: "We hope someday, having solved the problems we face, to join a community of galactic civilizations." In the light of our faith we are less optimistic about "solving the problems" on our own, and, while it would be delightful to "join a community of galactic civilizations" most of us have a more immediate hope of reaching the eternal world, and a final hope of a glorious community called the Kingdom of God."

If you don't like that letter how about trying to write your own?

"This World, with Devils Filled": Luther's Answer and Ours

EDITOR'S INTRODUCTION

ON OCTOBER 31, 1517, Martin Luther nailed his '95 Theses Against Indulgences' to the door of the University Church in Wittenberg. The Augustinian monk wasn't trying to incite a revolution so much as he was calling for a theological debate on the controversial practice of the selling of Indulgences. Luther's arguments, however, were run off on the newly invented printing press. Suddenly people all over Europe were talking about the brash young priest in Germany who had dared to challenge the authority of the Pope himself.

David Read's Reformation sermon largely bypasses the 500 year-old debate that Luther's protest sparked. Instead it seizes the occasion to champion what Luther himself was essentially championing: God's free, undeserved grace. Read sees grace escaping from the pages of the Bible and lighting up the beauty of the whole natural world. He sees grace in a child's anger-diffusing remark, in the courage of a stricken family at a memorial service, in the splendour of his city on a fresh fall morning. Above all, he sees God's grace breaking upon us in Jesus' revolutionary life and teachings, and especially in that awe-filled moment when "the embodiment of grace let himself be crushed by the very forces of which we are so afraid today."

"THIS WORLD, WITH DEVILS FILLED": LUTHER'S ANSWER AND OURS

A Sermon preached by David H. C. Read at Madison Avenue Presbyterian Church on Reformation Sunday, October 27, 1974

> Text: *"For by grace are ye saved through faith; and that not of yourselves: it is the gift of God . . . "* Ephesians 2:8
>
> Readings: Joshua 1:1–9; Ephesians 2:1–10; John 16:26–33

SEEN FROM FORTY THOUSAND feet this is a fair and beautiful world. The other day I flew in from the west coast over a pure and sparkling desert, then the folding, blue ranges of the Rockies with their misty turrets, then the quilted plains soaking up the riches of the autumn sun, till leveling down slowly over the flaming tints of New England. Even at five thousand feet New York itself is a dream city on such a day, and rises to meet you as a tapestry of streets and parks and bridges, as a glittering jewel in its silver setting of rivers and ocean. This is when you really want to shout: "The heavens declare the glory of God and the firmament showeth his handiwork." "The earth is the Lord's, and the fullness thereof."

Halfway across the continent the air traveler who can't spend all his time looking out of the window consumes the last unnecessary calories on his tray (I never knew what calories tasted like until I met airline food) folds up his table, and picks up the morning paper. In a few minutes it's a very different world he is seeing. Somewhere up in the Maritimes a storm has struck and pictures show families hopelessly digging out their belongings from the wreckage. In the Bronx a young woman has been found murdered in her apartment. School children in Boston and Brooklyn are scratching and stoning each other because some have black skins and others white. A picture of a mother and daughter from West Africa in the last stages of starvation cries out against the food that has already been wasted on this plane and calls out to the great breadbasket that stretches endlessly below us. He turns the pages. Human beings have been torn to pieces in Ireland in the name of religion. The Holy Land is the target of warring powers. Somewhere diplomats are conferring so that there may be some pause in the race for weapons that can destroy every living creature on this planet. Then page after page reports the suspicion and the cynicism with which we have come to regard the political scene. It's a different world the traveller sees when he looks again through that little window.

"And though this world, with devils filled,

Should threaten to undo us"

wrote Martin Luther, and we now know what he means. Fifty years ago these words would have had a curiously antique flavor. "With devils filled?" That's the way they used to talk, poor dears; we know better now: devils went out with Santa Claus: there's nothing wrong with the world that better education and a little Christian optimism won't be able to cure. Now we feel closer to Luther than to the blinkered idealists of the recent past. And to be closer to Luther is to be closer to the Bible. For the Bible tells us that this world, created to declare the glory of God, is a fallen world, and that humankind, made in the image of the Creator, has been enslaved by demonic powers. This doesn't mean that the world is bound for hell and that every human being is some kind of monster in disguise. But it does mean that there is a mystery of iniquity abroad that defies the simple solutions of human ingenuity. There is such a thing as sin which, as Karl Menninger has recently pointed out, has been strangely neglected by the modern Church.

Has there ever been a time since perhaps when Luther lived when ordinary men and women have been more baffled and dismayed by the virulence of human passions, the sheer irrationality of the evil things human beings can do to one another? Particularly in this country where ideals have glowed so brightly and hopes have been highest we are going through a period of shock, anxiety, and near-despair. We know exactly what Luther meant when we sang of "this world with devils filled" that "threaten to undo us." The trouble in the Church has been that we have wanted to hear the Good News without first taking a hard look at the bad. We have sometimes spoken as if our redemption was little more than a helping hand to humanity in its rise to perfection, and that the Son of God didn't really need to die to save us from our sins. It's time to see again in all its grim, demonic depths, the predicament of the human race, the fearful question to which the Gospel gives its answer. Luther, Calvin, Augustine, Paul, and Jesus himself would echo in this spiritual struggle the old military maxim: "Never underestimate the power of the enemy."

We need to be saved. Let's hear that word again with its full Biblical weight, without any undertones of sticky pietism. We need to be saved from evil in all its forms—individual, social, and cosmic. That's why Jesus taught us to pray: "Deliver us from evil." He believed the evil to be in us, in the world, and in an invisible sphere of the demonic. (The correct reading of the prayer is probably: "Deliver us from the Evil One.") The salvation the Bible speaks of is not some kind of religious emotion. It is health, total health of body, mind, and spirit, for the individual and for the whole human family.

The New Testament declares again and again that it is for this that we are being saved as members of Christ's Church. Being saved is being rescued, not only *from* the hell we make for ourselves, as *for* the colony of heaven God is establishing on earth.

It was because Luther found the answer to this question of salvation, first for himself and then for the Church and the world of his day, that he was able to sing: "Though this world with devils filled should threaten to undo us, We will not fear for God hath willed his truth to triumph through us." He found the answer in the Bible, where it lies still today. Nowhere is it more clearly expressed than in the seven monosyllables of our text: "By grace are you saved through faith." They summarize the whole content of the Bible. They express the dynamic of the Gospel which keeps springing to life again whenever the Church gets drowsy and over-organized. They offer to you and me today the only real antidote to anxiety and confusion. In them we hear the truth of the Gospel through which we can face the world, the flesh, and the devil unafraid. "We will not fear for God hath willed his truth to triumph through us."

"By grace. . . . " The view from forty thousand feet was not all an illusion. There is a glory in the natural world and in the works of man that reflects the joy of the Creator who still sees the universe he has made "and behold, it is very good," and also the dignity and aspiration of human beings created in his image. Neither Luther nor Calvin was blind to the beauty of the natural world, and each of them knew how to enjoy human company over, respectively, a stein of beer and a glass of wine. They were not the grim, sour-faced ecclesiastics of popular imagination. If they knew what it was to see a world filled with devils, they also knew how to see it filled with angels. The point is that, like the Bible, they took both the angel and devil seriously. That is: they saw the terrible force of sin in human nature but believed in the grace that can lift us up to our angelic destiny. In a demonic world they chose to live by grace.

Does that mean simply that the Gospel invites us to look on the bright side and throw our weight on the side of goodness in the human struggle? Can this Christian answer to our fears be adequately described in the words of Studdert Kennedy as "backing the scent of life against its stink"? There's truth enough in that to hold on to, but the word "grace" in Scripture and the life of the Church carries a profounder meaning. Sure, it's grace when we see this city sparkling in beauty on a fresh Fall morning; it's grace when a little boy disarms your anger with an absurd remark; it's grace when a stricken family gives thanks and takes courage in a memorial service here; it's grace when we hear the happy stories that never appear in the morning paper. But the Bible tells us that these signs of grace flow from the great rescuing love of

God, a love that shines through even the bloodiest pages of the Bible story, a love that comes to a climax with the coming of Jesus Christ. "We beheld his glory," says the apostle, "full of grace and truth."

When we use the words "the grace of our Lord Jesus Christ" we are not only thinking of the perfection of his life, the blazing signal that God has not given up on the Adam of his design. We are not only thinking of the way in which the love of God reached out through him to the lonely, the crippled in mind and body, the outcast, and the broken-hearted. We are thinking of his battle against the forces of the devil, his encounter with the evil in our world. This battle, this encounter, reveals what is most amazing about this grace. For it took the form of letting the powers of hell do their worst. The one who was the embodiment of grace let himself be crushed by the very forces of which we are so afraid today. He took the entire weight of human sorrow, anguish, and sin upon himself, and was crucified, dead, and buried. This is what Luther called "the right man on our side," the One who goes this length for our rescue. And ever since he came back triumphant from this mission against the enemy the grace of the Lord Jesus Christ has dawned upon the world as our hope and our salvation. "By grace are you saved . . .", by this gift of God, by this liberating love, by this victory over all the powers of darkness.

In his day Luther found a Church in which this grace was being obscured, even as it is often today in churches that celebrate his Reformation. It was, and is, obscured in two ways. First, there is the notion that grace is some kind of religious medicine dispensed by the Church. The impression is given that there is a kind of reservoir in the institution that is drawn on by its members, and that through the pipelines of its ordinances and activities we can get enough "religion" to keep us going. Luther, in his search for "a merciful God" made the great discovery that grace is supremely personal, the gift of a God who cares for each one of us. The grace that saves us is as personal—and as powerful—as the love of a mother for her child, as the communion of two close friends. The love that moves among a group of caring people is not something to be measured or rationed out; it is a free, spontaneous, accepting, forgiving, and delivering power that comes from the heart. So, I would say, grace comes not from the plans and programs of a religious organization, but from the heart of God. The services, the sacraments, the activities of a church are properly described as "the means of grace." They are not grace itself.

The second way in which grace is obscured is the persistent notion that somehow it has to be earned or deserved. The music exploded in the heart of Luther when he finally knew that nothing whatever was required of him to merit the grace of God: no penances, no mortifications—yes, and no smug sense that he had made the grade as a moral and respectable citizen. If there ever was a character who seemed able to rely on his own interior strength it was Luther who, when warned of the danger that awaited him at Worms, remarked: "If I had heard that as many devils would set on me in Worms as there are tiles on the roofs, I should none the less have ridden there." Yet this was the man who sang: "Did we in our own strength confide, our striving would be losing, Were not the right Man on our side, the Man of God's own choosing." It was this "right Man" whose grace alone forgave his sins, set him right with God, and nerved him for every struggle.

It is still a surprise for many people, even within the Church, when they really hear that the grace of God means that his love accepts them just as they are, that there is no scale of religious virtue to be climbed before they can know the grace of the Lord Jesus Christ, and the love God, and the communion of the Holy Spirit. So long as we retain one trace of self-justification, one little desire to earn our own salvation, we are at the mercy of these fears and victims of our pride. Grace is the great leveller—never more needed than in times when we tend to range ourselves with the good guys and blame all our troubles on the bad. "All have sinned," said Paul, "and come short of the glory of God." But all can be "justified freely by his grace through the redemption that is in Christ Jesus." "By grace are you saved . . . "

How then if there is nothing we can do, can we be really linked to this amazing grace? That's the big question today as at the time of the Reformation. There can be no quarrel among Christians any more about the answer. "By grace you are saved through faith." Catholic and Protestant may still have different ways of expressing what this means, but increasingly we converge on the ultimate truth. Faith is our total trust in this grace that meets us in the person of Jesus Christ. Every one of us knows that it takes two to be friends. I can offer you my friendship, my understanding, my sympathy, my love, but if this evokes no flicker of a response then nothing happens. Grace is the hand of God stretched out—and it waits to be grasped by our hand in faith. This faith can be expressed in a silent prayer of commitment and trust, in a common affirmation in creed or hymn, in an inward yielding to the Spirit of God. But it is also expressed by the direction of our lives, our concern for other people, our reflection of the love of Christ, our readiness to follow where he leads.

Here we come to the question that always arises when the Gospel of salvation by grace through faith is preached. Do you mean, it has been asked since the days of the apostles, that since there is nothing I can do to earn my salvation, I can just trust in this grace—and carry on in my own sweet way, caring nothing about the commandments of the Lord? Dietrich Bonhoeffer used to call this misunderstanding of the Gospel "cheap grace." The answer of the Bible is that the test of our faith is whether it issues in a real discipleship. If it doesn't it is not faith, and grace is not there. Listen again to the words of the epistle. "By grace are ye saved through faith; and that not of yourselves; it is the gift of God; not of works lest any man should boast." Our Christian activities in this devil-filled world are not the cause, or the price, of our salvation. They must follow genuine faith as the thankful answer of the forgiven sinner. "For we are his workmanship," the passage goes on, "created in Christ Jesus unto good works, which God hath before ordained that we should walk in them." In a new translation: "We are his handiwork, created in Christ Jesus to devote ourselves to the good deeds for which God has designed us."

So we come down from forty thousand to six feet above the ground. We go out again to face a world with devils filled. There is work to do. And we are called to do it with the joy of those who are being saved by grace through faith. In our anthem this morning you will hear the sounds of the devils: but through it you will hear the clear notes of the grace and the love that casts out fear. "Be of good cheer," said Jesus, "I have overcome the world."

The Resurrection of the Body

EDITOR'S INTRODUCTION

"We see through a glass darkly," said St. Paul. And that glass is so dark that even Jesus could not describe the conditions of life on the far side of death. All the Lord was prepared to do, Read reminds us in this Commemoration Day sermon, "is to give the absolute assurance that there *is* a resurrection, there *is* a heaven where God's will is done."

Still, most of us would like to know *something* about the nature of life in that heavenly sphere. Read for his part encourages us to follow the lead of the Bible in speaking at least about the resurrection of the body rather than the immortality of the soul. "Body" is the biblical word for the whole person. That whole person, the Gospel assures us, "is sown in humiliation but raised in glory . . . sown in the earth as an animal body but raised as a spiritual body."

But what does that mean? It certainly doesn't mean, Read hastens to say, "that these same bodies we have now are going to be put together again." It would, however, seem to mean that "in the new life beyond the grave we shall be the real people we are now, not phantom spirits identical in our invisibility; we shall be transformed but recognizably the same." This in turn would seem to imply that "we shall know others and be known by them in the life to come."

THE RESURRECTION OF THE BODY

A Sermon preached by David H. C. Read at Madison Avenue Presbyterian Church on All Saints Commemoration Day, November 3, 1985

Text: *"What is sown in the earth as a perishable thing is raised imperishable. Sown in humiliation, it is raised in glory; sown as an animal body, it is raised as a spiritual body."* 1 Corinthians 15:42–44 (NEB)

Readings: 1 Corinthians 15:35–49 (NEB); Luke 20:27–38

WHEN APPROACHING A TOPIC like the resurrection of the body or any other that has to do with the nature of life after death, I try to keep in mind the admonition of the great sixteenth-century Anglican Richard Hooker: "Dangerous were it for the feeble brain of man to wade far into the doings of the Most High . . . our safest eloquence concerning him is our silence . . . He is above and we upon earth; therefore it behooveth our words to be wary and few." Therefore in speaking about the resurrection of the body, my words will indeed be wary—and, within Presbyterian limits, I'll try to make them few.

Like all who have a bump of curiosity, I have from time to time wondered about conditions "over there," and asked the questions to which there seem to be no satisfactory answers. Gradually I have learned that we cannot possibly expect to understand much about life in a dimension beyond this mortal life of space and time. Even if someone were to return and attempt to describe it to us, we would be incapable of understanding. It would be like trying to describe the glorious fall colors to someone totally color blind. I realize now that this is why the Bible has so little to say about the nature of eternal life. The Old Testament has almost nothing on the subject. Jesus was very reticent. For instance, when confronted with the trick question about the woman who married seven brothers, one after the other, and was asked whose wife she would be in the resurrection, he replied that the question made no sense since conditions are so different in a dimension where mortal institutions like marriage no longer exist, and we shall be "like angels." That's as far as he would go in describing heaven; it's not very far since we have no idea of what angels are like. All Jesus would do is to give the absolute assurance that there *is* a resurrection, there *is* a heaven where God's will is done. "He is not a God of the dead," he said, "for all live unto him." That's a startling thought: for God there are no dead, those we call dead are alive in him.

We can be agnostic about the details of eternal life and refrain from taking literally the spectacular imagery of the Book of Revelation, and yet hang on to the ringing assurance of the Gospel that to know God now is to know him forever, and that Christ has conquered death. I would trade all the speculations of know-it-all preachers, or the evidences of psychic research, for these simple words of Christ: "In my father's house there are many rooms; if it were not so would I have told you that I go to prepare a place for you . . . I will come again and take you to myself that where I am you may be also." That's all I need to know about heaven—"where I am you may be also." Expand that thought, and do you need to know any more here and now?

But who is this "you"? We may be allowed that question. Is it the "you" that now exists, that strange combination of body, soul, and spirit? Or are we dissolved into something ethereal, invisible, and unrecognizable? The ancient Greeks held a doctrine of "the immortality of the soul." On the whole they held the body in contempt. It was something to be sloughed off at death to release the immortal soul. Eternal life was thus not a "communion of the saints," a fellowship of real people, but a community of souls in which individual personality is presumably lost.

Throughout the Bible we are seen as real people, each one of us known and loved by God. And since the body is the outward, visible means by which we can know and love one another it is treated with reverence and respect. "The Lord God formed man from the dust of the ground, and breathed into his nostrils the breath of life, and man became a living soul." The Bible portrays you and me as this mysterious body-soul creature, created and loved by God, and never speaks of the body, as the Greeks did, as a mere temporary prison for the soul from which we eventually escape. Therefore the eternal life we are promised is the recreation, the transformation, of the real you and me. Just as our souls are to be purified, so there will be new bodies through which they shine. For this Paul coined the paradoxical term a "spiritual body." It was, then, to proclaim the truth that in the life eternal we are not lost in some impersonal community of souls but raised up as real people, living persons, individual and recognizable, that the Church set in the Apostles' Creed these words: "I believe . . . in the resurrection of the body."

And gave a lot of Christian people trouble. In all my ministry I have had more questions about this than any other statement in the creed. Some bluntly say they can't accept it. Others confess that at this point in the creed they are tempted to cross their fingers. Well, it could have been omitted from the Apostles' Creed. The Nicene Creed simply has: "I look for the resurrection of the dead; and the life of the world to come." I usually find myself responding: "Well, you don't *have* to say it. You won't be thrown out of the Presbyterian Church for refusing to say it. But first let me ask if you're sure you know what it means."

It does *not* mean that these same bodies we have now are going to be put together again. Unfortunately, it was often interpreted in this way so that Christian people thought it all-important to have their bodies preserved and protected so that they could emerge at the right time and place and walk into heaven by the front door. When I was once in Jerusalem I was shown a graveyard reserved for those who could afford to be buried at the very spot where they expected Christ to come and revive them. This kind of thinking still infects the minds of those who attach enormous importance to the preservation of our mortal bodies, but can anyone who trusts in the God and Father of our Lord Jesus Christ really believe that he would differentiate in the life eternal between one who dies peacefully in bed and the other whose body is blown to pieces by a bomb? When I say "I believe in the resurrection of the body," I am not thinking of the literal reconstruction of the flesh and bones I now inhabit.

This is not just my private opinion. It is the point of this portion of Scripture we are listening to this morning. The Corinthians to whom Paul was writing were naturally trained to think like the Greek philosophers about the separation of the soul from this body. Therefore some of them when they heard about the resurrection assumed that the Church was saying that this old body would be put together again, and they were scandalized, just as many are today. Paul heard of these objections and didn't mince his words in replying. "You may ask, how are the dead raised? In what kind of body? How foolish!" (The King James' Version is nearer to the Greek: "Thou fool!")

He then concentrates on a simple illustration of the relationship of the body we have now to the body we shall have in the life eternal. He points out how, when we sow a seed in the ground it rots and dies: yet later it springs to life as a new and beautiful plant. "The seed you sow does not come to life unless it has first died; and what you sow is not the body that shall be . . . God clothes it with the body of his choice." Then he goes on to speak of the vast variety of these heavenly bodies corresponding to the variety we know here on earth. They are related to the earthly bodies but, he says, "The splendour of the heavenly bodies is one thing, the splendour of the earthly another." "What is sown in the earth as a perishable thing is raise imperishable. Sown in humiliation, it is raised in glory; sown in weakness, it is raised in power, sown as an animal body, it is raised as a spiritual body."

"A spiritual body." It is strange how this word of Scripture has been neglected by so many in the Church ever since. If we protest that we can't conceive what a spiritual body would be like, Paul's answer would be that of course we can't while we are still bound in this mortal life. What we can say about those who are in the new dimension of eternity is that, like the seed that has died, "God clothes it with the body of his choice." The plant is the same being (if I could put it this way) as the seed that has died, but it has now its unique and glorified body, just as the caterpillar is the same being as that magnificent butterfly that he will become.

"God clothes it with the body of his choice." This wonderful passage illumines for us the Christian view of life eternal. When we hear about this spiritual body that awaits us, this new clothing for the soul, we begin to realize how the doctrine of the resurrection of the body is richer and fuller than the affirmation of the immortality of the soul. It silences such questions as: "What age will we be in the resurrection life? Will babies be forever babies? Will the hundred year-old stay that way to all eternity? Will the handsome be frozen in their beauty and the deformed in their deformity?" God clothes us in the body of his choice—and I know that choice will be the best.

For me "the resurrection of the body" is an expression of my belief that in the new life beyond the grave we shall be the real people we are now, not phantom spirits identical in our invisibility: we shall be transformed but recognizably the same. Since it is with these bodies we have that we recognize one another it is my belief that we shall know others and be known by them in the life to come. It is this kind of life that awaits those who trust in the living God, and this kind of a life, far beyond our imaginings, that is now enjoyed by those whom we have loved here on earth and are now with Christ. As we worship this morning we are in communion, not only with our Lord, not only with one another here present, but with all the company of heaven who are gloriously and totally alive. "For this corruptible must put on incorruption, and this mortal must put on immortality, then shall be brought to pass the saying that is written, Death is swallowed up in victory . . . thanks be to God who giveth us the victory through Jesus Christ our Lord."

Thanksgiving:
The Smug and the Saintly

EDITOR'S INTRODUCTION

WHAT DOES A PREACHER say on Thanksgiving Sunday that hasn't already been said a hundred times before? Perhaps we shouldn't worry too much about repeating ourselves. We'll do well if we can just get the overall message straight and then stop before the pews start nodding. Still, it helps if we can come up with a new angle on the beloved old theme.

That's what David Read does in this sermon. With the help of a concordance, he conducted a little private poll amongst the characters reported in the Gospels as having given thanks. Surprisingly, he found, apart from Jesus himself, only two recorded instances of actual thanksgiving. The first is the classic story of Jesus' healing of the ten lepers with only one returning and falling down at Jesus' feet, "giving him thanks." The second expression of thanksgiving occurs when a Pharisee gives thanks to God that he is not like other men; "greedy, dishonest, adulterous, or, for that matter, like that tax collector." Read goes on to contrast the smug and the saintly. Both men are thankful but for wildly different reasons. The kind of thankfulness that the Lord prefers is obvious. Read's sermon, however, brings this old message alive in a fresh and captivating way.

THANKSGIVING: THE SMUG AND THE SAINTLY

A Sermon preached by David H. C. Read at St. James' Episcopal Church on Thanksgiving Day, November 22, 1984

Text: *"In that hour Jesus rejoiced in spirit, and said I thank thee, O Father, Lord of heaven and earth, that thou hast hid these things from the wise and prudent, and hast revealed them unto babes: even so, Father, for so it seemed good in thy sight."* Luke 10:21

JESUS SPEAKING—A SUDDEN EXCLAMATION of thanks to God. Seventy of his disciples had just returned from what could have been the first Christian mission. They had radiated the message of the Master and shared in his healing power. Now they were back to report and were ecstatic about the response of simple people and the signs of victory over the powers of darkness and disease. Jesus welcomes them joyfully. Then comes this flash of thanksgiving: "In that hour Jesus rejoiced in spirit, and said I thank thee, O Father, Lord of heaven and earth, that thou hast revealed them unto babes: even so, Father; for so it seemed good in thy sight."

This one glimpse into the soul of Jesus suggests that this was how he lived day by day. The bias of his mind, the instinctive movement of his heart, the inner melody of his life was thankfulness. From childhood he had absorbed the grateful spirit that rings through the Law and the Prophets of his people, and over his cradle hovered the song of praise: "My soul doth magnify the Lord, and my spirit hath rejoiced in my Savior." As he moved through the sunlight and the darkness, the joys and the agonies of his few years among us, his was a life of unswerving gratitude to his Father in heaven. We have many names of Jesus—the Lord, the Savior, the Man of Sorrows, the Liberator, the Man for Others. Do we forget that, beyond all others, he revealed this supreme quality of the saint—gratitude whatever happened. He was simply, purely, and, passing all understanding, the Grateful Man. So it is good to seek his presence as we reach another Thanksgiving Day as a people who try to be his disciples.

In preparation for this service I conducted a little private poll among the characters we find in the Gospels. With the aid of a concordance I sought to discover who among them were said to have given thanks. The result of my investigation was surprising. Apart from our Lord himself, I could only find two people of whom it was reported in so many words that "they gave thanks."

One of them is a favorite with all preachers on Thanksgiving Day and will, I'm sure, be occupying pulpits all over the country today. Luke tells us the story of the healing of ten lepers, and he notes that "one of them, when he saw that he was healed, turned back, and with a loud voice glorified God, and fell down on his face at Jesus' feet, giving him thanks" and, Luke can't help adding, "he was a Samaritan"—one of those whom many despised as illiterate and irreligious.

Somehow I had imagined that dozens of characters in the Gospel would be shown giving thanks to God. I'm sure many did, but their gratitude is not recorded. Yet here is this one cured leper who had what we might call the ordinary decency to turn back and thank the Healer. The sad disappointment of Jesus rings through the words: "Were there not ten cleansed, but where are the nine?" The other nine were surely rushing off to find their friends and spread the news of their cure. They were planning what to do with their new freedom and health. They were grabbing the gift they had been given with both hands—just as we do when good news comes our way, health, an unexpected gift, an experience of love, of beauty, or of sheer human kindness. That's where they are, the nine, living it up—and we disapprove.

But Jesus never lets us stay on the side lines disapproving. The last thing he wants is for a group of his disciples to gather in Church on Thanksgiving morning saying to ourselves: "Isn't it great to be one of those who returned to give thanks, and not to be out there with the nine who are thinking of nothing but having a good time with the turkeys and the booze?" "Where are the nine?" We have already confessed that, far too often, we are out there with the nine. Every one of us can call to mind right now good things that have happened to us for which we rarely pause to give thanks. We take for granted what our parents did for us, what wives and husbands do for us, the friends who nourish us in all kinds of ways, the huge network of people by whose skills and devotion food reaches our tables every day. We're not always ready for a "thank you" for the everyday courtesies we receive—the driver who holds back to let us join the traffic-stream, the bus-driver who stops to open the door again and let us in, the tired salesgirl who patiently answers our silly questions.

The saintly thankfulness of Jesus is reflected in this anonymous, one-out-of-nine, leper—about whom we know nothing except that he was "one of those," a Samaritan. For Jesus this simple grace of gratitude outweighed any judgment as to the religious or social status of this foreigner from beyond the pale.

The simple is the saintly. That's why I believe God welcomes today the genuine Thank yous that rise from grateful hearts whether in a service of worship, around the dinner table, or in the quiet of our room. Every pastor can tell you of the immense contribution made to any church by those who radiate a spirit of thanksgiving in all they say and do. We celebrate the various gifts of the Spirit that make a congregation into a lively and effective company of Christ. Among such gifts is this quiet and unnoticed one of constant thankfulness. Not only on Thanksgiving Day but often throughout the year, I find myself giving thanks for the thankful.

The second character who is recorded as giving thanks came as a shock to me. I found him in Luke's Gospel near the end of the story. There were the simple words: "God, I thank thee. . . . " And then what followed? "God, I thank thee, that I am not as other men are, extortioners, unjust, adulterers, or even as this tax collector." How about that for a prayer of thanksgiving? And is it at all that unusual? Jesus told the story of the Pharisee and the tax collector, we are told, for the benefit of those "who trusted in themselves that they were righteous, and despised others." (I am tempted to say that the prayer of the Pharisee sounds almost like a manifesto of the Moral Majority—but perhaps that would put me in the position of thanking God that I'm not like them.")

It's quite a trick of the devil to worm his way into our moments of thanksgiving to switch us from the saintly to the smug. If our gratitude is chiefly for material benefits, good health, and happy homes the temptation comes to listen to the voice that says: "You deserved it." There are traces in some of the psalms and in the book of Proverbs of that mood of self-congratulation, and we hear echoes of it today in what G. K. Chesterson described as the "easy speeches that comfort cruel men"—"I worked for it: I never fooled around: Thank God I'm where I am today." I'm not one who despises what is called the Puritan work ethic. I prefer it to the popular slacker-ethic or the chiseller-ethic. But Shakespeare's Malvolio is always hovering in the wings, so immensely grateful that he is not as other men are, like Toby Belch, for instance, with whose retort to Malvolio we feel some sympathy this Thanksgiving Day: "Dost thou think that, because thou art virtuous, there shall be no more cakes and ale?"

There was, I believe, a simple saintliness about those Puritans who gathered to feast in thanksgiving to God after that first hard year. They were not thanking God that they were not like those native Indians. Instead, they invited them to share their dinner. They were not thanking God that they were superior to every other people on earth, and therefore had been given a mighty land to conquer. They believed that they had been led to these shores on their pilgrimage as a people who humbly tried to serve their God and do his will and sought the promise given to Abraham that through them "shall all the families of the earth be blessed."

In these days of re-awakening patriotism, we need to remember that it can take two very different forms. There is the patriotism that consists in a deep and genuine love for the country of our birth or our adoption. This is the patriotism that rings through the Old Testament in the passionate attachment of the Jewish people to the land and its capital: "If I forget thee, O Jerusalem, let my right hand forget her cunning." This is the patriotism that inspired the noblest of the Greeks and Romans and made them seek the highest good for their people. It is the patriotism that has made the greatest leaders of our own country seek an America that is not only strong and courageous but also honorable, compassionate, and good. Thus we can give thanks to God today for all that we have derived from the good land we live in, and from the history of its great men and women to whose sacrificial lives we owe so much. To me, there is something sadly lacking in a man or woman who is unable to give thanks to God for their country, and I agree with Dr. Johnson when he writes: that man is little to be envied whose patriotism would not gain force upon the plain of Marathon, or whose piety would not grow warmer among the ruins of Iona."

The other kind of patriotism is totally different. It expresses a bigoted and lop-sided pride in one's own country combined with a mixture of fear and contempt for every other land. It says: "I thank God I am not like these other peoples with their strange languages and funny looks. I thank God that we are Number One." Such patriotism can be a mere disguise for ugly feelings of hatred and aggression that we would otherwise restrain. It was the false patriotism that the same Dr. Johnson had in mind when he called it "the last refuge of a scoundrel." Rudyard Kipling who was known as a vigorous and outspoken English patriot knew what this false patriotism could be and expressed it in his Recessional:

> "The tumult and the shouting dies;
> The captains and the kings depart;
> Still stands thine ancient sacrifice;
> A humble and a contrite heart."

It was the thankful response of the humble and the contrite that led Jesus to his own outburst of gratitude to God. "In that hour Jesus rejoiced in spirit, and said I thank thee, O Father, Lord of heaven and earth, that thou hast hid these things from the wise and prudent, and hast revealed them unto babes: even so, Father; for so it seemed good in thy sight."

May it be that spirit that we joyfully share this feast of thanksgiving, 1984, and now share in that "Eucharist" that unites us to the thankfulness of Christ.

The Season of Advent

Advent Parables:
Oil Crisis for the Bridesmaids

EDITOR'S INTRODUCTION

DAVID READ OFTEN SEIZED the season of Advent to preach a series of sermons under such titles as "Advent Voices," "Advent Answers," "Advent Encounters," "Advent Parables," and "Advent Grammar." This particular sermon, and the two following, are from his series "Advent Parables."

The Bible readings for this series are taken from the New English Bible translation, and one can see why. While the NRSV excels in elegance, there is nothing quite like the NEB for clarity and charm, especially when it comes to capturing Jesus' voice in the action-packed parables.

The sermon "Oil Crisis for the Bridesmaids" is based on the Parable of the Ten Virgins. This parable is especially topical as our world faces an over riding oil crisis. We simply don't have enough oil for our energy-drained, overpopulated world. At the same time, we have far too much oil as far as the ever-increasing, climate-damaging carbon deposits in the atmosphere are concerned. It is through this timely parable, then, that David Read brings the Advent message alive for us today.

The Bible readings are normally taken from the King James Version unless otherwise indicated.

ADVENT PARABLES: OIL CRISIS FOR THE BRIDESMAIDS

A Sermon preached by David H. C. Read at Madison Avenue Presbyterian Church on Advent Sunday, December 1, 1974

Text: Matthew 25:1–13 (NEB)

Readings: 1 Thessalonians 5:1–11 (NEB); Matthew 25:1–13

JESUS WAS A GREAT storyteller. That's one of the reasons why we read that "the common people heard him gladly." When he was talking, as he usually was, about life in the Kingdom of God, life under God's rule, what it means to reckon with God, in this world and the next, he told stories. The modern preacher is inclined to say things like: "The Kingdom of God is a concept of varying significance according as it is understood historically, sociologically, or eschatologically." Jesus said: "The Kingdom of God is like"—and then told a story.

Most of his stories are called parables. We tend to think that a parable is what we call today an illustration—one of these little stories that preachers work into their sermons to illuminate the point they are making. Last week, when speaking about hunger and making the point that anyone of us could find ourselves scrambling for bread if all supplies were cut off, I used an illustration from my experience as a POW. That wasn't a parable: it was an illustrative story. Jesus used illustrations too but the stories we call parables had another purpose and another shape.

Others think that parables are allegories. An allegory is a tale in which everything stands for something else. If that sounds confusing let me remind you of an allegory told by the prophet Nathan to King David. David had just had his notorious affair with Bathsheba, the wife of Uriah, whom he had then dispatched to the battlefield in such a way that he was bound to be killed. Nathan told the king a story about a rich man who had lots of flocks of sheep and a poor man who had only one ewe lamb which he loved like a child. When the rich man needed some roast lamb in a hurry he spared his own flocks and took the poor man's little pet animal. When David heard the story he was furious and said to Nathan: "As the Lord liveth, the man that hath done this thing shall surely die." And Nathan said to David, "Thou art the man." The rich man in the story stood for David; the poor man for Uriah; and the little ewe lamb for Bathsheba. Apart from some trimmings to the story, everything in an allegory like this fits. We say: "This stands for that, and this for that, and so on." Jesus used allegories occasionally, but his favorite form of story was the parable, and we may easily miss the point of a parable if we start allegorizing. When he made a point about prayer by telling the parable of the unjust judge "who cared nothing for God or man and finally gave in to the nagging of a widowed plaintiff," we get off on the wrong foot if we say that this judge stands for the God who listens to our prayers.

A parable is normally a story from real life which gets our attention by raising some unusual question, even evoking from us a protest about what happened. It is when we are pondering our question or our protest that a truth about the kingdom may begin to dawn on us. You can easily miss the point of a parable. An illustration is usually almost painfully plain and an allegory not hard to figure out. That's why Jesus spoke often about parables being "hidden" from the careless listener, found even his disciples slow to discover their meaning, and kept warning about the need to have ears to hear.

I've said all this because during Advent this year I want to listen again to four different parables of Jesus. When I say "listen" I mean that we should all let the parable speak to each one of us personally. It's much more important that you should hear the parable than the preacher, for not one of us can lay down the law and say: "This—and nothing else is what this parable means." It is part of my job to suggest what the parable meant to the writers and editors of the Gospels who were members of the first generation Church, and if possible, to get behind that to what Jesus originally intended it to convey. But no one can set limits to the power of these words to explode in the soul and challenge us to a new level of Christian obedience.

Here, then, is the parable, headlined in the King James' Bible as "The Parable of the Ten Virgins." Since the headlines in any Bible have no inspired authority, I'm offering you my own version: "Oil Crisis for the Bridesmaids" for that seems to me the nub of the story. Allegorists would immediately begin to play with the number ten—five and five—and find all kinds of hidden meaning in the numbers. I prefer to think that Jesus, telling a story about a wedding, from his own experience thought that ten was an average number of bridesmaids in what was obviously a first-class wedding party.

The first thing that strikes me is that he chooses a wedding party to illustrate the Kingdom of God. You will remember that Mark tells us that Jesus once said: "How shall we picture the Kingdom of God, or by what parable shall we describe it?" Well, more than once he deliberately decides to use the picture of a wedding. I'm not going to bore you with an elaborate description of the wedding customs of his day, but will just remind you that a marriage ceremony then not only lasted longer but was even more joyful and hilarious—not to say riotous—than any we know today. So Jesus must have surprised many of his hearers, and may surprise us today, by simply saying: "The Kingdom of God is like a wedding." If by the Kingdom of God he meant true religion, taking God seriously and living daily in his presence, this is not what the average man or woman would expect. From their observation of some aspects of Church life they would rather be inclined to say: "The Kingdom of God is like a funeral." "No," says Jesus, "like a wedding, a joyful, relaxed, love-dominated, uproarious wedding." This is what he came to offer everybody who would listen—a life of glorious freedom and fulfillment under God's rule, a life that has already the foretaste of the eternity where it will be fulfilled. "I am come," he said, "that they might have life, and that they might have it more abundantly." So he invites us to enter the Kingdom with the expectation that it will be at least as happy and refreshing experience as the singing and dancing at a glorious wedding party.

But the parable that begins on this startlingly happy note ends sadly. There's no getting away from that. Five of the girls missed the feast. They were arrayed in their finery and had with them the lamps which were an essential part of the ceremony of greeting the arrival of the bride and groom, but they neglected to take with them a supply of oil to replenish the lamps after the long wait. The Anchor Bible calls them the silly bridesmaids and the other five the sensible. When the crisis of the bridegroom's arrival in the middle of the night was upon them, the sensible naturally told the silly to run off and buy oil at the nearest store. If you protest that they were rather mean in not sharing what they had, I think Jesus would have answered: "I'm not telling you what they should have done, but what actually happened—so be quiet and listen to the story."

So, when they came back, "the door was shut." In these four words lie the tragedy of the story, and to my mind the point of the parable. We may not like the thought, but there's no doubt whatever that Jesus believed and taught that it is possible to miss the joyful experience of the Kingdom of God. It is possible to be so silly and so slack that when the critical moment comes the door is shut. Matthew ends the parable with the grim picture of the silly bridesmaids hammering at the door. "Sir, sir," they cried, "open the door for us." But he answered, "I declare, I do not know you." We are reminded of that other solemn saying: "Not everyone who calls me, 'Lord, Lord' will enter the kingdom of Heaven, but only those who do the will of my heavenly Father."

When Matthew inserted this story into his Gospel he probably had in mind the situation of the infant Church which was expecting an early return of the Lord Jesus in glory and judgment. A constant theme of the preaching in those days was that Christians should hold themselves in readiness for a sudden and dramatic re-appearance of Jesus to bring the present world order to an end and usher in his Kingdom in power. They believed firmly that the slack and the silly, the careless and the worldly-minded would then be shut out. Belief in this Second Coming of Christ has endured in the Church. We say that we believe "that he shall come to judge both the quick and the dead." Most conventional Christians have pushed that thought to the blurred edges of their belief, but it is significant that in times of great disturbance and insecurity, like ours, the doctrine of the Second Coming always reappears. I believe that it *is* true that history moves to a climax and that humanity, like the individual, faces in the end a death and resurrection. Whatever our thoughts may be about this Second Coming of Christ, we cannot escape the fact that we all face the crisis of death, and that there are other moments of crisis in our life and the life of nations, in which we are suddenly confronted with the reality of the Kingdom of God.

When Jesus told this story his hearers were confronted by the greatest crisis in world history, although the powers of his day, the rulers, the policy makers, the agitators, and the observers—seemed totally unaware of it. How many are aware of it today? The crisis was the advent here in our world of the Savior, the Son of God, the Word of grace made flesh, who was offering the Kingdom of God to all who would accept. He was the bridegroom and his invitation went out to all without distinction. He had not come simply to reinforce the ethics of the Old Testament or formulate some new code. He came to invite the religious and the irreligious, the respectable and the disreputable, the saint and the sinner, into his Kingdom. As he watched the crowds who had greeted him at first begin to fade away, as he saw the opposition mounting and the danger signals on every hand, his teaching took a more sombre turn, and his parables had the thrust of a rapier. As he moves to the Cross where he was to give his life in sacrifice for the whole human family and inaugurate the "new covenant" in his blood, he made his last appeal: "Here is your chance. Don't miss it. Don't wait till the door is shut."

If we feel like saying: "Well, I wasn't there when that great crisis struck, and the future crisis of his Second Coming means little to me," we still cannot escape the fact that he comes still in the great crises of our own experience. How easily we settle down to a minimum level of faith and hope, how subtly we allow our very familiarity with the truths of the Gospel to dull our spirits to the presence of Christ when he comes. There is an element of routine in Christian discipleship. The sensible bridesmaids, and not only the silly, "slumbered and slept" till the bridegroom arrived. But in that routine there is need for alertness, the preparedness, the expectancy of the true disciple. There was no oil crisis for the sensible when they suddenly awoke.

We say that the season of Advent is a preparation for Christmas. What do we mean by that? Is it a reminder that we should be buying those presents and mailing off these cards? Is it a preparation for conventional celebrations at home and in church? Advent means Coming, and the preparation above all others that is required of us is a readiness to meet the Lord as he comes to us. Who knows how he may come to the one who is alerted to the reality of his Kingdom and suddenly finds that the message of the carols is no ancient mythology but a piercing and glorious truth? Who knows how he may come to one who has been a typical agnostic if heart and mind are open at the moment of crisis?

"Don't miss it!" That's what this parable says to me. "Don't keep putting off the question of the Kingdom until it is too late, and the door is shut." It is Jesus who is speaking to us, this Jesus who keeps coming with his Kingdom in all the crises of our lives, this Jesus who has made possible for us a special meeting with him in the sacrament of his Supper.

Years ago it was a Presbyterian tradition to prepare for this Sacrament with prayer and fasting. Then the exercise was abbreviated to a Friday night service of preparation. It was a way of putting oil in the lamps so as to be ready for the bridegroom. With our custom of more frequent communion, in which I firmly believe, we run the risk of forgetting preparation, of even partaking of the bread and wine, in Paul's words, "not discerning the Lord's body."

Jesus comes to us here again this morning. He offers us this feast as a symbol of that great wedding feast that is his picture of the Kingdom. And his word again is: "Don't miss it; don't miss what I have to offer through indolence or carelessness or dullness of spirit."

> "King of kings, yet born of Mary,
> As of old on earth he stood,
> Lord of lords in human vesture,
> In the body and the blood,
> He will give to all the faithful
> His own self for heavenly food."

The door is open. Only if we are awake and alert can we meet this Lord, and know the joy of the wedding feast which is his Kingdom.

Advent Parables:
The Case Of The Troublesome Tenants

EDITOR'S INTRODUCTION

This Advent sermon holds ecological as well as Christological meaning for us today. When the owner's "own dear son" comes round to the vineyard to collect the rent from the vine-growers, they kill the son even as they had earlier killed the owner's messengers. What can the owner do now but come himself and put the tenants to death, giving the vineyard to others?

Ecological insensitivity is clearly one of the most obvious ways in which we prove today that we are irresponsible tenants of God's vineyard. And that irresponsibility, as we are slowly but surely learning from climate disasters, carries a death sentence for the offending vine-growers.

The climax of the parable, however, leaves us with the picture of the landlord shaking his head and saying "Surely they will reverence my son." Advent prepares the way for "the pleading of the Father who not only reminds us of our responsibilities, but offers us the companionship of his Son, and the renewing influence of his Spirit." Again the question is put to the vine-growers: "Surely they will reverence my son." David Read concludes this Advent sermon with the reminder of an even more basic question put to us at Christmastime: "Do you?"

ADVENT PARABLES: THE CASE OF THE TROUBLESOME TENANTS

A Sermon preached by David H. C. Read at Madison Avenue Presbyterian Church on December 8, 1974, Advent

Text: Mark 12:1–12

Readings: Isaiah 5:1–7; Mark 12:1–12 (NEB)

THERE WAS ONCE A church member who liked to come to worship every Sunday morning and always sat in the same pew. He loved to sing the most familiar hymns and to stand up and sit down at the usual times. Since he lived in a city where old buildings were always being torn down, in a country where old ways of thinking and behaving seemed to be rapidly disappearing, and in a world of great instability and insecurity, he liked to feel that there was one place at least where everything was as it used to be. So week by week as he worshipped the God of his fathers he expected to see the choir in the stalls, the Communion Table in the middle of the chancel, and the preacher, at the right time, in the pulpit. Then one day he came into church and found that everything was topsy-turvy. The choir had disappeared and their voices came floating down from the balcony behind him. The chancel was swept clean of the familiar objects and strange trappings confronted his indignant eyes. He had barely time to absorb all this when he found himself required to sing a hymn he had never heard before, and then, worst of all, to listen to a sermon delivered from his left and not his right, from a lectern and not a pulpit. At this point he reached for his coat to depart in protest when suddenly God said: "Just a minute. I fully understand that you like to worship me according to your habits and don't want to be distracted. We've a lot of good habits in heaven too, you know. But sometimes, just once in a while, it's good to break the routine. Even angels can get bored. I'm not just the God of your fathers, I'm also the God of your children—and they sometimes like a change. So just sit down again, and you'll perhaps hear my voice as you've never heard it before."

That, my friends, is a parable. It's not up to the standard of the parables of Jesus but the purpose is the same. Does anyone need an explanation? As with Jesus' parables we could argue for hours over the questions it raises but, since I wrote it myself, for once I can say with authority what the chief point of it is. It's just that occasionally all of us need to be shaken out of our religious routines, however good, so that we can hear God speaking in a fresh and vivid way.

Jesus used parables for exactly this purpose. The people he addressed were accustomed to sermons and expositions of Scripture and formal prayers. He never attacked these religious routines when they were sincerely performed, and was himself a regular worshipper at the synagogue. But to wake people up, to shake them into realizing that the things they professed to believe were really true, really demanding, literally a matter of life and death, he told stories—familiar stories with a new twist, original stories with highly controversial questions in them, stories to make people laugh, stories to make people cry, fascinating stories, crazy stories, simple stories, complicated stories, happy stories, shocking stories. And the parables often got through the defenses of the most sermon-proof class on earth—the ecclesiastics. After he told the story we are listening to this morning, we read that "they saw the parable was aimed at them."

It's ironic that we have succeeded in taming the parables of Jesus so that the very stories that should stab us spiritually awake have often been duly classified as the most familiar material in our Bible, whose content we know and whose meaning we know. One of our ways of doing this is to place the parable squarely in its historical setting. Sermon after sermon will explain just what the parable must have meant to those who heard it. We need this exercise, but it should only be preliminary to a brisk attempt to let the parable speak to *us*. When Matthew wrote "they saw that the parable was aimed at them" I wish he had added: "Do we see that the parable is aimed at *you*." These religious leaders had at least the insight to know that they were the target. Do we?

I can give you the historical setting and application in a couple of minutes. The thought of Israel as God's vineyard, his special possession entrusted to a people who were to be bearers of his message and witnesses to his truth, was familiar to Jesus' audience. The fifth chapter of Isaiah uses the metaphor dramatically. When Jesus spoke of the neglect of the vineyard by the tenants, he was echoing the constant theme of the prophets. And his hearers would immediately recognize these same prophets in the messengers that the lord of the vineyard sent. Some had even heard Jesus openly accuse them of their rejection of the prophets of old: "Woe unto you for you build the sepulchres of the prophets, and your fathers killed them."

When he went on to speak of the lord of the vineyard sending his own beloved son his hearers would know that he was making the audacious claim that he was the unique Son of God, and foretelling that they would also reject him and have him put to death.

The parable was spoken at a tense moment when Jesus was in Jerusalem for his last Passover Feast, and among his hearers were those who were planning to get rid of him. So when he indicated that disaster lay ahead for his people, but that out of it would come a new vineyard with new tenants they were stung to the quick. It was indeed a barbed story, told with amazing courage and prophetic insight. So much for the historical setting. Do we leave it there?

Nothing can be more smug and dangerous than to assume that we can leave this parable as a barb directed at the Jewish people of Jesus' time. We must confess that some of the most hideous pages in Christian history have been written by those who let the blame for the rejection of Jesus fall solely on the Jewish people, and have been deaf to his word of judgment on us all. Every single accusation that has been levelled at the contemporaries of Jesus—their blindness of God's presence, their evading of his law, their irresponsibility, their hypocrisy, their insensibility to human need—can equally be levelled in every age, including ours, against the community that calls itself Christian. Can we then, by the grace of God, see how this parable is aimed at us?

"A man planted a vineyard, and put a wall around it, hewed out a wine-press, and built a watchtower; then he let it out to vine-growers and went abroad." Here we have the usual realistic detail of a parable. If it were an allegory, as some scholars claim, we'd have quite a job figuring out what was meant by the wall, the wine-press and the watchtower. (I can just hear a sermon based on these three points!) We should also be left with the awkward picture of God as an absentee landlord. No, what's clearly conveyed here is the conviction that the human race, you and I, are not the owners of this world we inhabit but tenants. With one stroke we are in the middle of a major concern of our own day. Have we been behaving as responsible tenants of this fair earth or as owners who can deal with it, exploit it, quarrel over it according to our own sweet will? That's the burning religious question that underlies all our debates about ecology, conservation, and the distribution of the world's food supplies. Belief in God is often considered today as a personal idiosyncrasy with little practical consequence, like a taste for antique furniture or a fondness for vintage wines. Some believe; some don't—what does it matter? But this parable drives home the point that belief in God, genuine belief in God, must determine our behavior as occupants of this planet and our attitude to everything we have been given to use and to enjoy. If we believe in God we know that we are tenants here on earth, and not the owners. The strengthening of such a faith has practical consequences. To meditate and pray, to come with others to worship, to acknowledge our accountability, to receive pardon and to know the reconciling power of the Gospel—these things are not on the periphery of life but at the very center. If the human race is to throw overboard this allegiance as a useless relic of the past, with it goes the one great restraining influence against the despoiling of the earth, the exploitation of its resources, and a savage scramble for its diminishing returns. "You are tenants," says Jesus, "not lords of creation. To forget the owner is to open the floodgates to violence terror, and ultimate disaster."

Tenants. That's what we are, not only as passengers together on space-ship Earth, but as individuals. If I am asked: What's the difference between a believer and an unbeliever? I wouldn't lay stress on the capacity of one to accept a lot of doctrines that the other finds incredible. I would go straight to this question of responsibility, reverence, and thankful dependence. The choice is not between accepting and denying a bunch of theological proposi-tions, but between claiming complete dominion over our own lives and such of the world's goods as have come our way and acknowledging that life and all it has given us is the gift of God to whom we are responsible and must render an account: it is the difference between living as a tenant and living as the owner. That's all. And when the tenant idea takes possession it will determine a host of things—from our attitudes of conservation and world hunger to our use of the money and possessions God has committed to our care.

This is the basic thought behind Jesus' story of the troublesome ten-ants. These people behaved with complete irresponsibility. Worse still, they resented and resisted every warning they were sent. They not only refused to give the rent that was due but attacked the messengers and threw them out of the vineyard bruised, beaten, and even done to death. If this sounds like an improbable story we have to remind ourselves not only of the prophets of Israel to whom Jesus was clearly referring but of the way the world has treated—and still often treats, those who in the name of God cry out for a responsible and compassionate use of the riches of creation, or interfere with the selfish interests of any section of mankind.

Then comes the crisis, the center-point of the story. The lord of the vineyard, instead of immediately avenging his insulted and murdered mes-sengers, makes an extraordinary decision. "He had now only one left to send," the story goes on, "his own dear son. In the end he sent him. 'They will respect my son,' he said." As often in the parables of Jesus the natural response of those who are really listening is to say: "But that's crazy! What reasonable man would risk the life of his own son after he knew what these scoundrels had done to the messengers." It's so crazy that quite a number of commentators say that Jesus couldn't have uttered this part of the story. But this is exactly what he does time and again in his parables. He tells of someone acting so absurdly that we are forced to stop and ask: "What's the point?" Well, the point here reaches to the very heart of the Gospel. What we are being awakened to is nothing less than the absurdity of Christmas.

Have we let the conventional trappings of this season, our delight in the familiar carols and the unchanging tales of the angels, the shepherds, and the wise men, smother the fantastic, well-nigh incredible announcement of God's action in the birth of Jesus? What should the lord of the vineyard have done? we ask. Surely send a punitive expedition immediately. And what should God have done with his rebellious and murderous human race? Once in World War II, I was out for a walk outside my prison camp with a German guard. It was a beautifully, sunny, frosty winter day, and we both revelled in the quiet of a lovely countryside. Suddenly there was a droning noise, and a fleet of bombers appeared overhead. The fighters then swooped up to meet them, and the clear skies were criss-crossed with vapor trails as the machine guns opened up. One plane went hurtling down to the earth while the others went on to drop their bombs on the nearby town. The guard turned to me and shrugged his shoulders. "Mad," he said, "mankind is mad. The good God should have wiped them all out and begun again." That's what we may still feel like saying—except that we'd rather be around a little longer ourselves!

What should God have done? What he did was the unimaginable— to give himself in human form, his only son, born a helpless infant in the meanest surroundings at the very point in the world where the rivalries and tensions of the nations have been strangely focussed from that day to this. That's what he did. That's the kind of God we worship—one who "so loved the world that he gave his only begotten Son, that whosoever believes in him should not perish." If Jesus spoke of a crazy action by a distant landlord it should startle us into thinking how wildly improbable is the true message of Christmas. It is the ultimate appeal of a love "so amazing, so divine," that it demands "my soul, my life, my all." Our faith, then, is not simply in a Creator God to whom we owe obedience and respect. It is in a Redeemer God, who in spite of our disobedience has loved us so totally as to give himself in this Child who grew up among us: "full of grace and truth." "You are not your own. You are bought with a price."

"They will respect my Son." What fearful irony there is in these words on Jesus' lips a few days before they hanged him on a cross. "They will respect my Son." That he should dare to let such words echo, as they do, from the heart of the eternal God, is more than our minds or imaginations can bear. Yet from the Cross this love of God in Jesus streamed out into the world. And he is still here. Are we listening to him this Christmas? Do we still hear the pleading of the Father who not only reminds us of our responsibilities, but offers us the companionship of his Son, and the renewing influence of his Spirit?

The end is not yet. If the parable concludes with judgment it is to remind us that this gift of love was not in vain. Evil will run its course, but its doom is sealed. Last week at our full and lively meeting with our friends from Park East Synagogue, I was asked by one of them during the refreshments what Jesus meant by the question: "When the Son of Man comes will he find faith on earth?" (He was better acquainted with the contents of the

New Testament, I found, than many who are called Christians.) He said: "When Jesus first came he didn't succeed in establishing the Golden Rule on earth. Does he mean that if he comes again it will still be useless and mankind will go on quarrelling and fighting?"

There's not much leisure for a good theological reply between a cup of coffee and a kosher cookie, but I tried to say (with this sermon in mind) that we believe that, although indeed we have not responded well to the coming of Jesus, in the end his Golden Rule will prevail and evil will be vanquished.

That is the hope of Jew and Christian—that in the end the Messianic Kingdom will prevail. But for us worshippers here this morning what matters is our immediate response to the God who has again reminded us that all we have comes from him, to the God who is somehow pictured as that astonishing landlord who in the familiar version, said "Surely they will reverence my son." The question for us all this Christmas is: "Do you?"

Advent Parables:
The Forgiven Who Forgot

EDITOR'S INTRODUCTION

THE BROADWAY MUSICAL *GODSPELL* dramatizes Jesus' teachings and parables as recorded in the Gospel according to St. Matthew. The libretto for this highly entertaining show is lifted virtually straight out of Matthew's Gospel as translated by The New English Bible. There is no reason why this translation that works so well on stage won't also work well in the context of a worship service . . . if read with passion and animation.

Throughout his 1974 series of sermons on Advent Parables we find David Read exploiting the dramatic possibilities in the NEB renderings of some of Jesus' most action-packed parables. The story of the forgiven man who refuses to forgive others is particularly dramatic. And the message here is critical: "What God is willing to forgive us is infinitely more than anything we are called on to forgive in our fellow men and women."

This is the lesson that the forgiven in Jesus' parable forget. They forget the lesson because they forget that Jesus' teachings are based on his life. As Read reminds us, "We are to live a life of compassion, understanding, and love *because* this is the way God has treated us. We are to practice forgiveness among ourselves *because* God in his mercy offers to forgive us our sins."

ADVENT PARABLES: THE FORGIVEN WHO FORGOT

A Sermon preached by David H. C. Read at Madison Avenue
Presbyterian Church on December 22, 1974, Advent

Text: Matthew 18:21–35 (NEB)

Readings: Isaiah 40:1–11; Matthew 18:21–35

FIFTH AVENUE WAS CRAMMED with Christmas traffic. Loaded buses were
snaking their way through the log jams of cars and taxis while pedestrians
piled up at each red light. The shop windows sparkled with invitations to
buy anything from a rag doll to a mink coat. The skyscrapers were draped in
enough twinkling stars to delight the heart of Con Edison, and the crowds
surged along to the sound of tinkling bells and canned carols. Suddenly a
wisp of one of the carols caught my ear above the din.

> "Peace on earth and mercy mild,
> God and sinners reconciled."

For a moment the whole scene changed. These people on the sidewalks, these impatient drivers, these harassed salesmen, these elegant models, these stern figures behind the cash registers, these exuberant children,
these sandwich eaters in the drugstore windows—all became human beings
with the same needs, the same hopes and fears, as the shepherds at Bethlehem and the wise men on their camels. But, I couldn't help wondering, how
much of the meaning of Christmas—the word that is addressed to human
beings because they are human beings and not because they are executives
or taxi drivers or cashiers or models is getting through today? Did that busy
family negotiating the swinging doors into the big store hear that scrap of
song: "God and sinners reconciled?" If so, what on earth would it mean?
"Excuse me, sir," I imagined myself saying, "do you realize that this whole
festivity that brings you here is in honor of the birth of Jesus, and the birth
of Jesus meant that God and sinners were reconciled." "Some kind of a nut"
would probably be the response.

I was asked by a reporter on the telephone Wednesday what I felt was
the special emphasis of Christmas in this country this year. I didn't have the
quickness of mind to answer: "God and sinners reconciled," but I did indicate
that I felt the mood of the nation was more open to the understanding that
the real message of Christmas has nothing to do with our circumstances or
our relative affluence. It speaks of an assurance of God's love and care that is
even more real to us when conditions are difficult and material goods more

scarce. I don't want to mix with the crowd on the avenues as an old Christian curmudgeon deploring the gaiety and damning the commercialism, but I do long to see the Church really communicating the good news that God is still longing for his whole human family to accept the reconciliation that came with Jesus Christ. The anxieties and fears that lie behind the outward celebrations this year cannot be calmed by conventional words about peace and goodwill, or soothed by familiar tunes. They can only be resolved by the glad acceptance of the news that, as the New Testament says, "The grace of God has dawned upon the world with healing for all mankind."

This is a time for us in the churches not only to enjoy the old carols but to soak up their theology. Charles Wesley knew a good tune when he heard it, but he didn't write over 6,000 hymns just to provide words for the music. Like his brother John he was burning to convey the news of Jesus Christ, the inner music of the Gospel. And when he thought of Christmas and the angels' song the theme that exploded in his heart was that of our acceptance by the God we have so often ignored and defied: "God and sinners reconciled."

In recent years this theme has been too often pushed into the background. We give the impression that what the birth of Jesus meant is nothing more than the arrival of the world's best teacher of the way of love and peace. So our message becomes an exhortation to everybody to be more kind, more understanding, more compassionate, and more forgiving. How often have you been told that the world would be a different place if only we could spread the spirit of Christmas over the entire year. All this is true. We do celebrate the birth of the author of the Sermon on the Mount. We do need an infusion of the reconciling spirit and its diffusion throughout all sections of society. But the New Testament doesn't simply recommend a new way of life, or command a new kind of caring between human beings. It begins and ends with a triumphant word about what God has done, and speaks first and foremost of our reconciliation with him through Jesus Christ. Paul the apostle has much to say about how we should behave to one another, and his classic affirmation of Christian love still speaks to believers and unbelievers alike, but when he tells us that God has given us this ministry of reconciliation he goes to the heart of it with the words that "God was in Christ, reconciling the world to himself." "We pray you, in Christ's stead," he went on, "be reconciled to God." Behind all efforts at reconciliation in our world—in families, between races, and among the nations—there lies the question of our being reconciled to God.

The trouble is that for a long time in our culture this thought has not been very lively, even among Christians. How many in recent years have been desperately concerned about being reconciled to God? The flippant answer to the evangelist's question: "Have you made your peace with God?"

is "I didn't know we had ever quarrelled." The millions today who profess to believe in God are not given to admitting that they might not be on good terms with him. If they have some doubts about their sins it would seem that their attitude is like that of Voltaire who took the matter lightly: "Dieu? Pardonner, c'est son métier." "God? To forgive, that's his job."

That's what it looks like on the surface; but underneath the guilt has been building up. We know we are not the kind of people we ought to be. We know what a mess we are making of God's fair world, and how our human family is torn apart by hatreds, suspicions, fear, and violence. Increasingly, thinking people are aware that what is wrong cannot be put right by sociological or psychological techniques. It goes deeper. It has to do with our ultimate relationship to the God who made us, from whose commandments we have turned away in a titanic effort to be our own gods. This is the root of what the Bible means by sin—a word that has been trivialized by our pre-occupation with the specific moral lapses labelled "sins." The glory of the Christmas message of reconciliation begins to dawn on us only when we recognize that, individually and collectively, we are sinners. Our guilt before God, our indebtedness to him, is enormous.

Anyone who is serious about accepting the teaching of Jesus has to be willing to hear what he has to say on this very point. It's useless to say how much we admire his ethics unless we listen to the theology on which they are based. And that he makes crystal clear. We are to live, he says, a life of compassion, understanding, and love *because* this is the way God has treated us. We are to practice forgiveness among ourselves *because* God, in his mercy, offers to forgive us our sins. And this brings us, at last, to the parable.

I don't know any other story that Jesus told where the point is so obvious. As usual in his parables there is one point in the story where we are forced to sit up and take notice. In this parable of an oriental potentate who decided to have a day of reckoning with his stewards the spotlight falls on the man who owed his master an enormous sum—roughly the equivalent of ten million dollars. To his amazement he is totally forgiven and the debt cancelled. Then, on his way out of the presence his eye falls on a fellow servant who owed him a couple of hundred dollars. He grips him by the throat screaming: "Pay me what you owe." When the wretched man pleads for mercy he has him thrown into prison. The scene is compressed, pointed, and dramatic. Our attention is riveted on the disparity between the colossal sum this man is owed and the comparatively paltry sum he was owed, and on his astounding ingratitude and hardness of heart.

Could Jesus say more clearly that what God is willing to forgive us is infinitely more than anything we are called on to forgive in our fellow men and women? The almost incredible difference in the sum forgiven and the sum demanded is his way of saying that the mercy and reconciling love of God is so overwhelming that any forgiving we have to do must look trivial beside it. Have we yet learned to think this way? Let's put it in Christmas terms. This season often brings together family parties, and sometimes Uncle Joe may find himself sitting beside his sister Joan with whom he is not on speaking terms throughout most of the year. Once upon a time he handled the family finances in a way she considered totally unfair and unjust, and she wrote him a bitter letter. He was enraged, called her all kinds of names under his breath, and decided to break off all contacts. And now here they are and the hostess suggests that they sing a carol. "Hark the herald angels sing . . . God and sinners reconciled." If either of these two could for one moment realize the enormity of God's mercy celebrated in these lines, could really see how overwhelming is this reconciliation and forgiveness offered in this Jesus, could they possibly let that ancient feud loom up as something too great for their forgiveness, too vast for any reconciliation?

In this parable Jesus is pleading with us, not only at Christmas, but through every day of the year to keep in mind the vastness of our debt to this God of love so that we can see those offenses that rankle, those hurts we have nourished, shrink to their proper proportion. By our immediate shocked condemnation of this man in the parable we have judged ourselves. A Christian is by definition one who has experienced the forgiving grace of God in Jesus Christ. We receive it and give thanks for it every time we meet for worship. Then how, he asks, can we go on nourishing in our hearts grudges against other people, no matter how deeply we have been offended? There is no surer cure for an unforgiving spirit than a new realization of what God has done for us in the coming of the One who lived and died to reconcile us to the Father. Christmas is at heart a celebration of the mercy of God, the well nigh incredible gift of his Son to welcome us, in spite of all our sins, into the glad fellowship of the forgiven. "Blessed are the merciful; for they shall obtain mercy." The mercy we receive is the great motivation for the mercy we show. The Christian life is not so much a grim struggle to follow the commandment of love, as the spontaneous giving of love by one who knows how much we owe to the One who "so loved that he gave his only Son." This is what it means to live by grace—grace received and grace given.

The parable also makes it clear that it is impossible for anyone really to receive and experience the forgiveness of God if there is no willingness on their part to forgive. It is often asked what conditions are attached to the forgiveness of God. What must we do to be reconciled to him? The answer of the Gospel is "Nothing"—"nothing in my hands I bring." God's grace comes to us just as we are without waiting for any attempt to earn our salvation. It is sometimes added that, although this grace is freely given, it is conditional on our repentance. If this means that we must *want* to be forgiven, it is true. But in the Gospels I find only one condition spoken of by Jesus. And it's not so much a condition as a statement of fact. "You cannot be forgiven," he says and implies again and again, "if you have a totally unforgiving spirit."

Look again at what he says at the end of this parable. It ends roughly, you know, with this wretched man being condemned to torture. It's a parable, a story from real life, and that is the sort of thing that happened in such a society. But is there not a terrible truth lying behind these words? The unforgiving spirit, the one who harbors a grudge year after year, the man or woman who feasts on the venom of hate and bitterness, has indeed been delivered to the torturers. Jesus' words are forthright and awesome: "This is how my heavenly Father will deal with you, unless you each forgive your brother from your hearts."

A few weeks ago as we tried to face the fearful question of world hunger we found new meaning in the familiar prayer: "Give us this day our daily bread." I believe Jesus wants us to give new weight to the succeeding petition. After "give" comes "forgive." After thinking about our common human need for bread we concentrate on our common human need for forgiveness. "Forgive us our debts as we forgive our debtors." In effect he is telling us you cannot pray: "Forgive me my sins" unless you are in the position to say in all honesty: "as I forgive those who have offended me." Immediately after the Lord's Prayer in Matthew's version Jesus fastens on this one petition as if it were the one that we are liable to gloss over. "If you forgive others the wrongs they have done," he said, "your heavenly Father will also forgive you; but if you do not forgive others, then the wrongs you have done will not be forgiven by your Father."

Are we among the forgiven who forget? The one way in which the Christmas message of "God and sinners reconciled" can work like yeast throughout the year is for us to hear again, with all the authority of Jesus, the truth that the love, joy, and peace of the Gospel are granted to those who are willing to reflect this grace in their dealings with others.

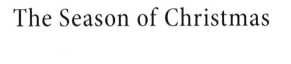
The Season of Christmas

Christmas Tales for All Ages

EDITOR'S INTRODUCTION

EACH YEAR ON THE Sunday before Christmas, David Read would abandon the custom of delivering a traditional sermon and instead offer the congregation a Christmas fantasy tale. His self-imposed rules were simple: (1) a genuine biblical theme must lie behind every Christmas fantasy; (2) the stories should have something for everyone, from the smallest child to the most sophisticated adult; and (3) they should link the "long ago" to the "here and now."

Simple rules, yes, but of course few preachers could produce such a homiletical feat and maintain it at such a high creative level. Read, however, wasn't showing off. He was simply trying to connect with people of all ages at Christmastime. In the process, he discovered that "the Good News can be heard through laughter such as many of Jesus' parables must have aroused."

Read's early Christmas stories were couched in prose, but increasingly they took the form of verse. What follows is an example of one of his Christmas tales in prose ("The Old, Old Man and The Baby"), and one in poetry ("The Poodle and the Stable: A Christmas Tale for All Ages").

Enjoy!

THE OLD, OLD MAN AND THE BABY

Christmas Eve, December 24, 1970

Reading: Luke 2:15–22; 25–35

ONCE UPON A TIME there lived a very old man in a little house not far from the temple in Jerusalem. His name was Simeon and no one ever called him anything else—not Mr. Simeon, or Lord Simeon, or MacSimeon, or O'Simeon, or Ben Simeon, but just Simeon. Sometimes a very little girl would call him Thimeon but, as he liked all children, he didn't mind. In fact, every time he went out of his house the children would come running from their homes or their games to go with him up the narrow street to the temple. And every day they would sing: "Happy birthday, dear Simeon, happy birthday to you!" for, you see, Simeon was so old that he had forgotten when his birthday was, and by singing this every day, they made sure that once a year it was bound to be the right day.

They had another song that they used to sing as they jumped around on the way to the temple. It went like this:

"Sing a song of Simeon,
Of love and hope and joy.
Sing a song of Simeon
And his little baby boy."

Now Simeon didn't have a little baby boy: he didn't have any children at all—that's why he loved to have so many around him. But he was always talking about a little baby boy. He would sit down on his doorstep from time to time and when all the children were around him he would tell them about the baby he was looking for. "One day," he would say, "a very wonderful baby is going to be born right here in our own country. He's not going to be born in a palace and have rich clothes and lots of people to wait on him, and he's not going to be born here by the temple where all the wise men are, and he's not going to be born over there in the citadel where the Roman soldiers live. There will be no trumpets blown to tell you that he has come into the world. His mother will not be a grand lady but will look like any of these girls you see passing up and down the street with the water pots on their heads."

And then one little boy would ask: "Then how are you going to find him?" And Simeon would smile into his long white beard and say: "That's my secret—but I'll know, I'll know." And then a little girl would ask, "What's going to be so special about this baby boy? Why do you want to see him before you die?" Simeon's eyes would light up, and he seemed to be look-ing a long way away. "He will love everybody," he said. Then a very stern, cross-looking man walked past, carrying a scroll of a book under his arm, and shooing the children out of his way. "Even the Pharisees?" "Yes, even the Pharisees." Then there was a loud shout and a clatter of hooves, and the children swarmed nearer to Simeon as a chariot came past driven by a big soldier with a long spear in one hand. "Even the Romans?" "Yes, even the Romans." Then they heard a bell ringing and at the end of the street a leper appeared and everyone was running away from him as fast as they could. "Even the lepers?" "Yes, even the lepers."

"But," said a little girl, "he won't have time to love everyone, and I'm sure if he were here now he'd be too busy to love *us*." "No," said Simeon, "he'll love you and you and you because he will especially like being with chil-dren." "What else will he do?" "He'll tell people about God and how they can talk to him, and how he takes care of them. He'll heal sick people, and he'll make cruel people kind, and greedy people generous. He won't be afraid of anybody, and he'll always speak the truth." "Then will everybody love him?" "No, they will not all love him. Some will even hate him, and before he is able to get old like me, they will kill him." Then they all groaned and said: "But that's a sad story. Why should all that happen to your little baby boy?" And Simeon would look very wise and say: "I don't know everything, but God has told me that it's not going to be a sad story and that someday men, women and children all over the world are going to be happy and sing songs because they have come to know this baby boy and the Man he became."

The children loved to hear Simeon talk about the baby he was looking for, but their fathers and mothers used to laugh, and tap their heads and say: "What? Listening to old Simeon again? It's time that old fellow went to join his ancestors." But Simeon didn't want to go and join his ancestors—not yet. And some days he used to take the children into his little house, where there was only a table, a chair and a bed, and show them an old Bible which he read every day. "That's where I read about the One who's coming," he would say, "and then I talk with God, and he has told me that I'm not going to die until I've seen him."

So Simeon got older and older. And new little children grew up to fol-low him up to the temple every day. He got to be ninety. Then ninety-one, and ninety-two, and ninety-three, and his beard got longer and longer and whiter and whiter, and sometimes the children had to help him up the steps. He always went to the same place. It was where the mothers came with little babies, just as they come with little babies here for baptism. He sat there watching, and then he would say, "Let me see the baby." And nearly always the mother would come over and lift up the shawl to let him look at her baby's face. Then Simeon would smile and say: "The Lord be with you," but when he came out into the street again he would shake his head and say: "No, that's not the One."

When he was ninety-four some of his old friends came to see him. "Simeon," they said, "the time has come to give up. There isn't going to be any baby like the one you're looking for. You needn't wait any longer. There are some lovely graves over there in the valley. Why don't you fold your arms and have a nice long sleep?" But Simeon just waved them away and got ready for another visit to the temple.

> When Simeon was ninety-five,
> They wondered why he stayed alive.
> When Simeon was ninety-six
> They said: "The old man's heart still ticks."
> When Simeon was ninety-seven
> They told him he should go to heaven.
> When Simeon was ninety-eight
> They said he was just obstinate.
> When Simeon was ninety-nine
> Something happened—hold the line!

. . . It was a cold winter evening, and Simeon was all muffled up in goatskins and sheepskins when he heard the children shouting outside the door: "Simeon! Simeon! There are three new babies at the temple." So, although he was very tired and very frail, Simeon pulled a heavy cloak around him and came out into the frosty street. Some tugged at his cloak from the front, others got behind and pulled and somehow they all arrived at the temple. In the dim sanctuary only one lamp was glowing, and they could see two mothers waiting, each with a baby in her arms. The children stood near the door and were suddenly very quiet.

Then a young mother stepped forward timidly and held up a little bundle. Simeon lifted up the shawl and gazed right into the eyes of a tiny baby. His own eyes began to shine as they always did when he looked at the children, but this time they became very bright, as if he were seeing right into the life of the baby—and far into the future. They all watched and strained their ears to hear what he would say. "Little baby," said Simeon, "You are going to grow up big and strong; you will be a great leader among men; you will be brave, although you will have to suffer much in the service of God."

When the children heard this, they couldn't help crying out: "Is it the One, Simeon? Is it the One?" But Simeon gently gave the child back to his mother and said sadly: "No, this is not the one. For he will not always be strong; he will not always be brave; sometimes he will tell lies, and sometimes he will lose his temper. He will be a great man—but this is not the One." Then he turned to the mother and said: "What is the name of this child?" And she said: "Simon." "That's like my name," said Simeon, "but it's going to be changed. When he is a man, they're going to call him Peter."

He sighed, and then looked expectantly at the second mother who was lifting up her baby to him. Again Simeon's eyes began to shine as he looked into the baby's eyes. The children and the mothers were hushed with excitement as the old man began to speak. "Little baby," he said, "you are going to grow up strong and beautiful. Many will love you, and you will have a great big heart of love. All over the world people will hear of the kind things you do." At these words a little boy became so excited that he began to shout: "This is the one! Simeon has found his baby boy!"

But Simeon smiled and said: "Alas, no. For this baby will not always love God. Sometimes there will be tears of sorrow, for this is not a perfect love I see. Besides," he added as he gently returned the child, "this is not a baby boy, it's a girl!" And with a twinkle he said: "What is the name of this child?" "Mary Magdalene," said her mother.

Slowly and sadly Simeon got up to go. Then he paused and said: "Didn't you tell me there were three babies? Where is the third? As if in answer, there was a little cry from a far corner of the sanctuary where the lamplight did not reach. And there on the ground a lovely young girl was kneeling with a baby in her arms. She was quietly praying, and as her lips moved a light seemed to shine around her and the child so that all around could see. She was simply dressed, and the baby had no beautiful shawl but was wrapped in a plain cloth. Simeon moved slowly across the sanctuary and knelt down beside them. Very gently he took the child, and suddenly his eyes filled with tears of joy. "It is the One," he said, "the One I've waited for all my life; the One who will be the leader of his people, the hope and light of the nations, the friend of children, the healer of the sick, the Savior who is Perfect Love." And with the child cradled in his arms he said: "I know the name of this child. You will call his name JESUS: for he shall save people from their sins."

Then, as they all gathered round, full of wonder and joy, he lifted up his eyes to God and said:

"Lord, now lettest thou thy servant depart in peace, according to thy word: for mine eyes have seen thy salvation, which thou hast prepared before the face of all people; a light to lighten the Gentiles, and the glory of thy people Israel."

Then the mothers with their babies went quietly out through the door and the children went jumping and laughing along the street to tell everyone the wonderful news. And, next morning, they found Simeon still in the temple. He was lying with his arms folded and his eyes closed, and on his face there was a smile of utter peace and contentment. And in the heavens the angels were singing and the trumpets were sounding for old Simeon had come to live with his God for ever.

THE POODLE IN THE STABLE: A CHRISTMAS TALE FOR ALL AGES

December 20, 1981, Christmas Sunday

Readings: Isaiah 11:1–9; Matthew 2:1–12

SOME DAYS AGO I was sitting in my study thinking about this Christmas story when I fell into a conversation with our dog Patches who always lies in her basket beside me when I am writing sermons. As you know, a conversation with a dog is always silent because they don't speak with their tongues but with their eyes, their noses, their ears, and their tails. So what Patches was saying was: "I suppose you're thinking about that story you tell at Christmas?"

I admitted that was in my mind. "This year," I told her, "it's going to be about a stable."

"Good," said Patches, thumping her tail, "I love stables—lovely, smelly places."

"But this was a very special stable," I said. "It was the stable where Jesus was born."

"I know all about that," said Patches with a faraway look in her eyes, "there were a lot of animals there, so it must have been a smelly stable."

"I hadn't thought much about the animals," I admitted, "though, now that you mention it, I have seen pictures of an ox and a donkey in that stable with Mary and Joseph and the baby Jesus."

"And chickens and pigeons and mice and rats," said Patches, licking her lips, "and, of course, a dog."

"A dog?" I asked.

"Naturally," she said, "did you ever hear of a farmyard without a dog? I'm sure if you look at one of the old Dutch paintings of that stable you'll find a dog. They even have them inside churches."

"There are some old tales about the ox and the donkey on Christmas Eve," I said, "but who ever heard of a dog?"

"It was a poodle," said Patches, pricking up her ears, "and if you'll close your eyes I'll tell you all about him."

So this was the story that Patches gave me, and I'm passing it on to you.

"Near a town in Judaea many winters ago,
Lay a farm, a poor farm, where little did grow
But some barley, some wheat, and a great many weeds.
They had only one ox and one ass for their needs.

So the wife of the farmer took in paying guests,
And at festival times there were many requests.
Thus they added more bedrooms outside and within,
And painted their farmhouse and called it an inn.
They made money this way, they were well patronized.
(In those days their products were not subsidized.)

"One night in December there came to the door
A poor man and his wife, travel-stained and sore.
They asked for a bed and the farmer said: 'Maybe
You think I don't see she's expecting a baby.
We cannot risk people like you round our table.
Be off! And make do with the straw in the stable.'

"So Mary and Joseph just ceased to implore
And trailed over the yard to the old stable door.
But now they were in for a series of shocks,
There stood in the doorway a ponderous ox.
So Mary said gently: "Dear ox, let us pass."
But he bellowed: "You think that I'd be such an ass—
Excuse me dear colleague, I hope you don't mind"
He said to an ass in the stable behind—
'Such a fool as to budge while I like where I am:
You can freeze in the yard, and I don't give a damn
If your baby is born in the slime and the mud,
Don't bother me now while I'm chewing my cud.'
So Hector the ox barred the way to the manger,
For Hector was selfish and hated a stranger
Who came to disturb him and give him a nudge.
So he chewed and he chewed, and he just wouldn't budge."

Patches paused and went to lap up some water.
"So that was the ox," I said, "and he wasn't very helpful."
"No" said Patches, "Hector just didn't want to be bothered. He used to say he was a peace-lover, but everybody knew whose peace he loved most."
"Like some people I know," I remarked.
"Like you," said Patches "when *you* want to lie back with a book, and *I* want a game with my ball."

"Get on with the story," I said, "how did Mary and Joseph get into the stable?"

"There was another door," said Patches, "and that's where Droopy was."

"Who was Droopy?" I asked her.

"The donkey," said Patches. "Listen while I tell you about her."

"Right there behind the other door
(Which I have told you of before)
Stood Droopy with her hanging ears,
And both her eyes were filled with tears.
She made no move to block their way
But sadly munched a bunch of hay.
'Droopy,' said Joseph, 'Please be kind,
For we need hay, and would you mind
If Mary here could rest till morning—
For there's a little child aborning?'
Said Droopy, 'So you want my hay?
I tell you, always that's the way
It goes. It's always *me* who's giving.
They are the ones who're really living.
I am the one who's always losing.
They are the ones who have the choosing.
So now you want my food for bedding?
It's in *my* bedroom that you're spreading
Your swaddling for the Babe who's heading
Here—the moment you were dreading.
Now when *they* celebrate a wedding
They make me carry portly brides
Who weigh like lead on my insides.
And never can I whet my whistle
Or munch upon a wayside thistle.
And when this donkey dares to venture
A Hee-haw! And expose his denture,
The children mock me as I pass,
And cry out: 'What a silly ass!'
That's what a wretched ass endures
My woes are so much worse than yours.'"

"So they still didn't have a place for the baby to lie?" I asked Patches.

"No," she said, "Droopy was so sorry for herself, she couldn't think about anyone else's troubles."

"Like some people I know," I said.

"Like *you*," said Patches, "when you have a cold in your head and don't notice that I've got a tick on my tummy."

"Get on with the story," I said.

"All right," said Patches, twitching her nose, "Now let me tell you about Percy."

"Percy?" I asked.

"The Poodle. Only a poodle would have a name like that. I told you there was a poodle in the stable. Let me tell you what he was like."

> "Percy was frisky and prancy and proud;
> Percy chased rabbits and rats in the dark.
> He was clever at begging and richly endowed
> With a piercing, long distance professional bark.
> Most people liked Percy. He was handsome and clean,
> And never had fleas, or distemper, or rabies.
> He liked little children and never was mean
> To kittens or puppies—and never bit babies.
> But Percy, alas, had one serious flaw;
> He was terribly, terribly, terribly greedy.
> When he held a big bone on the ground with his paw,
> He growled and he snuffled: his eyes became beady.
> No matter how big were the bones he was chewing,
> He would never leave any for those who were lacking,
> When he'd had enough and the kittens were mewing
> For scraps with a snarl he would send them all packing."

"Not a very nice dog," I said.

"Oh, he was all right," sniffed Patches, "but he had that one big trouble. He would never give away even what he didn't need."

"Like some people I know," I added.

"Like *you*" said Patches. "There's that cupboard in your room where I like to snooze. There are clothes in there you never use—and you've never given them away."

"Get on with the story," I said.

"All right" said Patches.

"Back to the stable
Where I hope you'll be able
To follow my fable,
And see how that poodle
Caused such a flapdoodle
Among the caboodle—"

"Slow down!" I ordered, "or I *won't* follow your fable."
Patches stopped panting and a dreamy look came into her eyes.
"It was wonderful," she said. "Listen."

"Hector stood chewing and blocking the door,
Droopy was sighing and grumbling some more,
When suddenly Joseph knelt down in the straw,
And, rejoicing, could hardly believe what he saw.
The baby was there, and his heart glowed with joy,
As he clasped in his arms an adorable boy.
'Mary, dear Mary,' he said, 'He is here—
The One you were promised: God's love has drawn near.
Now where shall we put him to shield him from danger?
Look, why don't we lay him to sleep in that manger?'
He lifted the baby and muttered: 'My darling,
your crib.' when exploded a terrible snarling.
From the manger there issued a volley of barks,
And some quite unrepeatable doggy remarks.
Now who do you think was this dog without mercy?
You've guessed it—none other than greedy, old Percy.
Now Percy had jumped in the manger that night
Just for fun, not to sleep—it was too rough and tight.
He hadn't the slightest desire for that manger,
But he wouldn't vacate it for this little stranger.
So he barked and he bristled like a cross porcupine,
And snarled: "You can't have it—it's mine, mine, mine, mine.
Anyone who comes near is in terrible danger
For I'm the original dog in the manger."

"Then what happened?" I asked. "You can't leave the story there, you
know."
"What happened," said Patches with her eyes shining, "was a miracle."

"I know it was a miracle when the Son of God was born," I said.

"Yes," said Patches, "but there was another miracle, a lot of miracles, and they have gone on happening ever since. Some have even happened to you. Listen."

> "Across the fields some distant bells were ringing,
> And in the stable everyone fell still,
> Except for angel voices softly singing
> Of peace and joy to all who have goodwill.
> Amid the straw a light began to shine,
> A light that drew some shepherds for their flocks,
> And Droopy in his corner ceased to whine,
> And kneeling by the manger was the ox.
> The poodle left the manger with a leap,
> And power-wagged his tail as if to show
> That those who really needed it could keep
> On using it for ever. Do you know
> A miracle like that when someone ceases
> To be so greedy or so cross and whining?
> It is God's Christmas Spirit that releases
> A power to change, a bright and inner shining.
> This is the endless miracle of mercy
> That makes all other miracles seem dim,
> So when we think of Hector, Droopy and Percy,
> Who are really us, you know, we pray to him
> That daily we may find afresh the grace,
> That comes when we meet Jesus face to face."

"We can all be like that," I said, "and not just at Christmas."

"Amen," said Patches.

"How Silently"

MAPC's Christmas Eve service in 1985 included extra Christmas music, the celebration of the Lord's Supper, and this brief Christmas meditation by David Read.

WE ARE A NOISY generation and we live in what seems like the noisiest city in the world. That may be one of the reasons you are here tonight. There's a stillness in a church on Christmas Eve—although I won't guarantee that before I've finished speaking we will not have heard a scream of brakes, a wail of an ambulance, or even the sound of a gunshot. We live with noise—roaring buses, clattering subways, screaming jets, rasping voices, the cacophony of pneumatic drills, klaxons and garbage trucks. And if we flee to the park for escape someone will be sure to follow us with a blaring stereo.

If we think we are the only generation to suffer from the din and distraction of a frenetic world, and complain that the glitter and the noise seal us off from a vision of the spiritual or the voice of God, we should have another look at the Bible. It's full of the fearful rumblings of nature, the clash of armies, the bellowing of tyrants, and the rioting of crowds. In one little psalm I find these cameos of discord and doom. "Though the earth be removed, and though the mountains be carried into the midst of the sea; though the waters thereof roar and be troubled, though the mountains shake with the swelling thereof. . . . the heathen raged, the kingdoms were moved. . . . What desolations He hath made in the earth . . . He breaketh the bow, and cutteth the spear in sunder; He burneth the chariots in the fire." Yet through these alarms and threatening noises we keep hearing of the God in whom we can trust. He is "our refuge and strength, a very present help in trouble . . . the Lord of hosts is with us; the God of Jacob is our refuge." It is He who "maketh wars to cease unto the ends of the earth." How does the writer find his God through the noise of this alarming world? Is he telling us that, no matter how loud the shouts of the secular powers, God can shout louder? Is he calling on believers to make more noise than the unbelievers?

Some seem to think so. For you must have noticed that in recent years religion, instead of calming the storms has often only added to the din. I'm not thinking of the attempt to compete with rock music at full blast, with canned carols turned up full volume. I'm thinking of the screaming voices on the air working up crowds to a frenzy with a waving Bible and shouts of "Hallelujah" and threats of Armageddon. Those who are seeking the signs of the spiritual in our secular bedlam are being offered a religion that can outshout the unbelievers, and add fuel to the fires of anxiety and distress.

I wonder if you know how this psalm I have been quoting ends? There is neither a bang nor a whimper. Instead come these calming and penetrating words from the Lord God almighty: "Be still, and know that I am God." The psalmist has found what you and I can find—what T. S. Eliot called "the still point of the turning world."

"Be still." What does that mean? At first it seems to offer little more than just one of these admonitions that we know to be excellent but feel totally beyond our reach. A doctor, psychiatrist, or pastor confronted with someone shattered by the stress of our noisy world, would feel cheated if the only advice given was just "Relax." Yet this is just what the psalmist means without benefit of the jargon of the textbooks of modern counselling. He means that we have to let another voice, a quiet but powerful voice, be heard through the din. All through the tumult and shouting of his poem he weaves in the thought of the God who is, after all, in charge. We can't relax at a word of command, but we can, perhaps gradually, learn to listen to the voice of the Lord who loves us. The prophet Elijah, in a moment of deepest depression, heard the roaring of the elements, and the rumblings of doom. And what are we told? "A great and strong wind rent the mountains, and brake in pieces the rocks before the Lord; but the Lord was not in the wind: and after the wind an earthquake; but the Lord was not in the earthquake; and after the earthquake a fire; but the Lord was not in the fire; and after the fire a still, small voice." It was when he was reached by the still small voice that Elijah recovered his faith in the sovereign God and went back to his appointed task.

"Be still." The word comes also to those who are searching desperately to find some answer to their search for a faith to live by, to those who are reaching out in all directions for answers to their religious questions, and also to those, like me, who try to offer all kinds of arguments for believing in God. At this point it is good to know that the words of this text can equally well be translated: "Shut up! And know that I am God." Many of us are plagued by the noise of our own thoughts when seeking God. Others allow their incessant "Why does God allow this?" or, "Couldn't God have made a better world?" or, "Why did this have to happen to me?" to keep ringing in their inward ear. To all of us when we allow these questions to dominate our minds the Lord may well be saying: "Shut up! And know that I am God." I don't know about you but I do need that reminder: *I* am not God.

Tonight we are beautifully reminded that God himself does not choose to win us over by making a bigger noise. The greatest event in history, the coming of God himself to the rescue of his human family was not accompanied by the evidences of his power and might. There was no mighty thunderstorm, no earthquake, no flames of fire, no Nuremberg rally when the Savior was born. It happened in an obscure corner of the Roman Empire. It happened in a little town, in a stable, in the body of a homeless peasant girl. The birth was not announced in flaring headlines, but in the hearts of simple people who could hear the sound of angels.

> "How silently, how silently,
> The wondrous gift is given,
> So God imparts to human hearts
> The blessings of his heaven.
> No ear may hear his coming,
> But in this world of sin,
> Where meek souls will receive him, still
> The dear Christ enters in."

And so, in this mid-Manhattan stillness, God speaks in the music, the story, and the bread and wine, saying to each one of us: "Be still, and know that I am God."

P. S. God Loves You

EDITOR'S INTRODUCTION

THIS WAS DAVID READ's final sermon before retiring after sixty-three years in the ministry. The Scripture readings that day included:

1. A consoling passage from the Old Testament in which the prophet Zephaniah encourages Israel to rejoice and exult with all her heart, knowing that the Lord is in her midst and "will renew her in his love."

2. A reassuring passage from Paul's letter to the Romans in which the apostle claims that nothing in all creation can separate us from "the love of God in Christ Jesus our Lord."

3. An emblematic Gospel lesson showing Jesus lovingly defending a woman of the streets who had anointed his feet with an expensive jar of perfume and dried them with her hair.

The sermon as a whole finds David Read fleshing out the message of God's indiscriminate love in Jesus' life, God's undeserved love in Jesus' death, and God's unending love in Jesus' resurrection.

P. S. GOD LOVES YOU

A Sermon preached by David H. C. Read at Madison Avenue
Presbyterian Church on December 31, 1989

Text: *"For I am persuaded, that neither death, nor life, nor angels, nor prin-*
cipalities, nor powers, nor things present, nor things to come, nor height,
nor depth, nor any other creature shall be able to separate us from the
love of God, which is in Christ Jesus our Lord." Romans 8:38, 39

Readings: Zephaniah 3:14–17 (RSV); Romans 8:31–39 (KJV); Luke
7:36–50 (NEB)

IF, BY A MIRACLE, there should be any in this church this morning old
enough, strong enough, and sufficiently long-suffering to have heard every
one of the 1490-plus different sermons I have preached from this pulpit
since 1956, they might tell you that I have cited this text probably more
often than any other. So let me use it again—not, as I am often tempted to
do at the end, but at the beginning. It could be, if you like, what Paul himself
called "a lovely legacy."

One day about thirty years ago I was driving with an old friend down
Park Avenue to see him off at Grand Central. He was Dr. D. T. Niles, a native of Sri Lanka, who, after years serving the Methodist Church in that
predominately Buddhist island, was at this time the Director of Evangelism
for the World Council of Churches. In that capacity he had come to Edinburgh when I was chaplain there to conduct a Christian mission—the first
time but certainly not the last that a missionary from the Third World had
come to evangelize Scottish students. So we had a lot to talk about as we
sped down the avenue, and that taxi driver must have heard more about
the task of preaching in a changing world than he wanted to know. As we
drew up at the station, and I said goodbye, not knowing that he had only
a few more years to live, he poked his head back in and said: "There's only
one thing to say, David, only one thing to say to a world like ours: God loves
you. That's all. That's what people need to know and that's what the Church
has to tell them. God loves you. Goodbye." After a vigorous discussion of the
preacher's task this was his P.S. And today it is mine to you: "God loves you."

Since it's a day for favorite texts, it also can be a day for favorite stories.
One of these, you will not be surprised to hear, is about the one whom I
consider the greatest theologian of this century, and he saw most of it. Karl
Barth, on his one and only visit to this country, was asked a question after
a lecture by an exceptionally daring student. "Dr. Barth," he said, "you have

written enormous volumes of your 'Dogmatics' with more to come. Could you summarize for us in one sentence what you are trying to say?" Barth thought for a moment, then smiled, and said in his hesitant English, "Ya: Jesus loves me/This I know/ For the Bible tells me so." There may have been a twinkle in his eye, but this *was* the basis and content of his theology—a living, loving God, and the Bible was his authority. And so it has been for me as a preacher and pastor: "Nothing can separate us from the love of God, which is in Christ Jesus our Lord."

If that sounds simple, so be it. Jesus was simple and liked simple people. God forgive me for the times I have forgotten that. But if it sounds simplistic and sentimental, then we've got it wrong. This Gospel of God's love is profound enough to exercise the minds of the greatest thinkers the world has ever known. It is strong enough to pierce to the depths of the human heart. As the apostle says: "The word of God is alive and active. It cuts more keenly than any two-edged sword, piercing so deeply that it divides soul and spirit, joints and marrow; it discriminates among the purposes and thoughts of the heart." The love of Christ is broad enough to include everyone from the saint to the tyrant; the billionaire to the beggar; the loved to the despised and hated; the idealist to the cynic; the adored to the forgotten. And it is vast enough to let us feel that we have only touched the hem of his garment and need eternity to explore the "unsearchable riches of Christ."

When I think today of preachers who have helped, and are still helping me to keep this Gospel of love central in my mind and heart and have persuaded me that nothing in all creation can separate us from the grip of God's love, I am amazed at their variety over the years. I think of Graham Scroggie, a Baptist whose preaching robe was wafted by an angel onto my shoulders on the 10th; and at the same time I am thinking of Bryan Green, an Anglican; J. S. Stewart, a Presbyterian; and, in recent years, Freddie Buechner, an agnostic turned Presbyterian; and Walter Burghardt, a Jesuit, whose latest book of sermons is by my bedside right now. I could add hundreds of names—and what an extraordinary assembly they would be at any party! Only one thing would link them together—a common conviction of the active love of God for his whole human family, and a desire that others would be drawn into the company of those "with eyes fixed on Jesus, the pioneer and perfecter of faith."

I've been thinking: For many today the announcement that God is love is an empty cliché—not a thought to stimulate the mind, a slogan to stir the blood and send us marching to make a better world, or a cry to wrench the emotions and send us dancing on the Berlin Wall. Hear what Shakespeare can do with four little words, as a bruised and battered Shylock slinks away from the kangaroo court of his enemies: "I am not well." We may ask: Is there anything to entice anyone to seek out a church today to hear some variation on the theme that God is love.

In this coming decade, probably the most exciting world-changing period to live in in modern history, is the church going to be out there on the margin, living on a cliche? Especially a highly controversial cliché, for who, taking a hard look at the kind of world we live in, with its confusions, its violence, its injustice, and the unfairness of "bad things happening to good people," would not want to dispute that a God of love is in charge?

But does not the Bible tell me so? Yes; the phrase occurs exactly once—in the first Epistle of John. But there it isn't a proposition to be discussed, it is a way of life to be accepted. "God is love; he who dwells in love is dwelling in God, and God in him." We don't come to worship to meditate on a proposition but to meet divine love that is alive, active, personal, seeking to draw us into the community of love which alone can give meaning, guidance, hope, and direction for our lives. We are not here, and the Church is not spread across the world, to discuss a cliche, but to find a conviction to live by. The Bible brings us the miracle of God in action. In its pages men and women like us meet him—in their homes, their joys and sorrows, their adventures and misadventures, in the silence of the desert or the thunder of Mount Sinai, in the voice of a prophet, or the song of a psalmist. You could say that in the Bible God is not a noun but a verb. He is alive; he speaks; he thinks; he cares, and he takes sides; he plans, and he reigns—but above all he loves. The message of the Bible is not "God is love" but "God loves you."

God loves you *indiscriminately*. That's what a deeply personal love means. God loves you as you are, without waiting for you to become a better man or woman. That's what Jesus shows us. He loved the happy family of Mary, Martha, and Lazarus. He loved Nicodemus the kindly, sincere Pharisee, and the eager young man who tried to keep the commandments and wanted to know how to get eternal life. He also loved the disreputable characters who stayed away from the synagogue and lived it up. He even went to their parties; he loved the flippant divorcee he met at the well; Mary Magdalene the call girl; the Roman officer whose servant was ill; the lepers, the bureaucrats and the tax collectors. He even loved the crowd, even the crowd that shouted for his death. No one is excluded from "this love of God which is in Christ Jesus our Lord." We can only exclude ourselves.

And the love of God is *undeserved*. Does anyone who has ever been truly in love imagine that they have won that love because of their lovable qualities, that they have earned the right to be loved? To use a favorite word from the New Testament, it's pure grace. Jesus wiped out any notion of earning our salvation. Paul caught the essence of the Gospel when he said: "It was while we were still helpless that, at the appointed time, Christ died for the wicked. Even for a just man one of us would hardly die, though perhaps for a good man one might actually brave death; but Christ died for us when we were yet sinners, *and that is God's proof of his love for us.*" John put it his way when he wrote: "This is what love really is: not that we have loved God, but he loved us, and sent his Son as a sacrifice to atone for our sin. If God has loved us, my dear friends, we must love one another." We don't love one another to enable God to love us, but *because* we cannot help responding to his love which is already given. The more we realize how much God has loved us, the more naturally, instinctively, and without self-congratulation, we express that love to others.

Then we discover that God's love is *forever*. There is a little word in the Old Testament—chesed—which has always bothered the translators. The King James Version often used "mercy," and, even more often that beautiful word that stays with all who were raised on this translation, "loving-kind-ness." But "chesed" means more than the mercy of God in coming to our rescue in time of need. It means more than the "loving-kindness" of a heav-enly Father. It contains the vibrant note of God's utter faithfulness, his un-breakable and unshakable commitment to his covenant of love. The scholars who sought to express this in the Revised Standard Version came up with an expression that is probably nearer to the original than any other—the stac-cato "Steadfast love." (Sometimes, you know, we must sacrifice beauty for accuracy.") This is what I mean when I say "God loves you." This is the faith in which the truest Christians I have known have lived and died—that the love of God is forever, like Shakespeare's words about real friendship, he has "Grappled us to his soul with hoops of steel." And that, my friends, is why I cannot, even while holding to the truth of a judgment to come, accept the doctrines of an eternal hell. The immortal hymn to love in first Corinthians 13 contains the words "Love never ends."

That thought brings light to those dark moments which come to nearly every believer when the love of God seems blotted out by some fearful, and apparently utterly meaningless series of personal blows to the heart. Liv-ing in confidence that God loves you is not always a joy trip through the accidents of life. Among my Christmas cards this year was an extra one the sender wanted to share with me. It contained simply these words that offer an accurate translation of a verse in our Old Testament reading this morning. It reads: "He is silently planning for thee in love." And those plans include the eternal dimension, for "eye hath not seem, nor ear heard, neither have entered into the heart of man, the things which God hath prepared for them that love him."

This is an open-ended sermon. There is so much more I could say about the love of God and how it is reflected and sustained in the community of love which is his Church. For this beloved congregation this is a time of transition—hardly an original remark, first made, I believe by Adam and Eve, as they left the Garden of Eden. Robert Burns, whose birthday, like mine, falls this month, said it once and for all: "The best laid plans of mice and men gang oft agley." My own plans are not set in concrete. Friends of mine in ministry have told how within a few years their plans for retirement were totally disrupted. I am content that he is silently planning for me and my family in love.

Much more important is the future of this church poised in this challenging city that is crying out for love, called to proclaim and live out the Gospel of God's love at a turning point in history. I believe that he is silently planning for you in love. And it is your trust in that love, your reflection of that love, which will not only keep the tradition of lively worship, and loving service that is the glorious tradition of MAPC, but will evoke new loyalties and wisdom during the time of transition, and kindle a new flame here on this corner, as every one of you fulfils the vow to serve this church "with energy, intelligence, imagination and love."

It remains for me to try to express the inexpressible—my simple, joyful thanks for the love, and amazing grace, that has sustained me as your pastor over these exacting but joyful years. Where else could Pat and I have found such a blessed company of saints and sinners from every walk of life whose friendship, loyalty, stimulation, humor, and love kept us going, and will go with us forever. These last few weeks we have felt as a family as if we were being carried out of this place on a tide of love. For the meticulously prepared and joyful celebrations, my profoundest thanks, for mistakes, follies, or failures in love, please, your forgiveness; and for all of us let this be an occasion for joy, hope, and the forward look—since nothing can separate us from the love of God in Jesus Christ our Lord.

Prayer: We thank thee, O God, for the truth of the Gospel. Help us to live as those who know thy love, in Christ Jesus our Lord. Amen.

The Season of Epiphany

The Christ We Admire:
The Christ We Worship

EDITOR'S INTRODUCTION

EVEN THOUGH DAVID READ was an extraordinarily gifted preacher he still had his share of critics. (Or perhaps he had his critics *because* he was so gifted.) A conservative minister once complained to me that Read was "theologically squishy," while a liberal minister let me know that he wouldn't walk across the street to hear Read preach. (In fairness to the liberal, when I sent him a copy of one of David Read's Christmas fantasy tales he quickly let me know that he would cross the street to hear that one.)

Read for his part wasn't trying to gain what counts in church circles as fans. He was simply doing his job which involved, as he saw it, standing in the pulpit with the Bible in one hand and the morning newspaper in the other. In this Epiphany sermon we find him fleshing out the social and political background behind King Herod's monstrous attempt to wipe out the infant Christ (the Bible side of the sermon). He then goes on to describe Jesus as "the one who gives us what only God can give today—forgiveness, reconciliation, and renewal within" (the contemporary side of the sermon).

THE CHRIST WE ADMIRE: THE CHRIST WE WORSHIP

A Sermon preached by David H. C. Read at Madison Avenue Presbyterian Church on Epiphany Sunday, January 5, 1986

Text: *"And he sent them to Bethlehem, and said, Go and search diligently for the young child; and when ye have found him, bring me word again, that I may come and worship him also."* Matthew 2:8

Readings: Isaiah 60:1–4, 18, 19; Colossians 1:13–20 (NEB); Matthew 2:7–12

"THAT I MAY COME and worship him." Herod, of course, was lying, which was quite in character. He had no intention of worshipping Jesus—or anyone else. The Herod family was one of the most notorious among the unscrupulous gangs of desperados who struggled for political power in the same section of the Middle East that is constantly in the headlines today. This Herod, in the last years of whose reign Jesus was born, is known to history as Herod the Great, perhaps because he re-built the ruined Temple in Jerusalem with a magnificent edifice which was the pride of the Jews and the envy of the Romans. The title also indicates that he was the most successful scoundrel of the five Herods who are mentioned in the New Testament.

Shakespeare could have done a lot with Herod, as he did with some of his famous contemporaries. It was Cassius who appointed Herod governor of Syria. Mark Antony and Octavius Caesar received him in Rome and then made him King of Judaea. Cleopatra objected to some of Herod's more brutal murders, but Antony confirmed him in office. When Octavius Caesar defeated Antony at the battle of Actium, Herod's star seemed to be setting. However, with his usual skill at diplomacy by assassination, he disposed of possible rivals, set off for Rome, and was confirmed in his kingdom by Octavius, now Caesar Augustus, the Emperor, sole master of the Roman world. I leave you to guess what Shakespeare would have made of this blood-stained tyrant with his ten wives and fifteen children, many of whom he disposed of by murder or execution. As for his trustworthiness one sober historian concludes: "Herod came to lack the ability to separate truth from lies."

This is the monster who, in Matthew's story, summoned the astrologers who were spreading the news that a king of the Jews was about to be born, and that they were being guided by a star to his birthplace. A king of the Jews! You can imagine what kind of a threat that was to Herod. He would stop at nothing to prevent any such child being allowed to live. And he didn't. For when, to his fury the child Jesus escaped his clutches, and the astrologers slipped off without seeing Herod again (the Bible says "they departed into their own country, another way." Wise men!) Herod ordered the infamous massacre of the infants. (A century ago scholars thought such a terrible edict so utterly impossible for a civilized man to put into action that it cast doubt on the whole story. We, alas, know better.)

Enough about Herod. I just wanted you to have the necessary background for understanding his orders to the astrologers: "And he sent them to Bethlehem, and said, Go and search diligently for the young child; and when ye have found him, bring me word again, that I may come and worship him also." I think we know exactly what he had in mind for the infant Jesus. And it was not worship. But the extraordinary thing is that worship is exactly what has been given to the one born at Bethlehem, worship first by some of his compatriots, like Simon Peter, the fisherman, who cried out: "Thou art the Christ, the Son of the living God," like Thomas the skeptic who fell at his feet sobbing "My Lord and my God," like Saul of Tarsus the theologian who solemnly wrote: "He is the image of the invisible God; his is the primacy over all created things." Then, as the news of this Lord and Savior spread out in all directions, Greeks began to worship him, Romans bowed in adoration at the risk of their lives, Egyptians, Ethiopians, Indians, then Gauls and Teutons, Russians and Britons, Spaniards and Africans in increasing numbers, in spite of all persecution, began to adore the Savior from Galilee.

How astonished Herod would have been if he had lived to hear of the millions who would in fact do what he pretended he wanted to do. People all over the world responded in hundreds of languages: "Bring me word . . . that I may come and worship him." The Church brought the word—and today more human beings than ever before are worshipping Jesus Christ. And on this feast of the Epiphany the words of the prophet ring out from every corner of the earth as they find their fulfilment in Christ. In spite of the gloom and despair that settle on an anxious world the divine Voice is heard in every language: "Arise, shine; for thy light is come, and the glory of the Lord is risen upon thee, for, behold, the darkness shall cover the earth, and gross darkness the people; but the Lord shall arise upon thee, and his glory shall be seen upon thee."

Who is this Christ whom the Church proclaims as the Light of the world? Anyone who has travelled to other parts of the world, anyone who has looked at the religious art in our galleries, anyone who has read books about the different Christian traditions knows that the figure of Jesus has assumed many startlingly different patterns over the centuries. You have only to compare a Spanish painting with its tortured Jesus on the cross with a triumphant Christ towering over an orthodox Cathedral, or Salman's Eagle Scout head of Jesus which is the icon of so many American Sunday schools with the fierce mystery of a Rouault, or to have received a Christmas card from Africa or

Japan with a black or Oriental baby Jesus, to become aware of the enormous diversity of the appeal of this Jesus of Nazareth. Yet one fact is crystal clear. With very few exceptions, the Christ who has been portrayed in so many different cultures is the Christ who is worshipped. His influence is not just that of a strong personality whose memory continues to haunt the human race. The luminous and transforming influence of Jesus, however he is portrayed, shines with a divine light. Alone among the great moral and religious figures who have left their mark on history, he evokes the worship that is due to God himself. Unlike Socrates, the Buddha, Mohammed, Confucius, Gandhi, he is not only admired. In the profoundest sense of the word he is worshipped. In whatever guise he comes, he speaks with the voice of God. As Charles Lamb once said: "If Shakespeare should come into this room, we would all rise; but if Jesus Christ should come in, we would all kneel."

In modern America this is not readily understood. We live in a society where the tendency is to play down the uniqueness of Jesus Christ. Most of us have—thank God—come to respect all great religious traditions that have enlightened our world, and we deplore any new outbreak of fundamentalist imperialism that threatens the peace and good will that lie behind all genuine piety, Christian or other. Thus many today content themselves with asserting an admiration for Jesus of Nazareth and would profess that his way of life is the one they would like to follow.

I am not about to write off this kind of admiration as misguided or hypocritical. Probably most of us here began our discipleship by responding in this way. So did the first disciples. Nor am I about to bombard you with theological arguments. (I'll leave that this morning to the tough little extract from the non-fictional writing of Dorothy Sayers printed in the bulletin.) I don't believe that you or I come to worship Jesus because someone has persuaded us that he is something more than a remarkable human being. It's more mysterious, more vital, more real than that. We come eventually to worship him because *he* has persuaded us—not so much by anything he said as by our encounter with him as a real, rescuing, welcoming, guiding power in our lives right now. Worship is not something that we can be dragooned to give. Worship is an inevitable response to that which meets us as the presence and power of God himself. And it can be refused. It was refused by Pilate, much as he seems to have admired Jesus. It was refused by that other Herod on what we call Good Friday. Do you remember the scene? "When Herod saw Jesus he was greatly pleased; having heard about him, he had long been wanting to see him, and had been hoping to see some miracle performed by him. He questioned him at some length without getting any reply . . . " Yes, we too can admire Jesus and question him—and find there is no reply. The young Herod was granted what his grandfather wanted—and he gave Jesus the mock worship of his cynical and self-centred heart. He "sent him back to Pilate dressed in a gorgeous robe." As Jesus implies "cursed are the impure in heart for they shall not see God."

This does not mean that our recognition of the divine and living Christ is dependent on our being good enough. Everyone knows that he did not summon the "righteous" but sinners. What we are being told is that we come to know and worship the Lord Christ when we are humble enough to know our need. The Christ we admire and seek to follow is the one who gives us what only God can give—forgiveness, reconciliation, and renewal within. It is not when we rack our brains trying to understand what is really meant by words we blithely sing at Christmas:

"Veiled in flesh the Godhead see,

Hail the incarnate Deity!" that we reach the point where we can adoringly say with Thomas: "My Lord and my God." It is at these moments when, deep within, we know that we have met with that great Source of life, that promiser of guidance, that amazingly kindred spirit, whom we call God, and all we can say is: "Glory be to the Father, and to the Son, and to the Holy Spirit." That is not a philosophical proposition but the response of the Church, the response of our hearts to the Christ we have come to worship.

This is why from time to time in our worship the chatter from the pulpit ceases, the music fades, and there is nothing here but you and I in our need. And in the silence Christ comes, not as a distant figure to admire, but as a living presence to adore. And with the inner ear we hear the Voice that says: "I am the bread of life; whoever comes to me will never hunger, and whoever believes in me will never thirst." It is the voice of the Jesus we know, and at the same time the voice of the eternal and universal Christ.

Growing with the Gospel:
Points at Which My Mind Has Changed

EDITOR'S INTRODUCTION

THIS PARTICULAR SUNDAY HAPPENED to mark David Read's 25th anniversary as the minister of Madison Avenue Presbyterian Church. The congregation had offered to invite a guest preacher for the occasion but Read demurred, concerned that the service might end up becoming too Read-centred and not sufficiently Christ-centred.

Read chose the hymns and proclaimed the gospel message that morning, but the members of the congregation did everything else. The sermon was based on the same text—Romans 1:16—that Read had used for his first sermon at MAPC in 1956. In describing how his mind had changed over the subsequent twenty-five years, he spoke about how his understanding of the gospel message had widened and deepened under the influence of Roman Catholic and Orthodox Christians, religious and secular Jews, and not least atheists and agnostics. Today David Read might speak about the need to address afresh the sin of racism, engage in greater dialogue with our Muslim neighbours, and address more radically the rapidly increasing and tragically irreversible problem of climate change.

Or maybe something else. What do you think?

GROWING WITH THE GOSPEL: POINTS AT WHICH MY MIND HAS CHANGED

A Sermon preached by David H. C. Read at Madison Avenue Presbyterian Church on January 11, 1981

Text: *"For I am not ashamed of the gospel of Christ: for it is the power of God unto salvation to everyone that believeth; to the Jew first, and also to the Greek."* Romans 1:16.

ON THE 15TH OF January, 1956, these were the words that I announced as the text of my first sermon from this pulpit. It's the same pulpit—but some will remember that twenty-five years ago it was over there. So, from my point of view I have moved to the left, but from yours I have moved to the right, so I leave you to figure out the symbolism of that! The text is the same, but I have resisted the temptation to give you the identical sermon, for that would be to betray a secret vow I made at that time. It was that each Sunday morning sermon in this pulpit would be a new one and each fully written out. This is now the 907th such morning sermon, and I am pleased to have kept that vow—with one exception, when I flew in from Berlin on a Saturday night. Of course, I know that I am thus exposed to the criticism of the Scottish beadle who remarked of a visiting minister's sermon that it was fine except for three things: (1) It was written, (2) it wasn't well written, and (3) it wasn't worth writing.

At the outset let me make it clear to the many friends who have been kind enough to join our congregation today that, for once, I have no responsibility for anything that happens this morning except the choice of hymns and the sermon. When I was asked if I would like a special guest preacher, I remembered the story of the seminarian who asked his favorite professor what he should preach about and got the answer: "About God and about twenty minutes." I wanted to avoid the risk of someone coming here to speak "about Read and about forty minutes."

I chose the text "I am not ashamed of the Gospel of Christ: for it is the power of God unto salvation to everyone that believeth" when I began my ministry here as an expression of my confidence in the historic Gospel and my determination to make the Good News of God's grace central in my preaching. That, with your encouragement, I have tried to do and intend to go on doing. In spite of lapses and inadequacies, known to God and to you, I still want to be able to say with St. Paul: "We preach not ourselves but Christ Jesus the Lord, and ourselves your servants for Jesus' sake."

As I think of twenty-five years of social, ethical, political, philosophical, and theological upheaval, loaded words and phrases flash through my mind like so many covers of "Time." Civil rights, riots, assassinations, the drug scene, the sexual revolution, situational ethics, the death of God, the Vietnam War, human rights, secular humanism, the New Left, the New Right, the New Theology, the Theatre of the Absurd, Vatican II, COCU, feminism—these suggest just a few of the hurricanes that have been roaring through these years. They have been testing times for any church seeking to witness to the power of God as a reality in our lives or the destiny of nations. Today I rejoice that, by the grace of God and the backing of a loyal, understanding, and stimulating congregation, I am able to say with an even greater confidence: "I am not ashamed of the Gospel of Christ: for it *is* the power of God unto salvation"—as the New English Bible puts it "the saving power of God for everyone who has faith." It has not lost that power.

"I am not ashamed." That is what the apostle said, and it seems an odd way to put it. I remember that, after that first sermon, a lady said to me with a touch of indignation: "I have never even *thought* of being ashamed of the Gospel." If she had really been listening to the sermon she would have discovered that it suggested several subtle ways in which any Christian can be overcome by the forces of secularism and unbelief. Have none of us ever been tempted to muffle our belief in the Gospel when discussing the great issues of the day, or when in the presence of those for whom religion is a kind of private peccadillo? Have we never, even for a moment, felt that this Gospel of God's love revealed in a crucified Jewish preacher two thousand years ago is almost an absurdity when measured against the political, economic, military, and technological powers that permeate our minds? With all that in mind I find that, twenty-five years ago, I said here: "Let them all come—scientific humanism, Marxism, logical positivism, behaviourism, 'I am not ashamed of the Gospel of Christ, for it is the power of God unto salvation to everyone that believeth.'"

What I went on to say then I believe more firmly than ever: "If there is one human need greater than any other it is for the 'power of God unto salvation'—that is, the divine dynamic that takes us as we are and moves us individually and collectively, toward the good life that God has planned for us. The Gospel is this power. It is not a technique for successful living; it is not a blueprint for immediate solution to social problems; it is not a moral code to which we are bound: it is a divine power that meets us at the point of our sin and helplessness and lifts us up towards 'the measure of the fullness of the stature of Christ.' This is the message of which we are not ashamed—that in this world where we are daily exposed to all kinds of forces and pressures that make for discord, despondency, and defeat, there is a silent, invisible power of God flowing to us through Jesus Christ that is able to cleanse and to heal and to reconcile, and to bring us through every trial and suffering, even through the last enemy stronghold which is death itself, to the kingdom where God's will is perfectly fulfilled.

The events of the last twenty-five years, and my experience with you here have not diminished my confidence in this Gospel. Rather, the significance of Jesus Christ and his stature as Lord and Savior have grown for me through the turmoil of these years. I am still not ashamed of the Gospel of Christ. But I *would* be ashamed if I had to confess to you that my understanding of this Gospel and how it should be proclaimed and lived has not nudged one inch since 1956. Dr. Barclay once remarked that he had seen a church with a notice proclaiming: "Here we preach and practice first-century Christianity" and said that he was more interested in preaching and practicing twentieth century Christianity—and I should like to think that my eye is now on the preaching and practicing of twenty-first century Christianity: I believe that next to having one's soul rooted and grounded in Christ, the most important gift of the Spirit is the grace to change one's mind.

So I have tried to discover what some of these points of change have been for me over these years. Some of you who have endured my preaching for a long time might have detected changes that I hadn't noticed. All I can do is to note a few of which I am aware, and summarize them—keeping that twenty minutes in mind!

The first has to do with the interpretation of this Gospel. Karl Barth said that the preacher is the one who stands with the Bible in one hand and the morning newspaper in the other. All true preaching is rooted in the Word of God revealed in the Bible. But the sermon is spoken to men and women living in the world of the daily newspaper. *Today's* paper—not last year's (which is why I don't ever write the winter's sermons during my summer vacation). The sermon then must deal, not only with what happened to Moses but what *is* happening to Mrs. Jones, or the multi-national corporation. I think you will find that over these years my sermons have not, I hope, been less concerned with the Bible but rather more with the morning newspaper.

This is a way of saying that I no longer believe that the Gospel can be preached, week after week, in fidelity to the Bible without reference to the questions that are agitating us and are reflected in the daily media. As you know, I do not believe that it is my duty to lay down the Christian answer to every controversial question, still less, to tell you how to vote. But I have learned from you that it is not enough to offer a Gospel that nourishes a private faith. It must be heard in the dimension of our daily life as responsible citizens. I now reject the distinction between Biblical and activist preaching.

A sermon, a church, a Christian whose faith flows from the Bible must be activist.

I am calling this "growing with the Gospel" and not departing from it. So it is with another point on which my mind could be said to have changed. This has to do with my attitude to other communions of Christians, to Judaism, and to those of other faiths, or of none. I remain, without apology, a Christian of the Reformed tradition. I still believe in Jesus Christ, not only as my Savior and Lord, but as the Lord and Savior of the whole human race. I am not an ecumenist of the stripe that says: "Any religion is better than mine." Still, it is not *my* religion in which I have total confidence: it is Christ. And it is his claim that I pass on when, as on Christmas Eve, I spoke of him as the one who came to save his people from their sins. I believe that is *all* people.

But I have learned that it is possible to have this conviction without isolating or offending those of other beliefs, that, in fact, there is much to learn from those of differing traditions. I have discovered what a great area there is for common conviction and common action among those raised in the great religions of the world—without either betraying or hiding one's supreme loyalty to Christ.

A special point of change has been for me my attitude to the other great Christian communions—the Roman Catholic and the Orthodox. The past twenty-five years have seen a revolutionary change in the relationships between Protestants and Catholics—and I rejoice in it. With my Scottish and Ulster heritage I tended at one time to think of Roman Catholics as a sinister quasi-Christian force always hovering near to lead good Protestants astray. And the Orthodox were so removed in time and space, so totally foreign in thought and practice, that they scarcely impinged on my Christian horizon. My mind began to change, not only when I found myself increasingly feeding on the theological insights and devotional riches of these communions, but when it dawned on me that, in this secularized and increasingly unbelieving society, what Christians hold in common is infinitely more important than the points that have so deeply divided them. Today it is for me much more important that I can join my fellow Christians in affirming the doctrines of the historic creeds, than that they hold some beliefs, and indulge in some practices, that may be offensive to our Presbyterian conscience. I am not ashamed, let me say, to confess that it is Roman Catholic theologians and Orthodox liturgies that often feed this Calvinist soul today.

But perhaps the greatest point of change for me has been in my understanding of Judaism as a living Faith. In Scotland I was raised to have the deepest respect for the people who not only gave us the Old Testament but our Savior himself. Looking back, I now realize how thoroughly Scotland was impregnated with the Judaism of the Old Testament. My recollection is of countless sermons on the great Jewish figures and endless singing of the psalms in the metrical version. But it *was* the Judaism of the Old Testament. There were so few Jews living where I was raised that I knew little or nothing of Judaism today. Even at seminary I was left with the impression of the enormous importance of the Old Testament (Hebrew was compulsory!), but little was said about the Jews who did not accept Jesus as their Messiah.

I need hardly say that to transfer my ministry from Edinburgh to New York was not only a cultural but a theological shock. For, unless one lives in a WASP ghetto, to be a New Yorker means constant contact with Jewish people in all walks of life—particularly in the arts and sciences. And I have had the illuminating experience of close friendship with rabbis. I have been enriched by a growing understanding of the spiritual riches of a living Judaism and respect for the people of the Covenant, and their place in the providence of God. I am therefore looking forward in my exposition of Paul's epistle to the Romans to the section where he deals, agonizingly, with his hopes for his own people in the light of his knowledge of Christ. You will notice that I have not so far mentioned the tail end of our text: "I am not ashamed of the Gospel of Christ; for it is the power of God unto salvation to everyone that believeth—*to the Jew first, and also to the Greek*." I hear these words, not just as a reference to the historical fact that the first Christians were all Jews, but as a reminder that we cannot be Christians unless in a sense we are Jews first—accepting the revelation that comes through the Old Testament. We have an immense amount in common, and at our critical point of difference—the recognition of Jesus as Lord and Savior, I find that my unmodified Christian conviction is no barrier to love and understanding when I am with believing Jews.

Has my mind changed also about the huge number of those around us who profess no faith at all? In one sense—No. I still long that people I know who are agnostic or atheist should come to know this "power of God unto salvation," or, since few would know what that means "this invisible spiritual power that meets us in Christ, floods our life with meaning, and lifts us up with hope and joy." Yet perhaps I have changed in that now I find the grace of God where I never used to think of looking for it. I mean that I now see the Gospel at work in unexpected places, and unexpected people, and realize that Christ is at work before I ever approach them, or preach a single word.

Today as I speak now to my own faithful congregation I must tell you that, if I have been able to expound the Gospel of God's grace over these years, it is you, by your support and your prayers, who have enabled me to do it. If I have changed my mind in any of these ways for the better it is you who have opened my eyes. For your love, your patience, your tolerance, your loyalty I continue daily to be grateful. So let me stretch that twenty minutes long enough to say with Paul: "It is not to be thought that I have already achieved all this. I have not yet reached perfection (You can say that again), but I press on, hoping to take hold of that for which Christ once took hold of me."

Prayer: Grant unto us, O God, a knowledge of that great power that thou hast given to us in Christ Jesus thy Son and enable us with loyalty and an open mind to follow after in Christ's name. Amen.

The Organ and the Vacuum Cleaner: A Note on "Creationism"

EDITOR'S INTRODUCTION

DAVID READ WAS CERTAINLY no fundamentalist with a tin ear for the poetry that colors the creation stories in Genesis. But he also wasn't the kind of person who uses a scientific theory like evolution as an excuse for imposing upon our children a dogmatic secularist view of life.

Read recognised, in other words, that just as poetry sometimes appears in the Bible by way of illumining the Why of things (why, for instance, there is anything at all, why we experience good and evil, and why we are given these years of life on this planet), science is needed to illumine the How of things (how this mysterious universe developed, how it works, and how we can harness its latent power).

This sermon encourages us to respect the different ways of thinking here. The Why question forces us to think *theologically* about God's creation while the How question forces us to think *scientifically* about the universe. We need to distinguish between these two approaches to truth and not shut ourselves off from either side: that is the advice that David Read's Note on "Creationism" offers.

THE ORGAN AND THE VACUUM CLEANER: A NOTE ON "CREATIONISM"

A Sermon preached by David H. C. Read at Madison Avenue Presbyterian Church on January 17, 1982

> Text: *"Where wast thou when I laid the foundations of the earth, when the morning stars sang together and all the songs of God shouted for joy?"* Job 38:4
>
> Readings: Job 38:1–11; Revelation 4; Matthew 6:5–13 (NEB)

LET'S STOP RIGHT THERE. Does anyone want to ask just what the foundations of the earth consisted of, and how God went about laying them? Do you want to know what particular tune the stars were singing and if indeed there was a sound that could have been scientifically picked up on a tape recorder and analyzed? Anyone with an ear for poetry and a delight in drama knows that the Book of Job is a masterpiece of literature dealing with the perennial agonizing question of the human heart: Why do the innocent suffer, why do good people often fare worse than the bad? Why is life so unfair?

This is not my theme today. I'm simply using this extract from the closing of the drama in which we are dazzled by the glory and mystery of the Creator and humbled by the Voice that asks: "Where wast thou when I laid the foundations of the earth?" and exhilarated by the image of the morning stars singing together and the sons of God shouting for joy. I am sorry for the unbeliever who cannot hear God speaking in those words; I am equally sorry for the super-believer who insists that he is revealing here the data for a scientific understanding of creation.

Yet we are now witnessing a fantastic replay of an argument that broke out a hundred years ago between those who insisted that the Bible, particularly the first chapter of Genesis, must be interpreted as literally as the evolutionary theory of Darwin's "Origin of the Species." There has already been one other replay under glaring arc-lights in this country in 1925 when a biology teacher in Dayton, Tennessee was charged with violating an act that made it unlawful to teach any theory "that denies the story of the divine creation of man as taught in the Bible." Since the leading prosecutor was William Jennings Bryan, and the leading defender was Clarence Darrow, the case did not lack for fireworks and the press had a field day. Since most of the theologians and preachers in the historic churches of Europe and the USA had long since settled down comfortably with the belief that there is no need for any such squabble, since the Bible and modern science are concerned with quite different questions, it is astonishing to find that in the 1980s we are being treated to a re-run of hoary arguments and bitter debate about a so-called alternative to the theory of evolution known as "scientific creationism." As you know, a Federal District judge has just ruled unconstitutional an act of the State of Arkansas which compels teachers to offer this "creationism" theory as an alternative to evolution.

In my opinion the judge was right in ruling that "creationism" is based on religious dogma and is not a theory that wins any support in the scientific community, except for those who embrace it for religious reasons. I would add the footnote, however, that the legal exclusion of religion from the public schools is a complex question. It is right to prohibit the teaching of a theory which is held only by those who hold to a literal interpretation of the Bible, but it is also possible that the theory of evolution could be taught in such a way as to impose on children a purely secularist philosophy of life—and that can be a religion too. I am glad for my son to be taught science by those competent in the field, whatever their religious views may be, but would not want to have him indoctrinated by a worldview that rules out belief in God. The theory of evolution has at times been reared into a total philosophy of life—indeed a religion—thus overstepping the limits of science. Good teachers, I know, whatever their religious beliefs or unbeliefs, make sure that they do not overstep that line.

Religion has to do with meaning, with the Why? of things—why, for instance, there is anything at all, why we experience good and evil, and why we are given these years of life on this planet. Science, on the other hand, is concerned with the How? of things, how this mysterious universe developed, how it works, and how we can harness its latent powers. So, although these two questions may at times overlap, there should be no conflict whatever between a belief that God is the Source of all that is and has given meaning to our human life, and whatever is discovered by science about the origin of the species or the age of the universe. Indeed some of the great Christian thinkers of our time have found inspiration for their theology in the story of life unfolded by evolutionary science. Notable among these has been the Jesuit Teilhard de Chardin who was equally skilled in theology and geology, and would have been astonished to hear that the findings of modern geology had to be rejected in favor of something called "Creationism" based on a literal reading of the first chapter of Genesis.

You have often heard me refer to the great Swiss theologian, Karl Barth, whose monumental scholarship and vibrant faith has left an indelible mark on the thinking and preaching of this century. I have just been reading a recently published collection of his letters. They reveal, as all good letters do, the human being who lies behind his work, and Barth was one of the most delightfully human of all scholars I have known—full of fun, delighting in good conversation, and good wine, and revelling in a hundred enthusiasms from playing with children to the music of Mozart. (He even asked the Pope to consider making Mozart a special kind of saint.) I confess I was comforted when referring to the index of his "Letters" to find no less than thirteen references to his pipe.

Among the letters is one to a grandniece. She was at college at the time and had evidently been troubled by some people who were insisting that since the Bible account of creation cannot be squared with the theory of evolution as science then one or the other must be wrong. This is what he had to say: "Has no one explained to you in your seminar that one can as little compare the biblical creation story and a scientific theory like that of evolution as one can compare, shall we say, an organ and a vacuum cleaner—that there can be as little question of harmony between them as of contradiction?"

I wish someone had been around to say that to me at a time when I went through this turmoil of trying to reconcile Genesis and evolution in scientific terms. Fundamentalists told me it couldn't be done and that therefore one had to deny all that evolution taught. Taken literally, the Bible data point to an age of about 4000 years for this world. Therefore if geologists talk of fossils indicating an age of several millions of years, one must fall back on a theory which was seriously proposed in the late nineteenth century, namely that God had placed such fossils in rocks quite recently in order to test the faith of modern Christians. On the other hand some were telling me that the two accounts could be reconciled. But this meant a series of mind-straining assumptions—such as that a vast period of time is implied between verse one and verse two in the first chapter of Genesis, and that each "day" of creation really meant some thousands of years. Soon I began to wonder how many more re-interpretations of Scripture would be needed to square the two accounts. It was an immense relief when it dawned on me that I was comparing, not just apples and oranges, but the apple as the scientist analyses it and the apple as seen by the artist in a radiant still life. I had indeed been trying to compare an organ and a vacuum cleaner. They belong to two totally different realms of human experience. It is nonsensical to compare them and to say, for instance, that an organ is better than a vacuum cleaner, that one does more for us than the other, that one is more real and true than the other.

Barth went on to his niece: "The creation story is a witness to the beginning or becoming of all reality apart from God, in the light of God's later acts and words relating to his people Israel—naturally in the form of a saga or poem. The theory of evolution is an attempt to explore the same reality in its inner nexus—naturally in the form of a scientific hypothesis. The creation story deals only with the becoming of all things, and therefore with the revelation of God, which is inadmissible to science as such. The theory of evolution deals with what has become, as it appears to human observation and research, and as it invites human interpretation." Barth ended his letter: "So tell the teacher concerned that she should distinguish what is to be distinguished, and not shut herself off from either side."

So much for Karl Barth—the man who did more than any other to restore the authority of the Bible in Protestant preaching in this age. Many of us learned from him how the Word of God can come to us with power and authority through the very human witness of the Bible. The opening of Genesis began to speak to me with new life as the Voice of God when I was liberated from the absurdities of treating these stories as a scientific textbook divinely dictated to Moses.

The glory of the Bible is that God speaks to us in it through history, poetry, drama, song, saga—every literary form through which the human spirit has expressed itself. What distinguishes this Book from all others is not some magic quality of inerrancy but the convergence of its content on the revelation of the one true God, and its climax in the coming of Christ. There were other sagas of creation in the ancient world, some of them remarkably similar to the Genesis stories, but what they lack is the Voice of this all-embracing one God, a God of holiness with a loving purpose in the creation and redemption of the world.

It is the organ music of this revelation that I want to hear in the Bible, that which confronts me with the reality and challenge of the Creator to whom I owe my allegiance humbles me with the realization of my own frailty and folly, and lifts me up to share in the joyful song of the angels—the glad shout of the angels in the book of Job at the moment of creation, and the soft music at Bethlehem at the moment of redemption. "Where wast thou when I laid the foundations of the earth. . . . and the morning stars sang together and all the sons of God shouted for joy?" I know I wasn't there, Job wasn't there, but I am moved to the depths by the God who brought all into being and yet is willing to converse with us, and listen to our protests as well as our prayers. This is a realm into which science cannot enter for that is not its purpose. It is not to the Bible I turn when I want to understand more about how things work, or to celebrate the technology that has produced the vacuum cleaner, the internal combustion engine, and the jet plane. So I am not the least interested in any doctrine of "creationism" that tries to make the Bible a sourcebook for geology or physics.

Like all of us here I am vastly indebted to the astounding and dedicated work of the scientist—not just for the vacuum cleaner but for the gifts of modern medicine and surgery, the inventions that have made existence less of a drudgery, the voyages into space that have rolled back our horizons, and the everyday things that have enriched our common life. (A new kind of hypocrite is the preacher who hammers out an attack on modern science on an electric typewriter, and speeds off in a jet plane to deliver it on television.) When I worship I can celebrate with the psalmist the achievements of human beings who were made "a little lower than the angels" and given dominion over the works of God's hands. But the essence of worship is the reminder that all human achievement is a reflection of the God from whom we come and to whom we go, the God who has made us to share in his creative power—and the God who sees how we can misuse it.

For the human brain that produced the vacuum cleaner has also produced the hydrogen bomb. The technology that can make the desert to blossom as the rose has not yet done much to feed the hungry half of the human race. The gifts of science are neutral. Many scientists today are deeply concerned about the use to which their discoveries are put, but it is not from science itself that they derive their ideals and their convictions, but from their ethics—and ultimately their religion. It is the great organ music of the Bible in which we hear of the creative power of God, the loving design of God, the redemptive power of God, and the joy that lies at the heart of the universe, that brings us the vision and inspires us with a humble and unquenchable hope. We don't need futile arguments about "Creationism" and Evolution. We need to go into the secret place of which Jesus spoke, and there talk intimately with the One who asks us: "Where wast thou when I laid the foundations of the earth?" and then invites us to listen to the morning stars singing together and all the sons of God shouting for joy.

Prayer: Open our ears, O God, to hear what thou art saying to us through the mystery of the world around us and the stories of the teaching of scripture; and send us forth humble yet joyful to serve thee and thy kingdom through Christ our Lord. Amen.

Life with Prayer in It

EDITOR'S INTRODUCTION

IT'S HARD STRIKING THE right balance in speaking about prayer, especially intercessory prayer. Liberal-leaning preachers are often tempted to interpret the subject along meditative and even aesthetic lines while conservatives may run the risk of treating prayer as a piece of pious magic. Yet pray we must if only because Jesus himself prayed—and summoned his followers to do likewise. And once we are praying we surely need help in understanding what we are doing—and why.

David Read's reflections on prayer in this sermon are mainly informed by the One who taught us to pray, taught us in words of course, but above all taught us by praying himself with a heart full of expectancy and love. Read tackles the subject convinced that "life with prayer in it" is not just a treat but daily rations for the follower of Jesus Christ. Jesus prayed, and following his example and instruction we may and must pray also. This sermon wrestles with the mystery that ensues.

LIFE WITH PRAYER IN IT

A Sermon preached by David H. C. Read at Madison Avenue Presbyterian Church on January 20, 1985

Text: *"What is the Almighty, that we should serve him? And what profit should we have, if we pray unto him?"* Job 21:15

Readings: Psalms 31:1–8; 19–24; Acts 4:23–33 (NEB); Luke 5:12–16 (NEB)

HAVE YOU EVER FELT like that? I'm speaking of a moment when, under the stress of some personal tragedy, or perhaps just out of the blue, you questioned the validity of your religion. You began to think the unthinkable. Who is this God I claim to believe in? The Man Upstairs? A childhood memory like Santa Claus? Or some nebulous Force that sometimes seems to be there, and sometimes not? And in what sense could my life be described as serving him? Then, what about these prayers that I have sent out in that direction? What good did they do? And why is this God not answering right now when I am beginning to question his existence?

Nearly everyone in this country has been raised with some kind of belief in God, and a poll would show that a vast majority are in favor of prayer whether they practice it themselves or not. There is very little dogmatic atheism such as is the official philosophy of the countries under Communist rule. Likewise there was almost no dogmatic atheism around when the Bible books were written. We may remember reading in the psalms "The fool has said in his heart, 'There is no God,'" but the one he is calling a fool is not the man or woman who is intellectually convinced that God doesn't exist and says so out loud, but the one who takes no account of God from day to day. The text literally reads: "The fool hath said *in his heart*: No God!" You get up in the morning: No God; you decide how to plan your day: No God; you ponder the news in the morning paper: No God; you wonder whether or not to respond to an appeal to help the starving: No God; you make big decisions—whether or not to divorce a husband or wife, whether or not to have an abortion; No God; and you turn in and go to sleep: No God. That's what I call practical atheism—and it's infinitely more common among us than the dogmatic atheism of the Marxists.

If this is your way of life you wouldn't be here this morning. Yet the chances are that you have had, or are having, your moments of doubt about the God you think you believe in and even more in the usefulness of your prayers. "What is the Almighty; that we should serve him? And what profit should we have, if we pray unto him?" In times of great distress you may have even wondered if it would make any real difference to your life if you gave up worrying about God and stopped praying altogether. If that has ever happened to you, you are not alone. Some of the most sturdy Christians who ever lived have confessed to this temptation, from Augustine, Pascal, Dr. Johnson, to Archbishop Temple, C. S. Lewis and other spirited believers of our own time.

There's the alluring—or is it frightening?—picture: No God; life without prayer in it. For some of us it may be literally unthinkable. Others may be thinking: "Well, there's old so-and-so. As far as I know he never gives a thought to God, and if I mention prayer to him he's probably going to laugh. And yet he does remarkably well, with a reasonably happy home, a steadily rising income, and never a day in hospital." This is exactly what Job is saying in his time of trial. His friends flock around to assure him that his troubles are due to some secret sin. They argue that God always rewards the virtuous and punishes the sinner. "Rubbish!" answers Job, and cites people he knew who were practical atheists and yet were enormously successful financially, had happy homes, positions of power, and were spared any lingering illness at the end. "Wherefore do the wicked live, become old, yea, are mighty in power? . . . They spend their days in wealth, and in a moment go down to the grave." Yet, these are the very people who have the nerve to say to God: "Depart from us; for we desire not the knowledge of thy ways. What is the Almighty that we should serve him? And what profit should we have, if we pray unto him?"

The man who wrote this book saw the problem as clearly as any of us. Yet we wouldn't be hearing his voice after all these centuries if he had not come through to an even deeper belief than he had before and a radiant confidence in a life with prayer in it. Neither would those Christians I have mentioned. So let me turn the page and look at the other picture—life with prayer in it. And my own private prayer at this point is to avoid the obvious, the trite, or the patently untrue.

First, I would claim that life with prayer in it is satisfying to the mind and spirit. It corresponds to our unique nature as human beings. It takes account of the mystery with which we are surrounded. It allows for the strange events that are inexplicable to the mind, and the dreams and visions that cannot be psycho-analyzed away. I have hundreds of books at home and sometimes let my eyes wander over them, remembering the special favorites, how many I have read—and which of the classics I have only pretended to have read. I know which ones to go to for the facts—about history, languages, science, biblical criticism, or whatever. I could live a life without prayer in it and enjoy all these books. But there are those others—those that come, as Wordsworth would have put it, "trailing clouds of glory, from God, who is our home." And I don't mean just religious books, but poetry, novels, biography, plays that have the dimension of eternity, that lift us from the mechanics of life to its meaning, that send "through all this earthly dress bright shoots of everlastingness." I am not saying that all such books are written by Christians with a conventional view of prayer, but if prayer is our opening into the mystery, our contact with a realm that lies beyond the calculations of the mind or the range of technology, then surely a life with no prayer in it leaves us "cabined, cribbed, confined," unsatisfied at the very center of our being. Isn't this what the psalmist felt when he came through his time of trial and sang: "Thou hast set my feet in a large room." Life with prayer in it is living in a large room that gets larger the more we pray.

Next, I would say that everything in my experience, what I have observed in men and women of prayer, and all I have learned from Christ, leads me to believe that this is the source of hope and joy, two qualities that are in short supply at the present time. To have hope for humanity, or for ourselves, while living in a world that has no access to the realm of the Spirit, no contact with that better way which Jesus called the Realm of God, must be hard going. We know the fearful threats under which we live, and there are fewer and fewer now who believe that the human race can extricate itself from them and move towards a hopeful and happier future without what has been called some "invisible means of support." For years the notes of hope and joy have been missing in the novels, the plays, the movies, and the art that reflects the life we know. Instead we have had cynicism, so-called realism, the anti-hero, black humor, and the demonic. But there are signs of change. Recent movies, for instance—and I am not speaking of just those with obvious religious motivation—have often left a different taste in the mouth. In one way or another they have reflected that other dimension where hope and joy break through.

"What profit should we have, if we pray unto him?" This sounds like the answer. I believe it is the ultimate answer, but I can hear someone saying: "It hasn't always worked for me. Often when I pray desperately nothing seems to happen. I don't find hope and joy flooding in in answer to my prayers." This is where we come up against what seems to us the terrible silence of God. We learn that there is nothing automatic, no instant response, in this life with prayer in it. We may give up, or we may go on to learn that prayer is opening our lives to a different world than the one we know. We expect God to respond on our terms and give us what we want. But his very silence on occasion should remind us that we are in touch with one who says: "My thoughts are not your thoughts, neither are your ways my ways." The adventure of life with prayer in it has its moments of sudden and startling answers to our prayers, but for the most part it consists in our attitude of trust even when God seems most silent in response. Does that mean we should not make specific requests in our prayers? What did Jesus say? "Ask, and you will receive." He set no limitations. I sometimes think that sermons and books on prayer are always telling us that we shouldn't think of prayer as asking but as trying to conform to the will of God. Sure, he taught us to pray: "Thy will be done," but he also taught us to ask for our daily bread, and what could be more down-to-earth than that? We are told we shouldn't just be beggars. But first and foremost we *are* beggars.

James Carse, in a stimulating new book on "The Silence of God" has this to say: "Childhood is a time of great dependence; that is to say, *need*, and therefore a time of begging from others. There is no more complete hunger than that of the newborn. They are asking not only for material sustenance they cannot obtain on their own, but they are asking for a great many forms of human touching of the very most fundamental and unconditional sort. Childhood is a state of the purest hunger for life. It is a state of being that can be comprehended as uninterrupted prayer." Isn't that why Jesus said we had to become like children to enter the Realm of God? We have to ask, and, said Jesus, "you will receive." "It will be given you" says the King James Version, but we are not told what that "it" is, what exactly will be given.

So I see life with prayer in it as the developing of a conviction that the Realm of God surrounds us pressing in on all we think and say and do, so we begin to live in that large room where anything can happen through God's answering love. This used to be called "the practice of the presence of God," whereby we come to refer to every detail, every decision, every relationship to him. But I see it also as a life that is punctuated by specific moments when we actively and consciously pray. If we have no discipline of this sort then the atmosphere of prayer in which we want to live will thin out and soon disappear. That's why it's worth persevering with whatever habit we have formed of deeply personal, uninterrupted talking with, and listening for God. This is how it was with our Lord in the record of his earthly life. As no one else he lived in that large room. The realm of God was near him, within him, all the time. His life had prayer in it from the moment of rising to the moment of sleep, and God was in his dreams. Yet he felt the need for regular times to be alone to pray. Unlike us, the busier he was the more time he sought for prayer. "Great crowds gathered to hear him," we read, "and to be cured of their ailments. And from time to time he would withdraw to lonely places for prayer."

It is Jesus who answers the mocking question of our text. "What is the Almighty, that we should serve him?" "My Father," says Jesus, thus giving to his church the first article of our creed, "I believe in God the *Father* almighty."

He is the one who cares for us with a parental love, willing what is best for us with an almighty wisdom that passes our understanding. Thus Jesus lived from day to day seeing God everywhere he went—in the eyes of an infant, in the lilies of the field, in the life that beat beneath the skin of a leper, in the uproar of a city mob, and in the silence of the mountains of Judaea, in the tears of the Magdalene, and in the grin of the Canaanite woman. And in his discipline of special prayer times he knew what it was to ask expectantly and in total trust. He knew what it was to have a request refused. "O my Father, if it be possible, let this cup pass from me." A few hours later he had to drain it. He knew what it was to experience the terrible silence of God when the cry was heard from the cross: "My God, my God, why hast thou forsaken me?" It is because he knew all this that this same cross became the door of hope for all who have met him as their risen Lord. And this supreme life with prayer in it was crowned with a radiant and infectious joy. To all who are groping towards such a life he says: "These things have I spoken unto you, that my joy might remain in you, and that your joy might be full."

"What profit should we have? This profit—the profit men and women could attest in our day, the profit of a satisfying life in the larger room, the profit of a hope that reaches beyond death to the largest room of all, and the profit of a joy that the world can neither give nor take away. I think of Dietrich Bonhoeffer, about to be hanged by the Nazis, saying: "This is the end: for me the beginning of life," and the comment of an agnostic fellow prisoner who escaped his fate: "I never knew a man whose God was so real and so near." I think of Mother Teresa ministering to the dying in the streets of Calcutta. Can anyone see her face or hear her words without thinking: "There is a life with prayer in it." You're not a Bonhoeffer? You're not a Mother Teresa? Neither am I. But I want that life with more prayer in it. Don't you?

> Prayer: Teach us, Lord, what it is to have prayer in our lives day by day and grant that we may trust, have greater patience, and experience expectancy and joy through Christ our Lord. Amen.

Amok in Eden: Ecology for Christians

EDITOR'S INTRODUCTION

CLIMATE SCIENTISTS HAVE LONG claimed that global warming is real, dangerous, and human caused. Some people have heeded their warnings, but many have simply closed their ears. Sadly, even many Christians have joined the climate change deniers in believing that with a little more prayer God will blow away the carbon dioxide that we keep dumping into the atmosphere.

It's not going to happen. Every year more and more evidence of climate change accumulates in the form of increasingly violent floods and snowstorms, droughts, hurricanes and forest fires. God has given us brains, and we had better use them to mobilize our resources into renewable energy, thus weaning ourselves away from fossil fuel dependence. If we don't, it may soon be too late to rectify the problem.

David Read's fifty-year old sermon on ecology reminds us that the Creator put the human creature in the Garden of Eden to till it and keep it. This remains our God-given task. The only difference is that if we refuse to heed the summons, we draw that much closer to mass extinction.

AMOK IN EDEN: ECOLOGY FOR CHRISTIANS

A Sermon preached by David H. C. Read at Madison Avenue
Presbyterian Church on January 25, 1970

Text: *"The Lord God took the man and put him in the Garden of Eden to till
it and keep it."* Genesis 2:15

EVERY SCIENCE FROM THEOLOGY to astrophysics has its own vocabulary
which the experts use as they pursue their researches and chat amongst
themselves. In these days of specialization it is difficult for any scholar to be
familiar with more than one or two of these technical languages, while for
the average man they are all varieties of double Dutch. Yet every now and
then a word or phrase leaks out from the study of the laboratory, and becomes (like the Vice President) a "household word." Whenever this happens
it's a sign that something has been going on behind closed doors that will
directly affect our lives or those of our children. For most of the time we are
content to let the specialists work away without caring too much what they
are doing, but when one of their technical terms begins to hit the headlines
we know that we had better sit up and take notice.

In the 1930's for instance if I had to use the phrase "nuclear fission" in
a sermon (which is highly unlikely since I had never heard of it) probably no
one present would have any idea what I was talking about. They would guess
that it was part of the vocabulary of the academic scientist engaged in some
erudite research. But in 1945 it was a household word, and any preacher using
it knew that he was talking about matters of life and death. The threat which
everyone heard in the words "nuclear fission" had the side effect of releasing
a technical theological word into the popular vocabulary—eschatology, the
science of "last things." A few years before no one would have dreamed that
this area of doctrine which was usually tucked into the short last chapter of
standard theological textbooks would ever arouse popular interest.

It is my guess that there are other technical terms which are hovering
on the edge of our daily vocabulary.

For years they have been common currency within the narrow walls
of their particular science but are now invading the popular media because
of their implications for your life and mine. For instance, there is DNA. I
remember first hearing of this as an innocent in biology some years ago
from an expert and being astonished at what I heard. For what sounded
like an academic piece of research on the acids found in the nucleus of cells
functioning in what is called "the transference of genetic characteristics,"

clearly meant that a breakthrough had occurred which could mean that within the lifetime of most of us it would be possible to decide what kind of people were going to be born. So in the near future almost certainly DNA will be as familiar a term as TNT—with even more explosive implications. For the biological revolution is upon us and enormous ethical decisions will have to be made.

At the present moment the technical term that has broken through to us and has become familiar in a matter of months is "ecology." Not long ago this word belonged to the specialists in biology or anthropology. Why now do we see it in the headlines? Any dictionary will tell you that it is the science that deals with the inter-relationships of organisms and their environments. That can sound a learned pursuit that we can happily leave to the expert. But when you translate it into the specific field of man and his environment and apply it to the world we know, you will soon be talking about the air we breathe, the water we drink, the food we produce and the machines we use. Ecology, in fact, talks of many urgent things that can be literally a matter of life and death for us and our descendants.

Every single citizen who has a voice in a democracy ought to be as concerned with ecology as with the mighty matters of justice, liberty and peace. For this—as much as nuclear war—is a question of human survival. Only slowly and comparatively recently have we awakened to the facts of air and water pollution and the exploitation of natural resources. Now the alarm bells are ringing. President Nixon has spoken of a "now or never" fight against the pollution of the environment and warned that by 1980 huge areas of the country may be unlivable. The dailies and weeklies are carrying articles about the poisoning of our cities by vehicle exhaust, the pollution of our rivers with chemical waste, the raping of the land by the indiscriminate use of chemicals and pesticides, and even the threat to the oceans with their no longer endless supply of edible fish. The TV shows us jet planes' smoke across our cities and oil-drenched birds dying on the beaches. At last we are waking up and beginning to shout: "Why?" Why must the mania for so-called progress mean the sacrifice of our human rights to breathe fresh air and drink unpolluted water? Why must the drive to go faster, produce more unnecessary goods, get quick results, or quick profits take priority over the basic health of ourselves and our children? Why can the astounding skills of modern technology and the enormous funds that direct their use not be applied to rescuing mankind from the desperate dangers that are now apparent? And why can we not voice adequately our demand that man stop running amok in the Eden God has given us?

These are questions any enlightened citizen must ask. If you ask me what particular interest the Church has in this matter, the answer is, first, that the Christian community has an immediate concern in whatever affects the life and health of mankind, and loving our neighbor surely means not polluting his air or poisoning his crops. But there is also a specific question of Christian doctrine at stake, and it is that I want to speak about now.

Everyone knows that Christians have certain beliefs about God and certain beliefs about man. It is on the basis of these beliefs that we try to order our lives and make our decisions in the modern world. But there is also such a thing as a Christian belief about our environment. May this not be one of the neglected areas of our faith? How many sermons have you heard on the natural world which is our habitat, on our responsibility for the soil, the sea, the plants and the animals? How many hymns celebrate the creation and remind us of our kinship with the elements and all living things? (The one that does it best—St. Francis' "All Creatures of our God and King"—with its celebration of sun, moon, wind, clouds, fire, water was omitted from our hymnbook.) With all our Mother's Days how much thought have we given to our duty to Mother Nature?

"The Lord God took the man and put him in the garden of Eden to till it and keep it." The Jewish and Christian teaching on man's relation to his environment are based on the belief that the natural world is a home given to man by God to till and to keep. He is a trustee and will be held accountable for his stewardship. Throughout the Bible there runs a sense of reverence for God's creation. The books of the law spoke of such things as care for the soil and the animals: "For six years you shall sow your land and gather in its yield; but the seventh year you shall let it rest and lie fallow, that the poor of your people may eat, and what they leave the wild beasts may eat. You shall do likewise with your vineyard and your olive orchard." The book of the Psalms is filled with joy and gratitude for the natural home in which man lives. The prophets had a vision of the kingdom in which the wolf and the leopard and the calf and the kid are happy and safe, and when "all the trees of the field shall clap their hands." Jesus could beckon the spring flowers round the Lake of Galilee and declare that any one of them was more wonderfully decked than "Solomon in all his glory." Paul, who seemed less sensitive to the beauty of nature nevertheless felt his kinship with all creation and saw it sharing in the final redemption of mankind. "The creation itself will be set free from its bondage and decay and obtain the glorious liberty of the children of God."

The early Genesis chapters set out the doctrine in story form. Adam— that is, mankind—is given the Garden of Eden—that is, the ideal environment that God has planned for him. He is put there "to till it and keep it." In the other creation story there is an emphasis on man's dominion over the creation. He is to "be fruitful and multiply, and fill the earth and subdue it;

and have dominion . . . " This doctrine of man's dominion is the theological basis for the vast enterprise of exploration and control which has marked the whole era inspired by the Jewish and Christian Scriptures (which is why it was not an empty gesture of public relations when the astronauts broadcast from the Genesis story as they circled the moon). But the doctrine of man's dominion needs to be balanced by this other one of man's obligation to till and to keep the Garden God has given him. The subsequent story of the Fall, which speaks of man's expulsion from Eden, in no way changes the original command. The suggestion is rather that nature herself has partaken in this distortion and decay and that mankind, having rebelled against God will be tempted to mutilate and destroy the works of his creation. The process of redemption, the winning back of all mankind to the Father-God, must then include a new reverence for our earthly home and a compassion that spans the whole of creation.

The theology of ecology can be simply stated. The world is not a treasure chest to be rifled and exploited; nor is it a playground which man can run amok. It is a temporary home granted him by God to be tilled and kept and explored with respect and responsibility. The word, "home," is the key. It is the very word we use when we say "ecology." For "ecology" comes from the Greek "oikos" which means home. Ecology is the science of our home. So it really ought to be a household word. It is the word used in the verse: "In my Father's house there are many mansions," so Christian ecology will stretch beyond the secular environment to the eternal world. But that should never mean that in Christian eyes our material environment is of little account in the eyes of God.

The sad fact is that the Church has neglected its doctrine of nature, its theology of ecology. At one time its concentration on the eternal world was so intense that no one seemed to care about this temporary home. St. Francis was almost a lone voice with his celebration of nature and kinship with the animals and elements of this world. In more recent times we have been so obsessed with our human problems and our duties to one another that we have forgotten to cultivate a due reverence for all creation. Only now do we see that such neglect brings with it an aggravation of these human problems and a fearful nemesis as we face the penalties incurred by those who wreck the home that God has given them.

For Christians, then, ecology is an urgent question involving the heart of our faith. It should, indeed, be part of our worship as we sing the glory of God's creation, as we confess that we have behaved like vandals in the Father's house, as we hear the word of forgiveness promised to those who change their minds, as we meet with the Son of God who shared this earthly home with us for thirty years, as we give thanks for the gifts of food, shelter and earthly beauty, as we dedicate ourselves to a new reverence for the world around us and pledge ourselves to work for its conservation and renewal.

The Christian view is summarized by Joseph Sittler's words quoted in a thoughtful article on this subject by Edward Fiske in the New York Times: "Reason says that destroying clean air is impractical. Faith ought to say it is blasphemous."

How then do we respond as Christians to the present crisis? First, I suggest we have to be willing to learn the facts as to the pollution of our air and water, the destruction of natural resources and the attack on the Gardens of Eden that still remain to us in this age of ruthless progress. Then we have to realize that there will be a cost to be paid, perhaps in terms of gross national product if we are to call a halt to industrial devastation. Above all we have to awaken, as Christians in a democratic country, from the torpor that accepts any pollution or destruction as the inevitable price of progress, or the unstoppable activity of an anonymous "them." Last week's Time Magazine carried a story of a little island that I know. Hilton Head off the coast of South Carolina is a lovely place that has been recently threatened by an industrial development that could pour toxic effluents into the surrounding water. Local action by concerned citizens is at least halting the construction and promoting strong protective legislation. It is not true that an awakened public conscience is helpless in these matters, and the time has come not only for the Church to speak, as I have tried to do this morning, but for Christians to act.

"The Lord God took the man and put him in the garden of Eden to till it and keep it."—To till it, not to rape it; and to keep it: this is a strong word in the Hebrew. It means to protect, to garrison, to defend. Scholars have often wondered against whom man is to defend his Garden of Eden. Now we know.

Am I a Racist?

EDITOR'S INTRODUCTION

RACISM IS MOST CERTAINLY a wicked prejudice. But it is also an absurd prejudice. Why should the color of one's skin matter in the least when skin color is based simply on how close or far away one's ancestors happened to live in relation to the equator? Or based on interracial marriage with the offspring of those whose ancestors *did* happen to live closer to the equator. Still, once the prejudice takes root, all kinds of other prejudices often follow. These racial prejudices are as rational, David Read notes in this sermon, as "the Nazi doctrine of the superiority and right to dominate of the so-called Aryan stock."

Yet even if we are agreed that racism is an utterly irrational prejudice, there is still a great temptation for whites to force Blacks to accept equality on the grounds that Black people accept the prevailing ways of the white culture. This way of solving the problem overlooks the fact that African-Americans have developed their own culture and unique expression of human worth over the years. What we need to do now is simply replace prejudice and rationalization altogether with happy and healthy relationships with one another regardless of skin color. People of all shades of the rainbow need to realize that, in the words of Read's text, "the Lord seeth not as man seeth; for man looketh on the outward appearance, but the Lord looketh on the heart."

AM I A RACIST?

A Sermon preached by David H. C. Read at Madison Avenue
Presbyterian Church on February 8, 1970

Text: " . . . *for the Lord seeth not as man seeth; for man looketh on the
outward appearance, but the Lord looketh on the heart.*" 1 Samuel 16:7

I HAVE CHOSEN THIS Scripture as a guide for our thinking on race relations
this morning for two reasons.

First, because it reminds us in plain language that God is not concerned, as we are, with physical features such as the color of our skin, but
with the man within. He looks through to the heart. And secondly, because
I want to speak from the heart—to your hearts. By that I don't mean talking sentimentally or playing on emotions of pity, fear or guilt, but trying
to understand our own inner convictions, our experience, our prejudices
and our share in the tensions that threaten the nation today. It would be
easy to speak smoothly and impersonally about Christian attitude to race,
about how we are all brothers under the skin and to congratulate ourselves
that membership in this church has always been wide open to all races. But
the fact that any controversy in which race is a factor touches off violent
expressions of opinion among us should be a warning signal that everything
on this front is not sweetness and light. There is not one of us who does not
have to ask himself some searching questions if we are to be honest in the
sight of the Lord who "looketh on the heart."

This is why I propose to you the question: Am I a racist? A few years
ago the question would scarcely have made sense to me. Like many of you, I
assumed that I was color blind, that I treated everyone as a fellow human being whatever race they happened to belong to. Like many of you I was aware
of the injustice done to the black community in the United States beginning
with the abomination of slavery and continuing through years of open and
covert discrimination. And like many of you, I welcomed the remarkable
advance made in recent years towards equal rights for all citizens both in
law and in fact. I was shocked by the occasional explosions of brutality and
murder and also by the violence and rioting that followed in their wake. I
believed that men and women of good will of both races, inspired by Christian compassion and hope were on their way to achieving a society of real
freedom of opportunity and mutual respect.

In all this I was sincere—if somewhat naïve. How could anyone call me
a racist? (My picture of a racist was of a lunatic in a white shirt thirsting for

negro blood.) But some things have been happening in these recent years that have shattered many of the assumptions and illusions of white people with good intentions. And we are being forced either to rethink or react. By reacting I mean the mood that says: "This thing has gone too far. I'm all for black people having equal rights but now they seem to want priority in everything. And just when we were ready to drop all insulting epithets and welcome them as brothers they turn round and cover us with abuse. After we have struggled to end segregation they seem to want some kind of apartheid for themselves. The only thing to do is to put the brake on and stamp out this new militancy before it turns the country into a shambles."

This reaction of the not-so-silent majority is understandable. And, before I plead for its rejection in favor of re-thinking, let me say that I believe a crime is a crime whether committed by white or black, and that it is folly to ignore the existence of those—not necessarily black—who desire the destruction of this nation. But nothing could better serve that end than the kind of reaction that raises the racial temperature, escalates violence and promotes the emergence in this land of what the Kerner Report called "two societies, one black, one white—separate and unequal." We may disagree with some conclusions of that report, but who can deny that the spectre already exists in a nation where blacks are mainly huddled in the center of the cities while whites live in the suburbs and where both live with mounting tension and violence? If we react to the present situation with fear and anger we are helping to ensure that this spectre becomes a frightful reality. Here is surely a point at which our commitment to the Gospel of Christ should give us a deeper insight than is provided by the casual gossip of the world around us and provide a grace that can overcome our natural passions and prejudices. With God looking at our hearts we need, not to react, but to rethink.

Our rethinking begins with the question: "Am I a racist?" A recent dictionary defines racism simply as "the notion that one's own ethnic stock is superior." If that is all it means, then racism might appear no more sinister than our natural tendency to think that our hometown, our nation, our school, our hospital, our football team or even our church is superior. What you might call local loyalties run very deep in human nature and begin the moment the child says: "My father is bigger (or stronger, or richer, or funnier) than yours." But pride of race is a much more vicious thing, for it divides men and women only too often on the basis of the color of their skin. It is also based on an illusion; for there is no such thing as any pure race in the world. We are all mongrels. Nor is there any scientific foundation for the idea that certain human groups are inherently superior, intellectually or morally, to any other.

Racism assumed its ugly overtones with the Nazi doctrine of the superiority and right to dominate of the so-called Aryan stock, and the world is still reeling from the appalling practical consequences of this myth. With such pictures in our minds, you and I tend to recoil in horror and indignation from any suggestion that we might be tainted with racism. I think almost all of us here would claim, whatever our views may be on current controversies, that we treat fellow citizens of a different color with full respect and without any sense of racial superiority. Therefore, we are puzzled and shocked when the statement is made that this is a racist society we are living in and are hurt by the accusation that we ourselves are racist.

I don't think the situation will be improved either by our angry rejection of this word or by an orgy of breast-beating and over compensation. I don't want to be called a racist if I say a black brother is talking nonsense any more than I want to be called an anti-Semite if I disagree with a politician who happens to be a Jew. (In fact, if I pretend to agree with my brother simply because he happened to be black then I *am* revealing a racist attitude.) What we have to do in the light of the God who "looketh upon the heart" is to rethink some of our assumptions.

If, for instance, we listen to what is being said to us by the voice of black power, disregarding the more extreme and hysterical notes, we may begin to discover why our good intentions in the area of civil rights were not perhaps as entirely good as we thought they were. For has there not been an underlying assumption that the ideal we were striving for was the integration of the black into our white society? We said, in effect: "You have too long been denied the privileges of our white culture. Come along in and share them with us." And that presupposes that there is an essential superiority about our way of life. It ignores the fact that there is a black identity to be sought and found, and a black culture not to be suppressed but accepted on equal terms with the other ethnic traditions that make up the richness of our common Americanism. If today an exaggerated black nationalism seems threatening or even to be a repudiation of the principle of integration, we have to remember the hidden racism of our own assumptions. Loving our neighbor as ourselves doesn't mean giving him the privilege of becoming *like* ourselves. It means, among other things, having the patience to let him discover the real self that he must love before he can truly love us.

Then, there is the awkward question of whether or not you and I who disclaim all racial bias are actually enjoying advantages that have come to us through centuries of white control of economic power and social advantages. This is the point where our Christian conscience, consciously or unconsciously, is disturbed. Am I a racist at second-hand because I am profiting from a system in which color has been a factor in keeping millions in the poverty and hopelessness of the ghetto? The Kerner Report was explicit about this: "White society is deeply implicated in the ghetto. White institutions created it, white institutions maintain it, and white society condones it."

When the Lord looks on my heart and asks about this, I don't want to spread a smoke screen of rationalizations—all of which you know. I want to understand, and I want to act. And I don't want to act on the basis of what is called "reparations." This seems to be a futile and endless procedure for every section of the human race to start calculating their debts and submitting bills to one another for various enormities and injustices of the past. I want to act on the basis of present challenges to our conscience and the possibilities of positive results. This is why I am happy that even in a small way our church is beginning to listen to our neighbors in the near north and to respond in the practical questions of housing and social investment. The Christian rethinking of this aspect of racism doesn't mean wallowing in guilt feelings but doing the thing that God shows us to be the practical expression of the Gospel of healing and reconciliation.

" . . . For the Lord seeth not as man seeth; for man looketh on the outward appearance, but the Lord looketh on the heart." If our Christian faith is real within us we shall soon discover the tension between "outward appearance" and the "heart." When our Lord sent his disciples out to be the salt and light of the world he knew that they would be under pressure from the world of "outward appearance." He himself experienced to the full the prejudices of his day, the popular judgments that were based on religion or race. Color doesn't seem to have been an ingredient in the racism of Biblical times, but other "outward appearances" certainly were. When we read that "when Jesus was entered into Capernaum, there came unto him a centurion . . . " the familiar words may blunt the impact of this encounter. Here was a Jew approached by a Gentile. Here was a Palestinian approached by an officer of the occupying army. The "outward appearance" of this situation was ominous. You can imagine how Roman officers would speak about "these natives" in their comfortable clubs. And you can imagine the epithets applied to the Roman soldiery in the dark lanes of Jerusalem. "Lord, my servant lieth at home sick . . . " "I will come and heal him." That was the conversation—and it was as great a miracle as the healing.

Christ saw beyond the outward appearance to the heart—and it was the heavy heart of a good man who cared for his servant and would do anything to help him. What does he see as he looks into our hearts in this time of racial tension? Does he see smouldering suspicions and ugly fears? Or does he see a true desire to understand, a patience that will endure the vituperation of racism in reverse, a humanity that sees past the outward appearance, and a hope that will not abandon the vision of a nation where the wounds are healed, the races reconciled and a new and liberating unity in diversity created for us all?

This is the first time I have spoken here as a white preacher to a nearly white congregation, and I should like never to have to do so again. I have thus spoken because it seemed to me to be false to deal with this theme on any other basis. I am white; most of you are white; and I have sought God's Word to us. But there is no white Gospel or black Gospel. And this is not a white church—for there is no such thing in God's sight. The word of healing is addressed to all; for we are all sinners, and we all need the grace that comes to us from this God who "looketh on the heart."

The Psalm on the Avenue

EDITOR'S INTRODUCTION

FEW SERMONS WOULD SEEM to be preached today on the twenty-third Psalm. This is surprising given the enormous popularity of the Psalm. But maybe that's the problem. The 23rd Psalm is so popular that preachers may think that nothing remains to be said about it. Yet surely plenty is left to say as this sermon demonstrates.

First, however, note the Bible readings that David Read uses by way of creating the context for this sermon. A reading of the 23rd Psalm itself is naturally included, and this in the beloved King James Version. (Why try to improve upon perfection?) Then there's a reading from Peter's epistle with its consoling conclusion: "You had wandered away like sheep. Now you have returned to the one who is your shepherd and protector." And finally the Gospel reading from Mark: "And Jesus when he came out, saw many people, and was moved with compassion toward them, because they were as sheep not having a shepherd: and he began to teach them many things."

Thus the stage is set for a sermon on the psalm that "may well be the best-known religious lyric in the world," and is certainly the best-loved psalm in the Christian Church.

THE PSALM ON THE AVENUE

A Sermon preached by David H. C. Read at Madison Avenue
Presbyterian Church on February 15, 1987

> Text: Psalm 23
>
> Readings: Psalm 23; 1 Peter 2:21–25 (TEV); Mark 6:30–34

THE TWENTY-THIRD PSALM MAY well be the best-known religious lyric in
the world. It is certainly the best-loved psalm in the Christian Church. Originally sung in the Temple in Jerusalem and learned by heart by children in
simple homes like that of Mary and Joseph in Nazareth, it has winged its way
through the centuries in hundreds of translations, and been sung in every
mode of music in great cathedrals, tiny chapels, conventicles of persecuted
Christians on hillsides with guards alert for the presence of the enemy, at
royal weddings, and in the mud and squalor of a battlefield. Phrases from it
are woven into the great literature of every land and also into the chatter of
the avenue today. Who has not heard of "green pastures," "the valley of the
shadow," or some play on the words "My cup runneth over"?

In my native Scotland the psalm, in the metrical version, has become almost a national anthem, and its phrases are as familiar to even non-churchgo-
ers as those of Robert Burns. A story went around the POW camps in World
War II about two Scottish prisoners. One said to the other: "I'll bet you ten
marks that you can't recite the Lord's Prayer." "Done" and off he went: "The
Lord's my shepherd. I'll not want," and through the whole psalm. The other
handed over the ten marks saying, "I never thought you'd make it."

What has given this Hebrew psalm this tremendous grip on the hearts
of people of every age, every language, every walk of life, in every century,
including ours? Some answers are obvious. It uses vivid images. It's beautifully
constructed and the words are simple and concrete. And it packs so much
practical theology into six little verses that its spiritual riches are inexhaustible. I must have read it or heard it thousands of times, yet preparing this
sermon revealed to me how much I had missed, and how much there was still
to come. If you are wise enough to memorise the whole psalm, you'll find that
there is nothing better with which to fill a boring moment in a waiting room,
or, better still, those sleepless hours we all have from time to time.

The psalm on the avenue? This title doesn't literally mean that I commend an inward muttering of this Scripture as we weave our way through
crowds on the sidewalks, dodge the swerving cabs, and are deafened by
roaring suburban busses (although I did just that last week for obvious

reasons). I'm simply saying that the content of this psalm has as much to do with our deepest needs, the hopes and fears of the modern New Yorker as it had with King David in his oriental palace or a peasant on the Galilean hills.

Not long ago we were being told that in our search for relevance preachers should avoid images like the shepherd and his sheep. (Someone even produced a new variation which began "The Lord is my parking lot attendant.") Although it may be helpful to be reminded of some ancient customs that would be familiar to those who first heard the psalm, I am assuming that you know what a sheep is and have at least seen a picture of a shepherd. You may even know that shepherds in the Middle East lead their sheep and don't keep them in front of them with the aid of expert dogs. They had no dogs. Now are we ready for the psalm?

"The Lord"—that's the God in whom we believe with different degrees of conviction. The word here is the most powerful four-letter word in religious history. The mysterious "I AM" with which the Bible reminds us that he cannot be described (not even *with* the pronoun "he"). God just *is*. We must use images. And here is one that has burned its way into the Christian heart ever since Jesus said: "I am the good shepherd." For us it is impossible to repeat this psalm without the thought of him. It doesn't matter whether our first thought is of God the Father or of the Son who revealed him since the words of Christ are "He who has seen me has seen the Father."

"The Lord is my shepherd." The psalmist chooses this particular metaphor to transmit the greatest discovery of his stormy life—that we have a God who cares, cares as a good shepherd cares for his flock. If that sounds a very familiar thought that is only because most of us have in the back of our minds (or the depth of our souls) the assurance of Jesus that not a sparrow falls to the ground without God's noticing and that the very hairs of our head are numbered. The image of the Shepherd, or rather the Shepherd-King, was familiar in Egypt and other ancient lands, but the King predominated, and that King was usually too occupied with his affairs—hurling thunderbolts, getting drunk, or fighting with other divine Kings—to care much about the human race. More sophisticated religions had more refined ideas of the divine, so refined that, like their equivalent today, they lacked any message of a deeply personal care for people like you and me.

In one verse the psalm brings the kind of assurance that we long for, whether we live in a tent in the desert of Sinai or Madison Avenue, New York. God cares—and since he cares, "I shall not want." As the Coverdale Bible translates in the Anglican Prayerbook, "Therefore shall I lack nothing." "Lack nothing?" Is this some kind of promise that we'll never be in want of any kind? Is this the modern religion of success—all these tales about becoming a Christian and then finding all kinds of goodies falling into our lap?

No, it is a promise that I shall not be in want of anything I really need, whatever happens. That's why the psalm goes on to describe all that can happen to us—good and bad—as we go forward trusting in the Shepherd-God. There are dangers ahead, real dangers we cannot wish away. So first we are told about the need for the moment of stillness, the refreshment of our souls.

"He maketh me to lie down in green pastures: he leadeth me beside the still waters. He restoreth my soul." We shall respond to God's presence, be armed with his grace, only if we make room in our crowded lives for the stillness when we can hear the word "I am God: I am with you." Just as from the uproar of the avenue we sometimes let our thoughts drift off to some favorite island, some lovely loch, some murmuring stream, so we can make room for the time of prayer, the service of worship where God waits to restore our soul. A busy city doctor once told me he came to church to get his "batteries recharged." That's a modern image, and it's what the psalmist meant by "He restoreth my soul."

Something else happens when we pray or worship. We can't help reflecting on the direction our life is taking. Am I just drifting? Have I learned to live with bad habits that used to trouble my conscience? In the choices I have to make do I ask first: Is this the right decision or is my question: Which will be easier or more comfortable? That's when the Shepherd-God comes alongside and moves me in the right direction. The "paths of righteousness" may not be a familiar phrase out there on the avenue, but isn't the choice between right and wrong, what we call the ethical issue behind story after story in our daily paper? Don't we need the guidance of the Shepherd-God in our homes, in our schools, in Congress, and on Wall Street?

The psalmist is a realist too when he thinks about the way ahead. There will be trials. There will be dangers. There will be loneliness and pain. It is not all "green pastures and still waters." He sees ahead the "valley of the shadow." What he wrote was the "dark shadows," and he conjured up the picture of the flock on their way home passing through a dark defile where dangers lurked, and they might be ambushed by robbers, or seized by wolves.

Without the shepherd they would be lost. They needed his staff to pick their way in the dark through the rough places, and his rod to beat off any attackers. The psalmist knew about the valley of the shadow, and so do we. And this is where the psalm, for me, reaches its climax. If I were to extract one phrase as a heading and a summary, it would be this: "I will fear no evil: for thou art with me."

Have you noticed how the writer who has been speaking of the Shepherd-God in the third person—"He leadeth me." "He restoreth my soul" now slips into the second? "*Thou* art with me." This happens in all true prayer. We may meditate on the nature, the promises, the gifts of God, but the moment comes when we must talk as we talk to an intimate friend. I can say to myself "God will be with me in the valley of the shadow." But it is different to be able to say: "I will fear no evil for *thou* art with me, thy rod and thy staff they comfort me." This is a deeply personal psalm: that's why it meets our needs.

"I will fear no evil: for thou art with me." For the Christian the divine presence is Jesus Christ, the "good shepherd" who gave his life for the sheep. We fear no evil for the one who is with us has known the very worst that can happen to any one of us and has come through. His enemies, who are our enemies, could not defeat him—even that "last enemy" which is death. The resurrection light shines right through the valley of the shadow. Therefore, it is not surprising that the Christian Church accepted a scribal change in the original text and translated "through the valley of the shadow of death." No one escapes that valley, and it is when we are there, or even approaching from a distance that, more than ever, we need the grace to say: "I will fear no evil: for thou art with me; thy rod and thy staff they comfort me" (remembering that "comfort" here means "strengthen and protect").

Now in the last two verses the picture changes, without disturbing the unity of the psalm. Suddenly we are at a banquet. The sheep are gone (except, perhaps, in the form of mutton). We can think of some glorious feast of the Shepherd-King with an abundance of good things and every comfort provided for the guest—an image of the heavenly banquet which awaits the end of our pilgrimage. Didn't Jesus say at the Last Supper: "I will drink no more of the fruit of the vine until that day when I drink it new in the Kingdom of God"? But we may rather think of the traveler stumbling through the valley of the shadow and emerging to see the lights of a tent set up in the desert, and being welcomed and copiously refreshed at the table. God, like the Prodigal Father of the parable, lavishes his hospitality on his returning child.

"Thou preparest a table before me in the presence of mine enemies." The banquet is not pie in the sky but pie right here where the enemy is still real and near. That's why our service of Holy Communion is not a sad memorial but a celebration of the Victor. We can joyfully meet with him even when the darkness may be closing in. I felt that powerfully once when I found myself singing with some Scottish troops on a field in Flanders with enemy bombers droning overhead: "My table thou hast furnished in presence of my foes." The anointing with oil and the brimming beakers were the symbols of welcome all over the Middle East, and they speak here of the royal welcome and limitless refreshment offered by the Shepherd-King, even when the enemy is near.

But they also speak to the Christian of the end of the road. As the psalm closes it picks up the quiet, but confident, note with which it began. "The Lord is my shepherd; I shall not want." No; not even when I pass through the veil to a totally new dimension of life, for "Eye hath not seen, nor ear heard, neither have entered into the heart of man, the things which God hath prepared for them that love him."

At a time when our future is being painted in grim terms, and the end of the world as a bang or a whimper, and when that fact is being used in the scare tactics of religious orators who claim to know all about heaven and hell, what could be more steadying and satisfying than these calm and confident words of the psalmist: "Surely goodness and mercy shall follow me all the days of my life; and I shall dwell in the house of the Lord for ever." What more do we need?

Prayer: We thank thee, O God, for the inspiration of thy Word coming to us across many centuries and through many lives. Grant that we may walk forward in the paths of righteousness knowing that thy goodness and mercy will follow us all our days, and we will dwell in the house that thou has prepared forever. Through Christ our Lord. Amen.

The Season of Lent

Root Questions for Lent:
What Makes Me a Christian?

EDITOR'S INTRODUCTION

David Read's Lenten sermons normally took the form of variations on a single theme. The first question that he raises in "Root Questions for Lent" is "What Makes Me A Christian?" The answer, he suggests, has to do with our response to the summons of Jesus: "Come to me, all whose work is hard, whose load is heavy, and I will give you relief."

Almost all of us feel that our work is hard and our load is heavy. But why believe that Jesus gives us relief? Read recalls his own life experiences in answering this question. First of all, he was born into a family that predisposed him to believing in Christ. Then he intellectually experienced the persuasive power of the Christian faith. Next, he responded to the emotional power of the Gospel. Finally, he took an actual leap of faith, thereby personally testing the weight of Christ's promises.

The question now becomes: Is this leap of faith vindicated by divine reality, or are David Read and others like him simply taking a leap into the dark? That question, surely, can only be answered in the process of taking the leap of faith ourselves. And this is something, Read observes, that could occur that very morning as Communion is celebrated and Confirmation takes place.

ROOT QUESTIONS FOR LENT: WHAT MAKES ME A CHRISTIAN?

A Sermon preached by David H. C. Read at Madison Avenue Presbyterian Church on March 4, 1977

Text: *"Come to me . . . "* Matthew 11:28

Readings: Joshua 24:14–18; 2 Timothy 1:3–9 (TEV); Matthew 11:25–28 (TEV)

FOR THE BEGINNING OF Lent I have selected the simplest text in the entire Bible. "Come to me. . . . " and for the first root question that every church member is almost sure to ask more than once between the age of nine and ninety: "What makes me a Christian?" The text is simple but not easy—for it demands that we discover who it is that has the right to say to everyone of us: "Come to me," and it requires a lot of self-examination to give an honest answer to the question: "What makes me a Christian?"

"Come to me." Jesus had been visiting the towns scattered around the Sea of Galilee, preaching and healing. Everywhere he had found people in need—not only the crippled, the blind, the epileptic, and the lepers—but the poor, the overworked, the anxious, the scared, and the depressed. As he tried to help as many as he could, he sensed an even greater need. And that had to do with their religion. To him believing in God is a lifting of the load, a giving of inward strength, and a helping to bear other people's burdens. What he found was that the official religion of the day was actually adding to their troubles. For they were told that to please God they had to keep to the rules—and these rules were very strict and complicated. Some felt that they couldn't make it so they just dropped out of religion altogether—whereupon the religious authorities labelled them "tax gatherers" (which was a term of abuse in those days) and "sinners", and they spent their lives with the unhappy thought that God had no further use for them. Others tried to keep the rules, but for tired, hardworking people religious duties could be like the straw that broke the camel's back. Believing in God was made to seem like one extra load they had to bear. It was too much. Almost the only people that Jesus found with a spontaneous and joyful trust in God were the children. That's why he liked them to come clambering around him as he talked.

It was to a crowd in one of these towns that Jesus spoke one day and startled them all by saying: "Come to me, all whose work is hard, whose load is heavy; and I will give you relief." (Another translation is "I will refresh you.") What he was saying was: "The kind of God I represent doesn't want to add to your load but to help you carry it. The religion I stand for is not worry but wings—wings to lift you up. It's not something to be carried but something to carry you. 'Come to me and I will refresh you.'"

That was revolutionary—for more than one reason. First, it transformed their idea of God from that of a stern taskmaster to that of a Father who loved them and was ready to forgive all their sins and welcome them into his Kingdom where they would find strength and joy and peace. Second, it was revolutionary because Jesus used the word "all" in his invitation. For "all" meant more than the respectable, the devout, the meticulous keepers of the Law. It included the dropouts, those who had been turned off religion, the kind of people who say "Leave me alone with all that mumbo jumbo," and those on whom the pious turned their backs—tax collectors, prostitutes, even Roman soldiers. "Come to me *all* whose work is hard"—and whose isn't? (Even ministers have been known to think their work is hard.) In the third place, this was a revolutionary call for who else in the wide world has ever been known to say: "Come to me"? Yes, I know that dictators arise who try to attract a whole nation, and even some scholars or leaders of cults have been so sure of themselves that they seem to be saying: "My philosophy has all the answers. Come to me and learn of me." But has anyone dared to invite all, every conceivable type of person who has this burden in every part of the world from that day in Galilee to March, 1979, saying "Come to me"? No other religious leader has used these words—not the Buddha, not Mohammed, not Joseph Smith, not Mary Baker Eddy, not even Mr. Moon. The most they will say is: "I will show you the God to whom you must come." Jesus said: "Come to me" and with these words he makes the unique claim that he expressed when, on another occasion, he said: "Anyone who has seen me as seen the Father."

Those who have, in one way or another, responded to this amazing invitation are called Christians. You don't find the word in the Gospels, but the Book of Acts tells us that it was given to those who had come to Jesus by the people of Antioch as a kind of nickname. And it stuck. In the early days the label "Christian" stuck out like a sore thumb. If you admitted to being one you risked losing your job, or your friends, or even your life. Much later when the Gospel had spread all over Europe the word covered whole nations. Virtually everyone was baptized on entering the world and people spoke of a Christian nation, a Christian civilization. Where are we today? Things are changing. You are more likely to be asked the question: "Are you a Christian?" than your father was, or your grandmother. The question used to mean: "You're not a Jew, are you? Or a Muslim? Or an agnostic?—then you must be a Christian." Now it is veering back to the original meaning: "Are you a believer in Christ? Are you, in fact, one who has come to him?" And what is your answer?

If, as I hope is true for many here, your answer is Yes, then you must now be prepared for the next question: Why? Why are you a Christian? Have you ever had to answer that one? I have. So let me try to summarize my answer in the hope that you also will try to formulate your own. For there is no one answer that is totally correct. And I hope that if there is anyone listening who is thinking: "I'm not sure that I *am* a Christian" will find this a helpful exercise, and perhaps hear in a new way these words of Jesus: "Come unto me."

(1) The first thing I would say is perhaps not what you would expect. It would be tempting for me, as a preacher, to offer all the arguments for be-lieving in Jesus Christ as Lord and Savior. Why am I a Christian? "Well, you see, I first of all went into all the reasons for and against believing in God. Then, when I was convinced, I made a thorough study of the rival claims of all the great religious teachers of the world and decided that Jesus had more of the truth than any other. Then I analyzed all the doctrines in the creeds of the Church and satisfied my mind that they were acceptable. That's how I came to Jesus. That's why I am a Christian." Absolute nonsense. The first reason I must give is the honest one: I was born to a Christian family and a Christian tradition.

Does that shock you? Well, it may sound like a thin reason, but it's the truth. Do you honestly think that if I'd been born in an Indian village, or in Cairo, I would have worked my way by sheer study into the Christian faith? When Karl Barth, the theologian, one of the greatest minds this century has produced, was asked by a University colleague why, with all his intellectual brilliance he came to accept the Christian Gospel, he replied: "Because my mother told me." Many though not all, who are here today would have to say that family background had a lot to do with the fact that they are Christian.

And why not? What my mother told me, what my schools taught me has to do with what I believe about the stars or the atoms, about Julius Cae-sar or King Tut, microbes and medicines. I couldn't have discovered these things on my own, and it has never occurred to me to question their truth simply on the grounds that I inherited this kind of knowledge. So I accept the fact that I was baptized as an infant and taught to pray to Jesus at an early age and recognize that this is most certainly one of the reasons why I am a Christian.

(2) But of course this can't be the whole story. Lots of people who were baptized and raised in the Christian faith either renounce it in later life or just drift away. And lots of people today are coming to Jesus in their maturity although they have no background in the faith whatever. Obviously the very first disciples had no such ancestral pressure to make them Christians. They came to Jesus on their own. And sooner or later that has to happen to us.

I may have been taught to say on going to bed:

"Gentle Jesus, meek and mild,
Look upon a little child.
Pity my simplicity;
Suffer me to come to thee,"

but it was not very long before my critical mind got to work on these words. Jesus, I discovered as a teenager, was by no means "meek and mild," and I had no intention of confessing my simplicity or asking him to "suffer" (which was a word I had never understood) me to come to him. From there it was a short step to begin questioning all I had been told about God, about Jesus, about prayer, and about the Church.

Now, of course, there were always people who would tell me not to ask those questions. "Just shut your eyes and believe," they would say—but I couldn't. I had to think through the religious teachings I had inherited. And in my late teens I began to find the arguments of skeptical writers much more appealing and the church I was dragged to a bit of a bore. Fortunately I later made contact with people who seemed equally as clever as those skeptics and yet who believed. I don't mean that all my doubts fell away or that I found it easy to bring my religion into focus with all the other activities of my mind. The thinking-through process went on right through college days and—most stringent of all—through a seminary training, and I hope the process never ends.

So one of the things that I have to say when asked the question: "What makes you a Christian?" is that I have, in the end, found the Christian interpretation of the universe, the Christian ethic, and the Christian image of God more intellectually satisfying than any other religious or philosophical position that I have come across. It's not that I was argued into the faith, or that I have not still many questions to which God seems unwilling to give me the answers. It's just that I have to say that, once I have responded to Jesus' invitation to come to him, a lot of things seem to slip into place in my mind and make sense. So I am a Christian at least in part because, like Paul, "I am persuaded." In these days when we are not encouraged to use our critical faculties in the field of religion and almost any absurdity seems to be acceptable without any examination, it is good to listen to the commandment to love the Lord our God "with all our minds," and, as the New Testament says, "to be able to give a reason for the faith that is in you."

(3) But it would be misleading to give the impression that it is my mind alone that makes me a Christian. Equally as important as my thinking is my feeling. Why should we be ashamed to admit that our emotions are

deeply involved in our Christian faith? When Good Friday comes around I don't find myself here in church thinking of the doctrine of the atonement or philosophizing about the sufferings of Christ. I see him on his cross again. I hear words like: "Father, forgive them, for they know not what they do." I am like Zinzendorf, the European aristocrat who found himself one day gazing at a picture of the crucifixion and heard a voice say: "All this have I done for you. What hast thou done for me"—and then became one of the great Christian leaders of his day. These haunting words of Jesus "Come to me" are not just spoken to the mind. They are an appeal to our hearts from the heart of the living God. This is why Jesus continues to haunt this generation with his appeal. It speaks to something very deep inside us. Once you really hear his "Come to me" you will have no rest until you respond. And for those of us who feel that, in a sense, we have already come, there is that other terrible question he once put to his disciples when all around seemed to be rejecting him: "Will you also go away?"

Just last week I heard a small group of representative New Yorkers, of varied church allegiance or none, speak very personally of the moments when the light seemed to come on, and they were responding to this appeal of Jesus. No one spoke of arguments or doctrines. Everyone had something to say about a curious and deeply emotional response to the Spirit of Christ. If we can get worked up about a political issue, if we can let ourselves go in delirious support of our favorite football or baseball team, if we can be moved to tears at a movie, a play, or a concert, why should we be ashamed to admit that Jesus Christ makes a deeply emotional appeal and that we really mean it when we sing:

> "When I survey the wondrous cross,
> On which the Prince of Glory died,
> My richest gain I count but loss,
> And pour contempt on all my pride."

(4) But I have left something out. Yes, my background helped to make me a Christian. Yes, my thinking has led me in that direction. Yes, my feelings are mysteriously aroused by the story of Jesus. But none of this would make me a Christian unless I answered this invitation: "Come unto me." If a man says to a woman: "I love you. Will you marry me?" she may say to herself: "I know from my background about this marriage business, and I think it's what I want to do;" or "I've been thinking about this man, and I'm convinced he'd make a good husband;" or "Gee, he really turns me on!" But she will not become his wife until she says the magic words "Yes, I will." A boy or girl at Confirmation gratefully remembers the family background and early teaching. You have

been through a course in which you had to use your minds. You have, I hope, felt the tremendous appeal of Jesus in the depth of your heart. But there is a moment when you say: "Yes; I will." It is ultimately this movement of the will, this open commitment that makes you or me a Christian.

Every time we have a service of confirmation in this church, I am aware of older people present who are saying to themselves: "I wish I could have an opportunity to do just this: to say simply and openly, "Yes, Jesus Christ is my Lord and Savior." It can be done, of course, anywhere and at any time.

Often what is lacking in people who confess that they want to be Christians but find their faith wobbly and unreal is just this—that they have known the appeal of the background, the mind, and the emotions, but have never deliberately used the will and said that simple "Yes." There is one opportunity that God gives us regularly to do just that. When you are offered the bread and wine with which the crucified and risen Christ comes to each of us the very act of taking, eating, and drinking can be our Yes.

For here again at the Table Jesus says: "Come to me." And to partake in faith is our "Yes, Lord; I come."

> Prayer: Speak thine own word, Lord Jesus, to those bowed before thee now, and may this be a time when each of us says and renews our Yes to thy great appeal, for thy name's sake, Amen.

Strong Stories for Lent:
The Cross of Moses

EDITOR'S INTRODUCTION

THIS STRONG STORY FOR Lent finds Moses excoriating the children of Israel for exchanging the one true God for the pagan worship of a golden calf. Convinced that God is calling his people to a new and faithful life totally different from that of the surrounding tribes, Moses literally takes the bull by the horns, grinds it into powder, mixes it with water and forces the rebellious Israelites to drink it.

"There's a fierceness in this story," David Read concedes, "that we shouldn't try to soften, and a savagery in another account that slips into this chapter about the bloody purging of the people that we shouldn't try to excuse." Even so, the blood-curdling story does more than sound the note of judgment. It also and especially signals the promise of grace as Moses proceeds to make atonement for his people's sins: "Oh, this people have sinned a great sin, and have made them gods of gold. Yet now, if thou wilt forgive their sin—; and if not blot me, I pray thee, out of thy book which thou hast written." Thus Moses is seen not only as leading God's people through the wilderness, but as anticipating the grace of God in the *new* Moses, the One who allows "the whole weight of our sins (to) blot out his name from the book of life," and addresses us all from the Cross, saying, "Father, forgive them; for they know not what they do."

STRONG STORIES FOR LENT: THE CROSS OF MOSES

A Sermon preached by David H. C. Read at Madison Avenue Presbyterian Church on March 13, 1977, Lent

Text: *"And Moses returned unto the Lord, and said, Oh, this people have sinned a great sin, and have made them gods of gold. Yet now, if thou wilt forgive their sin—; and if not, blot me, I pray thee, out of thy book which thou hast written."* Exodus 32:31, 32

Readings: Exodus 32:15–24; 30–33 (NEB); Romans 9:1–5 (NEB); Mark 14:32–36

A SHORT STORY I once came across was based on the alluring supposition that the prayers of a Christian congregation were all immediately granted. As I remember it the climax came when they rose to sing the classic hymn by Isaac Watts called "There is a land of pure delight." As soon as they voiced the words:

> "Could we but climb where Moses stood,
> And view the landscape o'er"

the entire congregation found itself transported to Mount Pisgah which commands a magnificent view of a large tract of the territory of modern Israel.

Well, in a sense I am going to transport you to the land of Moses this morning, and the fact that the borders of Israel are high up on the agenda of the State Department today should remind us that in the Bible we are not reading of some never-never land and that Moses is no legendary figure like Hercules or Jack the Giant-killer. The figure of Moses belongs with the cluster of outstanding leaders who have left an indelible mark on human history and, in particular, with those who are associated with a great movement of liberation for their people. Moses raises for us the perennial questions about such leadership. Granted that history teaches us that the aspirations of any people for liberty from bondage, for a better life, for satisfying goals, tend to focus on one charismatic figure, what kind of person do we want him to be? With how much power can any human being be entrusted? How can we prevent a great liberator from becoming a despot who again enslaves his people? Hitler was indeed the man who liberated his people from what he called "the shackles of Versailles." Lenin and Stalin were thought of as liberators of the Russian people from the old regime. But into what slavery of mind and conscience did these men lead their people. What, then, are the qualities needed in one who is endowed with this mysterious gift of leadership, and how should he be related to the people whose loyalty he commands?

The answer of the Bible rings out from the stories of a vast and varied list of leaders—Abraham, Joseph, Moses, Deborah, Gideon, Samuel, Saul, David, Jesus, Peter, Paul, to name a few, with contrasting types like the Pharaoh, Jezebel, Nebuchadnezzar, Cyrus, Herod, Augustus, and Nero. The character and ambitions of such as these are analyzed in scores of histories and biographies, but what the Bible sets before us as the primary quality of a true leader is often ignored. It can be stated quite simply: *the true leader must himself, or herself, be led by God.* As these great personalities pass before us in the pages of the Bible, they are all being judged by this criterion:

Were they—to use the language of our Pledge of Allegiance—"under God?" There are no illusions about human nature in these Bible books, no suggestion that anyone at all can be entrusted with immense power over others without the safeguard of a humble dependence on a holy God. We talk of the need for *responsible* leadership. But to whom is human power—political, economic, military, technological—ultimately responsible—answerable—if we should lose belief in the sovereign God who is our final judge? The Bible exposes the claim of every tyrant to be seeking only the good of those whom he controls. The cliché that "power corrupts" is the sober testimony of history. The leader must be led. The power must be subject to the one great Power who requires that we "do justly, and love mercy, and walk humbly with our God."

Moses was pre-eminently such a man. In the story I have selected from the thirty-second chapter of Exodus, he appears not only as a charismatic leader dealing with a crisis in the Great March of his people to the Promised Land—and behaving with all the vigor, decisiveness, and even ugly temper of any of the world's great heroes—but also as the utterly devoted servant of the Lord his God. This is where the narrative differs so spectacularly from that of any secular history book. What puzzles and even repels the modern readers, this constant refrain of "Moses said to the Lord" and "the Lord said to Moses," is in fact the key to the inner meaning of Moses' leadership. Just how Moses talked with the Lord, and exactly how God communicated with him is of little importance. For the Bible narrators it was natural to cast it all in the form of an intimate conversation—and I, for one, would rather have it that way than listen to condescending talk about the "primitive anthropomorphism of the earlier strata of the Pentateuch." (Incidentally, a book by a Princeton scholar, reviewed in last week's "Time," proclaims the startling theory that it was not until after the time of Moses that human beings developed consciousness and the power of thought, and that before then they were directed entirely by inner voices telling them what to do. The left side of the brain is said to be for speech while the right side produces the inner commands. I note this only to suggest that we don't really know what kind of communication went on between Moses and the Lord.)

What matters is the intense conviction of this leader that God was calling his people to a new and fruitful life totally different from that of the surrounding tribes, a life both disciplined and free. Unlike the prevailing polytheism the religion of this people was to be rooted in an unswerving loyalty to the one true God whose will was made known in the way of life spelled out in the Ten Commandments. What was happening away out there in the desert was a revolution that was to change the course of history. What Moses discerned was that the God who had liberated them from slavery and made known his will was the one supreme Lord and that to defect from him was to betray their calling to reflect his justice, his compassion, and his purity. What infuriated him when the Israelites lost heart in the desert trek, when they rebelled against his leadership, when they took the opportunity of his absence one day to create for themselves a pagan image in the shape of a golden calf, was their refusal to believe that they were being called to a new and holy life. The issue of polytheism was not a theoretical or theological question. The point is simply that if you make your own gods, or collect an assortment of other peoples' gods, you have no standard of right and wrong. Polytheism is as much at issue today as it was in that ancient desert. It is the ethics of polytheism we are hearing whenever there is talk about the total relativity of moral standards. So when Moses came down from the mount with the tables of the law and found his people cavorting around the golden calf, he lost his temper.

Joshua heard the noise and said: "I hear the sound of battle in the camp." Moses said: "That doesn't sound to me like a shout of victory or a cry of defeat. It's the sound of singing." And so it was—nothing less than a pagan orgy. "When Moses came close enough to see the people dancing, he became furious. There at the foot of the mountain he threw down the tables he was carrying and broke them." It tells us something about the strength of leadership in this man that he walked into that orgy and literally took the bull by the horns. He ground the golden bull into powder, mixed it with water and forced people to drink it. There's a fierceness in the story at this point that we shouldn't try to soften, and a savagery in another account that slips into this chapter about the bloody purging of the people that we shouldn't try to excuse. What we have here, in contemporary terms, is the blazing loyalty of this leader to his God, his passionate desire to lead them to the promised land, and the courage with which he posed the fatal question: "Who is on the Lord's side?"

The Moses who looms out of this story as the God-intoxicated leader of his people has not only been for the Jewish people the towering symbol of devotion to the divine Law; he has hovered over Christian history as a sign of the enduring validity of the Ten Commandments and as the great Leader of the people of God. Moses and Elijah, representing the Law and the prophets, are never far away from the Gospel story. The verse from the Prologue of John's Gospel—"for the law was given by Moses, but grace and truth came by Jesus Christ"—might seem to write him off as belonging to a superseded religion, but neither Jesus nor his apostles banished Moses to the limbo of forgotten heroes of the faith. In fact, the Church increasingly saw in him the prototype of the "leader under God," and found in his passionate determination to guide his people, despite all their complaints and rebellion, "through Hell and high water," to the Promised Land, an allegory of the pilgrimage of the Christian Church. Moses with his pleading with God for his people, Moses with his utter loyalty to the God of the Covenant became a symbol of the Christ who was to come. So Paul could even tie Moses into the life of the Christian with such words as these: "I want you to remember my brothers, what happened to our ancestors who followed Moses. They were all under the protection of the cloud, and all passed safely through the Red Sea. In the cloud and in the sea they were all baptized as followers of Moses. All ate the same spiritual bread and drank the same spiritual drink. They drank from the spiritual rock that went with them; and that rock was Christ himself."

We begin to see that there is more to this story of Moses than merely an example of a "leader under God," a man who, like Jesus, passionately believed that nothing mattered more than doing the Father's will. At the end of this chapter from Exodus we come across a passage that is so memorable and moving that it seemed to me as I read it again that the shadow of the cross of Jesus fell across the page.

The words of Moses to the people after this fearful confrontation around the golden calf and his violent denunciation of their apostasy throw another light on the nature of his leadership. His temper has cooled and there emerges that other quality that makes a true leader in the sight of God—a mighty compassion, a suffering with and for the people whom he serves. "And it came to pass on the morrow, that Moses said unto the people, Ye have sinned a great sin: and now I will go up unto the Lord; peradventure I shall make atonement for your sins."

The ensuing prayer of Moses to the Lord is for me the high water mark of the Pentateuch. Nothing in the Old Testament short of the fifty-third chapter of Isaiah with its picture of the servant of the Lord who "was wounded for our transgressions" can compare with this. It was, of all things, a peculiarity of punctuation in the King James' version that first drew my attention to this verse. It is the only place in the whole Bible where you find an unfinished sentence and a dash. "Oh, this people have sinned a great sin. . . . Yet now, if thou wilt forgive their sin—" Within that dash lie all the agony and uncertainty of a faith that totally yields to the will of God but is not sure if he is really the God who will forgive, the God of mercy, the God of pardoning love. "*If* thou wilt forgive"—if, if, if . . . Is this God of the Covenant, this God of utter holiness, this one and only God a forgiver, or is he not? Perhaps not. Then the love of Moses for this disobedient and unlovely people breaks out in the astounding words: "and if not, blot me, I pray thee, out of thy book."

Here is leadership of a kind the world can scarcely imagine—a compassion, a willingness to suffer with, that goes the length of laying his own life on the altar of sacrifice. You could even say that within that dash in our Bibles Moses descended into hell, willing to be blotted out with the very people he had tried to guide and save. Do you see now why I can talk about the cross of Moses? He's not just the leader who drives his people forward in the name of God. He's the one who so identifies himself with this human family that he is willing to endure the suffering, even to accept the last fearful penalty of their sins.

What a contrast with that other leader in the story—Aaron, Moses' spokesman and friend. While Moses was wrestling with the Lord on the mountain, Aaron's identification with the people took another form—one quite familiar to us as the spokesmen and friends of Jesus. When the people demanded an idol he just went along. He probably said: "Well, Moses has been away a long time, and these folk are getting restless. They might as well have this golden calf. To me it's just an idol, but if it keeps them quiet, let them have it." Compassion? Yes; the easy compassion that has no depth of understanding. And how feeble and foolish does Aaron look when Moses returns! Isn't there something familiar about the shamefaced excuses he makes for his lack of real leadership, real compassion? "Don't be angry with me; you know how determined these people are to do evil. They said to me, 'We don't know what has happened to this man Moses, who brought us out of Egypt; so make us a god to lead us.' I asked them to bring me their gold and their ornaments . . . I threw the ornaments into the fire—and out came this bull!" You can almost hear Moses saying "Oh yes?"

How like the disciples of Jesus, yesterday and today. Our leadership quickly loses power when the Master seems far away. Our compassion so easily takes the form of acquiescence in whatever idols are in vogue. But just as Moses reappears, the Moses who is willing to be blotted out with the people whom he loves, so Christ reappears to us this Lent and calls us to the kind of leadership he represents. "If anyone will follow me let him deny himself, *and take up his cross*, and follow me." This is the supreme Leader given for the whole human race, the One for whom the world waits, the One who emerged from the story of Moses and the race of Moses. He was the leader sent from God to fill that blank in the prayer of Moses. For he spoke with a total and sublime assurance that word of forgiveness for which we hunger. He spoke it as he walked the streets and met with the sick in body and in mind. He spoke it to every kind of person who looked and found in him the reflection of the Father's love. And he spoke it from that cross where he was letting the whole weight of our sins blot out his name from the book of life: "Father, forgive them; for they know not what they do."

This is the leader to whom we turn this morning. And he asks us, as the members of his Church, to go out and be leaders, with courage and conviction "under God," and in our hearts the compassion of his Cross.

Prayer: Lord, we would offer ourselves as followers of him who not only loved thee with heart and mind and soul but loved us so much as to give himself for us. In his name make us to be leaders and grant us guidance in all that we do through him. Amen.

Roots of a Living Faith: The Grip of a Loving God

EDITOR'S INTRODUCTION

WHEN POPE JOHN PAUL II visited New York City in 1979, David Read preached a cheering sermon on John 3:16 under the title "God's Love—a New Pope and an Old Text." Nine years later we find Read returning to the same beloved text to preach this Lenten sermon.

Earlier Read had called John 3:16 "the most familiar and best loved text in the entire New Testament." It is certainly a beloved text in evangelical circles, and even amongst many mainstream congregants. However, not a few mainline preachers wince over this text, surrounded as it is by so many legalistic sounding verses (e.g., John 3:18: "Those who believe in Christ are not condemned; but those who do not believe are condemned already, because they have not believed in the name of the only Son of God.")

Forget the legalism, Read says in effect. There will always be signs of human over-kill in our fallible Bibles. Focus rather on the light that shines in the darkness. And the light that shines through this particular text reminds us that "we can shake the hand of Christ in prayer and Holy Communion and know that whatever may happen to us we are in the grip of the loving God."

ROOTS OF A LIVING FAITH: THE GRIP OF A LOVING GOD

A Sermon preached by David H. C. Read at Madison Avenue Presbyterian Church on March 13, 1988, Lent

> Text: *"For God so loved the world, that he gave his only begotten Son, that whosoever believeth in him should not perish, but have everlasting life."* John 3:16
>
> Readings: Numbers 2:4–9; Ephesians 2:4–10 (NEB); John 3:14–21 (NEB)

IF I WERE ASKED by a friend who was not a member of any church—one of those genial agnostics who have no desire to attack anyone's religious beliefs or to dismantle the traditional expressions of faith in this country but are frankly puzzled how any intelligent person today can be a believer—to say in a few words what a living faith means to me, what would I reply?

That's the question I have asked myself in preparing this sermon. I'm talking of an intimate conversation between two friends, not of a public meeting where I am expounding or defending the contents of the Christian faith, or a sermon which, you must have noticed, is seldom limited to "a few words." At such a time one gets down to the roots. All the familiar pulpit phrases, all the scraps of conventional apologetic vanish as I seek an honest answer to an honest question: "What does it really mean to you?" Peeling away the onion skins of religious tradition, habits of prayer and worship, creeds and confessions, outward professions of faith in baptism, confirmation, and ordination, what's at the heart of it all? In Ibsen's play "Peer Gynt" his hero is shown doing just that. One by one the layers come off and litter the stage until the tragic moment when he stares at us and says "There *is* no heart."

For me there is. And the shortest, simplest way to say what it is, is the title of this sermon: "The Grip of a Loving God." That's what I discovered to be the living center of my faith. To put it differently: this is the magnetic north to which my spiritual compass keeps returning, no matter how wildly it may have swung. There is Someone there in charge of the universe, who brings a cosmos out of chaos, and is in charge of me and the entire human family. And the nature of this immortal, invisible Spirit is Love—not love as a glimmering ideal a billion miles away, but active love. At the heart of my faith is this One of whom the Bible says not only: "God is love" but that "God *so* loved that he gave . . . " And the living center of my faith is that the universe, the cosmos, the human family, my life and yours are in the grip of this loving God. And it is Christ, above all, who brings me this confidence.

Now let me bring you another scripture. This time it is not from a page in the Bible but from a wall in Grand Central Station among the graffiti. It hit my eye last week as I was making for a subway with this sermon on my mind. There, scribbled at eye level was this terrible question: "Why does God hate the homeless?"

All the way back here I sat in the subway car with this question ringing in my mind. It was as if a voice from the other New York was challenging my simple faith. It was saying: "All very well for you with a comfortable home and regular meals to be sure you are in the grip of a loving God. What about me?" A fair question. No use thinking, "Well, I did once have some years without a real bed or full meals," for I knew then that there was at least a fifty-fifty chance that I would get out of a prison camp and back to the comforts and securities that most of us take for granted. What must it be like if it seems that nobody cares, not even the Almighty? Would that drive me to the conclusion that God actually hates the homeless?

But perhaps it was not one of the homeless who had phrased this bitter question. In my experience it is not so often the sufferer who curses God as the spectator, the one who does care and is enraged by the apparent carelessness of God. There flooded into my mind the great communion of the saints, known and almost totally unknown—men and women who go through the most fearful agonies of mind and body without losing their ultimate trust that they are in the grip of a loving God. The psalmists knew what it is to be surrounded by all kinds of enemies. "Look upon mine affliction and my pain. Consider mine enemies; for they are many; and they hate me with a cruel hatred. . . . " Then come the words, "O keep my soul, and deliver me. . . . for I put my trust in thee." The twenty-second psalm begins with the words: "My God, my God, why hast thou forsaken me?" and the twenty-third with: "The Lord is my shepherd; I shall not want." Of all peoples the Jews might have most reason to feel that God hated them—from the time of the exile in Babylon to the Holocaust in our day. Yet, it was from their exile that came the most moving expression of the mercy and compassion of their God, and from his experience in an appalling death camp that Dr. Frank wrote of his experience of the presence of God.

By the time I got off that subway, my thoughts were right back to the text I gave you this morning. For if ever there was one who went through the worst life can do to us totally confident that he was in the grip of a loving God, it was the Christ who echoed from the torture of his cross the agony of the psalmist—"My God, why hast thou forsaken me"—and then died with the words "Father, into thy hands I commend my spirit" on his lips. Did God hate the One he called his Son? The miracle of the Gospel is that he was there giving himself totally to his human family with an inexhaustible and everlasting love. God *so* loved us that he gave himself to rescue us from the network of evil that is our sinful world.

> "We may not know, we cannot tell
> What pains he had to bear;
> But we believe it was for us
> He hung and suffered there."

Sometimes it takes a children's hymn to express a truth that baffles the brain but grips the heart.

"For God so loved the world, that he gave his only begotten Son, that whosoever believeth in him should not perish, but have everlasting life." Luther called this text "the Gospel in miniature." It has been the most quoted text in the Christian world. No other sentence in the Bible has been so explored by the keenest theological minds, yet it has a way of reaching the simplest of God's children. It is the lode-star of the saints and yet has penetrated to the most dissolute and blaspheming. It soars with the music of the great composers but can also speak directly to the despairing. It is being spoken to the homeless by those in the churches and the Salvation Army, who are translating the love of which it speaks into food for the hungry and homes for the homeless. And it comes to us in the context of a conversation between Jesus and a scholarly and influential Pharisee.

Are these the words of Jesus? As often in John's Gospel we are not sure when he is giving us the actual words of the Lord or reflecting on the deep meaning of what he said and did. It makes no difference—except for those who love their little certainties and welcome those Bibles which print every word they believe can be attributed to Jesus in red. (I heard recently of a customer in a religious bookstore who asked: "Have you got one of those Bibles where there's red print for all those bits you don't have to take literally"!)

For me this is a word of God in which the Spirit speaks directly to us all—all, that is, who, as John says, are open to the Light. This is the God who has us in his grip—not a Divine Idea, not a remote and perfect Potentate who watches from outer space while human beings run amok in this little corner of the universe, not simply a "Judge eternal throned in splendour," or an implacable Fate totally deaf to the cries and protests of people like us. "God so loved," and he goes on loving. It is the mystery and tragedy of our freedom to reject that love. This is what drove Paul to tell everyone he could reach in a world as skeptical and despairing as ours that "God has *proved* his love toward us in that, while we were yet sinners Christ died for us." And it is what drives me to come back again and again to his ringing affirmation that "neither death, not life, nor angels, nor principalities, nor powers, nor things present, nor things to come, nor height, nor depth, nor any other creature shall be able to separate us from the love of God which is in Christ Jesus our Lord." That's what I mean by being gripped by the love of God.

This time around two words leaped from this text with power to kindle my mind and stretch my soul. The first is "world"—God so loved the *world* (the Greek word is cosmos). What a vast inclusive word that is and how often preachers and evangelists have tried to shrink it into the dimensions of our social, religious, and racial prejudices. We may sing "In Christ there is no east or west," but do we actively believe that God today loves the east— the east of the Communists, the east of Islam, the east of business rivals, as much as he loves us and those like us? And then, doesn't the cosmos include a lot more than the human family? The Book of Jonah was written long ago, not, as many think, to challenge us to believe that Jonah was swallowed by a fish and regurgitated or else perish everlastingly, but to tell his Hebrew compatriots that God loved the people of Nineveh as much as he did his chosen people and would save them if they repented. They did repent and were delivered much to Jonah's annoyance. But I love the last four words of the Lord's rebuke to Jonah: "Should I not spare Nineveh, that great city, wherein are more than six score thousand persons that cannot discern between their right hand and their left hand; *and also much cattle?*" The animal world is in the cosmos and anyone who watches the nature films on TV is reminded that in their beauty and even their savagery they are also the objects of God's love, as is the whole cosmos, what we coldly call our "environment." "Not a sparrow," said Jesus, "can fall to the ground without your Father's knowing." What an all embracing love is reflected by this revelation of the Son of God who is not only our Savior but the cosmic Christ!

But the thrust of the text is, of course, toward the human family— made in the image of God and charged with the care of this cosmos. If that word expands our minds and dazzles our imagination, another word here suddenly brings us up against the real challenge of this text. It's a very ordinary word, a capacious word, like cosmos. But it's a very personal word, even a limiting word. "Whoever." "Whoever believes in him." The grip of the loving God is known by those who trust in him, those who respond to the light of Christ. It's not an automatic distribution of divine grace to everyone. When I offer my hand in friendship, when we pass the peace in our service here, you are perfectly free not to take it. I've never known that to happen, but it's obvious that many live from day to day without accepting the grip of a loving God. "By grace," says the apostle are you saved *through faith.*" The promise of our text, the promise of the Gospel is that "whoever believes, whoever responds to the light of Christ, will not perish but have everlasting life." The obverse of this cannot be evaded. We are told that the light has come into the world but that some have "preferred the darkness because their deeds were evil." Jesus never underestimated the power of the Enemy who beckons us toward the way that leads to the death of the soul.

We cannot really hear this Scripture unless we let it force us to ask: Am I among those who respond? Am I resting my life on the reality of this loving God who offers me everlasting life, "whoever" I am—religious or irreligious, satisfied or dissatisfied, powerful or weak, gifted or deprived, young or old—or am I not responding? We can't earn this eternal life by any effort to be more religious. We cannot claim it as a prize for good behavior. But we can respond to the Light. We can shake the hand of Christ in prayer and Holy Communion and know that whatever may happen to us we are in the grip of the loving God.

Prayer: Strengthen us, again, O Lord, that we may truly trust in thee, through Jesus Christ our Lord. Amen.

Root Questions for Lent:
"When I Survey the Wondrous Cross"—
What Then?

EDITOR'S INTRODUCTION

IT'S TEMPTING FOR WORSHIP leaders to fall into the habit of using the same translation for the Scripture readings every Sunday. This may be the King James Version or the NRSV or an even more contemporary version. What ministers tend to forget, however, is that all of these versions are *translations*, taken from the original Hebrew in the Old Testament or Greek in the New. Some of the translations work better than others depending on which passage is read, and the occasion at hand. Only sheer prejudice or indefensible laziness finds preachers using the same translation week in week out, year in year out.

David Read for his part favored the contemporary versions, ranging from the J. B. Philips translation to the New Jerusalem translation, the Revised Standard Version, the Revised English Bible, Today's English Bible, and especially The New English Bible. But given the right passage he would occasionally fall back on the Shakespearian eloquence of the King James Version. Generally, however, Read favored the NEB for its remarkable clarity and charm. Nobody likes to be thought of as a stick-in-the-mud kind of preacher. And one way of escaping from that mud is to use more than one translation for the Scripture readings.

ROOT QUESTIONS FOR LENT: "WHEN I SURVEY THE WONDROUS CROSS"—WHAT THEN?

A Sermon preached by David H. C. Read at Madison Avenue Presbyterian Church on April 1, 1979, Lent

Text: *"And sitting down they watched him there."* Matthew 27:36 (KJV)

Readings: Isaiah 53:3–7, 10; Philippians 2:5–11 (NEB); Matthew 27:33–38

"THEY" WERE THE SOLDIERS. Permission to sit down was granted, for a crucifixion could take a long time. Why did they "watch him there"? It looks as though we are being told that, instead of averting their eyes from a horrible sight, they gave way to that shameful instinct that lurks in all of us and forces us to look at something terrible—like the rubber-necking motorists who slow down to gaze on a messy accident. I am sure that happened at Calvary, for there was a crowd around the cross besides the soldiers, a crowd of people who didn't have to be there, drawn by a morbid desire to see an execution.

But Matthew here is not accusing the soldiers of enjoying the spectacle. The word "watch" he uses means "keeping guard." Their orders were to be on the alert for any trouble. Pilate knew that there were armed terrorists in Jerusalem who might use this occasion for a strike. He also knew that at other crucifixions friends of the victim had succeeded in releasing him before he was dead and smuggling him away to be revived. They may even have had the idea that, in his agony, Jesus might utter some words that would betray a plot against the Romans. Who knows? In any case the instruction was to watch. I see these anonymous soldiers with that steely, alert, and piercing look in their eyes that we see almost daily in the photographs of these equally anonymous security agents that surround a president or a prime minister on tour.

"They watched him there." The power of imperial Rome was not too grand to neglect the slightest possibility of insurrection, even in this insignificant land on the fringe of its dominions. They had to make sure that this troublesome character really died and was buried. Innocent or guilty, they wanted to be rid of him once and for all. There must be no sudden rush to his rescue, no smuggling away of Jesus to revive him, no possibility of a Jesus cult to cause trouble, no hidden Ayatollah to pull the strings of revolution.

It is not for us, sitting down in our comfortable pews to watch him there, to sneer at the anxious Roman governor or condemn his hard-hearted execution squad. If we had been part of a Roman family living in that insecure and dangerous colony might we not have supported vigorous action against all suspects, even if an occasional one was innocent? If we had been part of the Jewish establishment might we not have agreed with Caiaphas, the father-in-law of the high priest, when he advised his colleagues that "it was expedient that one man should die for the people"? You know the argument—better let one innocent man be put to death than have a revolution in which thousands would be killed. Yes, yes—keep watch and make sure that Jesus dies.

What all human authorities, and especially totalitarian ones, forget is that no instrument of coercion has ever been devised that will so keep watch over the human spirit that a new and liberating inspiration can be crushed into the ground. Later, when the Roman world was disturbed by the followers of this Jesus who was executed the most savage campaign of persecution was unleashed against them, but the Gospel could not be obliterated in the sands of the arena. History indeed proved that "the blood of the martyrs was the seed of the Church," and it was the followers of Jesus who outlived the decline and fall of the Roman Empire. The wielders of power in every age forget one other factor in the human story—the silent and pervasive action of the living God. For them today as in Roman times, God is a name to be cynically invoked, as Hitler did at the end of every speech, as an ally of the powers that be. They do not reckon with the God of whom the prophet wrote: "It is he that sitteth upon the circle of the earth, and the inhabitants thereof are like grasshoppers; that stretcheth out the heavens as a curtain . . . that bringeth the princes to nothing." The grasshoppers thought they were gods on that day when Jesus died, but God was moving in a mysterious way at Calvary when his Son was lifted up to die. The grasshoppers are dead, and the name of Pontius Pilate completely forgotten if it had not found its way into the creed that honors the death and resurrection of Jesus Christ. We have surely learned that you cannot set a watch on the Son of God. You cannot hold him impotent on that cross. In every age he breaks loose and people like you and me hear those piercing questions: "Is it nothing to you, all ye that pass by?" "Were *you* there when they crucified my Lord?"

Among the root questions that we are asking this Lenten season, there must be this one about the meaning of the Cross. There are other questions which we share with adherents of other faiths, questions about God's nature, about prayer, about love in action, about suffering. Only the Christian has to come to terms with the Crucified. A neutral student of comparative religion must find it astounding that the faith which still claims the allegiance of a greater number of human beings than any other has at its center a young Jew who was executed two thousand years ago. And, stranger still, this incident is not hushed up or explained away. The very instrument of his execution is reared up in every corner of the world; wherever Christians worship, this terrible death is celebrated and kept in remembrance by a universal rite whereby bread and wine "show forth the Lord's death," and, far from being ashamed of this terrible end of their Master, Christians actually sing: "In the cross of Christ I glory."

From the beginning the leaders of the Church knew that this is where Christianity has something new, something astonishing, something almost unbelievable to say. The story of the crucifixion, familiar though it may be to those of us raised within the Christian fold, has always been shocking, and even repulsive, to the most religious and to the skeptics an absurdity. "We preach Christ crucified," said St. Paul, "unto the Jews a stumbling block, and unto the Greeks foolishness, but unto them which are called, both Jews and Greeks, Christ the power of God, and the wisdom of God."

So, on our journey to Good Friday this year, once again we "watch him there." And the question is: Are we truly among those who see in the Crucified "the power and the wisdom of God," or is there some religious sensitivity in us that still finds this Cross too crude, too horrible, too impossible to reconcile with our idea of the love of God; some skepticism in us that wants to dismiss all the fuss about atonement, the shedding of blood, the "wondrous cross," as mere foolishness derived from the lurid imagination of St. Paul—"Crosstianity" as Bernard Shaw used to call it?

If you find such questions troubling as you "watch him there," or as you receive the symbols of his broken body and shed blood, let me first assure you that there is no one authoritative, satisfying, and exhaustive interpretation of the Cross that is binding on everyone who wants to be a disciple of Jesus and true member of his Church. Too often, in the name of the Gospel, some particular theory of the atonement, some dogmatic statement of exactly what happened at Calvary, has been forced upon a questioning soul. In the New Testament there is unanimity that this was the crucial event in the story of Jesus (that's what "crucial" literally means), but its inner meaning is explored and understood in a great variety of ways. Mark surveys the Cross in one way, John in another, Paul again sees a little differently, so does the writer to the Hebrews, and the author of the Revelation. All are agreed that the death of Jesus was a world-shaking, world-changing event, without which the Resurrection would merely have been a curious story of one man being brought to life again after he was dead. On the day of Pentecost Peter spoke for them all: "God hath made that same Jesus, whom ye crucified, both Lord and Christ."

"When I survey the wondrous cross"—what then? Let me this morning relay to you the most vital and extraordinary thing that the New Testament declares, and the Church has gone on believing. When I survey the cross, when I "watch him there," I am beholding the most moving, and almost incredible demonstration of the love of God the world has ever seen. If I were to forget all that the Church has taught me and see the best man the world has ever known so miserably put to death, I would want to say: "When I behold what you call 'the wondrous' cross all I see is one more example of how the powers of this world make martyrs of the saints, one more ghastly spectacle of the suffering of the innocent." But instead I hear one witness telling me that "God so *loved* the world that he gave his only Son"— gave him up like this—that *whoever* believes in him should not perish but have everlasting life." And I hear another saying: "Why, one will hardly die for a righteous man—though perhaps for a good man one will even dare to die. But God shows his *love* for us in that while we were yet sinners Christ died for us." And yet another has this to say: "In this the *love* of God was made manifest among us, that God sent his only Son into the world, so that we might live through him. In this is *love*, not that we loved God, but that he loved us and sent his Son to be the expiation for our sins."

When we "watch him there" no two of us in this congregation will have an identical response, just as, when we receive the elements of Holy Communion, no two of us have exactly the same experience. But there is one dividing line that must be passed before any of us can hear the Gospel that is sent from the Cross. So long as we behold nothing more than a martyrdom, the wretched death of a good man, the Cross can be nothing but Bad News. For any of us to hear Good News in this terrible deed we have to find in it, however mysteriously, the love of God. According to the New Testament God was not far away, a spectator of this dreadful death, like the soldiers who sat down to watch him there. At that very moment when the darkness fell, and a cry of desolation was heard from the victim on the cross "God was in Christ reconciling the world to himself." That is the Gospel. The long line of ritual sacrifice by which an estranged humanity had sought to appease the holy God was over. God himself had provided the one supreme and final sacrifice. He had met us in the very depth of our alienation and despair. God had come. The way into the Holy of holies was open. For when Jesus died "the veil of the Temple was rent in twain from the top to the bottom"—and this unimaginable love had drawn us in.

That's what I see: not a good man abandoned by his God, but a good God whose love has come reaching to the depths in the Son on whom is laid "the iniquity of us all." In moments of crisis the Cross is no theological problem: it is the mighty symbol of the love of God. I have spoken as a chaplain to men who were dying of starvation in a prison camp, and found that I could speak of little but the Cross of Christ. I have talked with those who were desolate from the loss of a little child, and only the Cross could speak to them of the love of God. No words can fathom this amazing grace that every kind of person has found when, perhaps for the first time, they really "watched him there."

"When I survey the wondrous cross"—what then? Only an immense gratitude for this breaking of the heart of God in such a searching love: only a new resolve to let that love be somehow, somewhere reflected in my care for others: only a hunger for that bread and wine that unite me with his Cross and nourish me in that love. The blind Scottish preacher, George Matheson, expressed it for us all:

> "O Love that wilt not let me go,
> I rest my weary soul in thee;
> I give thee back the life I owe,
> That in thine ocean depths its flow
> May richer, fuller be."

"The Stones Cry Out":
A Palm Sunday Challenge

EDITOR'S INTRODUCTION

MATTHEW'S GOSPEL OBSERVES THAT not only did Jesus speak in parables but "in all his teaching to the crowds . . . he never spoke to them *without* a parable" (13:35). The closest thing we have to parables today in our proclamation of the Gospel is the sermon illustration. Not surprisingly, such illustrations are almost as popular with the crowds (or what passes in our churches today as crowds) as Jesus' parables. The only problem is that we're not Jesus. We're not in control of the message the way he was. We tell stories to illustrate the message of the gospel. He told stories because he *was* the message. When our pulpit stories fail to illumine the gospel, they are told for no good purpose, however interesting they may be as stories.

In this Palm Sunday sermon, David Read tells a story that *does*, I suggest, illumine the text and thus illustrate the gospel. Granted, it is a powerful story in its own right, drawn from one of Read's hair raising experiences as a chaplain and POW in World War II. Still, the story truly illumines "the overwhelming power of the God who comes in the blood-stained humility of Jesus." A good example of, among other things, an illustration that works.

"THE STONES CRY OUT": A PALM SUNDAY CHALLENGE

A Sermon preached by David H. C. Read at Madison Avenue Presbyterian Church on Palm Sunday, March 26, 1972

Text: *"Some Pharisees who were in the crowd said to him, 'Master, repri-mand your disciples.' He answered, 'I tell you, if my disciples keep silence the stones will shout aloud.'"* Luke 19:39, 40

IN A RECENT ISSUE of the "New York Times" an article by a rabbi raised again the spectre of Auschwitz and concluded that atrocity on such a scale and suffering of such intensity finally erased the possibility of believing in the Biblical God. Under the heading "Faith After Auschwitz" letters have been printed from other rabbis pointing out that, in spite of the uniquely cold blooded and scientific nature of that holocaust, nothing new had been added to the agony of faith. The paradox remains that the Jewish people who have again and again been the victims of suffering and atrocity to an almost unparalleled degree are the very people through whom the world has learned of the God of justice and mercy. How to reconcile such faith with the brute facts of the torture of the innocent and the random massacres of history is a problem at least as old as the Book of Job. And in the end it is not at all changed by the ghastly arithmetic of Auschwitz. It is personal. One happy child suddenly struck with cancer or killed by a drunken driver—and you have the right to ask me: Where is your God of love?

If I am to go on believing it is not because I can explain such things, because some clever writer has proved that there is some beautiful plan behind these horrors. Nor is it because I will not face the fact that such things happen. We may have trained ourselves to reduce the tragedies of war, earthquake, famine and fire to little pictures on a TV screen that are quickly obliterated by a commercial, but there is always the moment when the reality strikes again. In the new movie version of Vonnegut's "Slaughter-house Five" one is exposed to the stark reality of the bombing of Dresden. There it is. One moment a beautiful city with women shopping and children playing in the streets. The next moment we are in the blazing ruins, a char-nel house, an inferno of smoke and ashes. If we keep silent the very stones cry out. Vonnegut disinfects the scene with his peculiar brand of fatalism, "So it goes," and the movie is shot through with a redeeming compassion and cathartic humor. But the Christian cannot escape the question: Where is the God of love?

For me the answer is not a philosophy, not a detachment. As the problem is in the end personal, so must the answer be. The divine voice mustn't be in the clouds but right there where the stores cry out. My faith must be in a God who was there, who is there and will be there. I need at this point a God of flesh and blood, a God with a heart that beats, a God who speaks our language in distress and in joy. He's not going to be a God I discover at the end of a chain of argument but one who awakens recognition by the compulsion of his love. He will be one lowly enough to ride into my heart on a donkey and yet with such majesty that the very stones cry out.

Yes; this is what Palm Sunday says to me, and if I may share a memory with you, with especial force because of what "Slaughterhouse Five" brought back to mind. In this movie at one point a shaggy line of American POW's guarded by German teenagers in uniform trails past another pen of prisoners who gape at them through the wire. I think I recognized them as Russians, and a vivid image flashed into my mind.

It was Palm Sunday, 1945—March 25th. I was standing in a wired-off compound in Stalag 9A in the west of Germany conducting a service. A few days before I had left a small and quiet officers' camp fifty miles farther east and had come to this vast concentration of some 10,000 prisoners—American, British, French, Polish, Russian and others, each sealed off from their neighbors. The congregation in front of me were squatting on the muddy grass. Few were strong enough to stand. These were men who had just been marched five hundred miles from their camps in the east and had been shot up by our own planes on the way. Some were dying of exhaustion and starvation. The only note of hope that morning seemed to be the distant organ voluntary that was played by the guns of the Third Army advancing towards us from the west.

What do you preach about to such a congregation at such a time? Jesus. Which Jesus? Not the starry-eyed idealist; not the sentimental Jesus; not the revolutionary Jesus; not even the teacher and the healer. You speak about one who rode into the darkness unafraid, one who submitted his stainless life to the obscenities of men, one who let the whole tide of pain, absurdity and desolation wash over him—and one who lets it all happen to him *for our sake.* For this Jesus has deliberately exposed himself to the enemy to draw their fire. This Jesus has taken on himself the ultimate agony of men astray from God, and gone through hell for us. And this Jesus is the one who still comes to us as he did to Thomas, "the doors being shut," and shows us his wounds. It is this appeal to the very center of our being, person to person, that compels the recognition: "My Lord and my God."

My words that day were carried by a bitter wind across the heads in front of me, and the bright Spring sunshine almost seemed to mock the feeble effort to preach the love of God in Christ. It was one of these moments when Nature seems totally indifferent to the agonies of men. You wonder—does all this make sense? Let some cosmic dice decide whether we live or die. So it goes. Then I knew as never before the presence of Christ. The men in front of me knew it too. They told after—all kinds of men. It was a presence that did not depend on the preacher's words. It was a presence that did not depend on their being understood. For I glanced round for a moment and found another congregation. On the other side of the barbed wire, peering through, was a silent, reverent, wondering line of Russian prisoners.

What does it take to recognize Christ? I don't know; but one thing Palm Sunday will always mean to me is the overwhelming power of the God who comes in the blood-stained humanity of Jesus. There is no doubt that in his mind the climax had come, and he threw aside the caution with which he had hidden his Messianic claim upon the people. He didn't want to be hailed as the popular preacher of Galilee. He didn't want to be mobbed as the healer and miracle worker. Above all, he didn't want to spark an insurrection that would hoist him onto the throne of his fathers. So he constantly told his disciples to say nothing about his being Messiah, and even told those whom he healed to go away and keep quiet. He did not choose to be recognized as the great Teacher of Righteousness who would be revered for generations to come. He did not choose to be recognized as a thaumaturge who could turn stones into bread and leap safely into space from the pinnacle of the Temple. Nor did he choose that moment on the mountain top when his three closest disciples saw him transfigured with supernatural light and heard the divine words: "This is my beloved Son: hear him." "They kept it close," we read, "and told no man in those days any of those things which they had seen." He waited, waited till the moment came when they would know what kind of Messiah he was to be, and when in total surrender to the powers of darkness he would win the victory of love.

Now he casts off all restraint and invites the recognition of the world. Yes, now in this pathetic parody of a royal entrance with a common donkey for a mount instead of an imperial charger, with dusty palms and filthy clothes under him instead of a red carpet, with delirious peasants for a royal escort, now he claims our response and our allegiance. How can we escape the force of the words he used when the anxious, security conscious Pharisees pleaded with him to restrain the enthusiasm of his disciples? "I tell you, if my disciples keep silence the stones will shout aloud."

Just now, when the figure of Jesus has again broken out from the sanctuaries of the Church where all too often his disciples have kept silence, and thousands are asking: Who is this? anyone really concerned about an answer must reckon with a word like this, "I tell you, if my disciples keep silence the stones will shout aloud." Don't you hear in these words the authentic voice of Jesus, in the brief and gloriously poetic phrase? What else can it mean but that right there when he is entering the gates of hell is where we see the answer to our agonies and hear the heartbeats of our God?

This is no popular philosopher, no local Savior, no temporary prophet speaking. He hears and accepts the hosannahs of his disciples. He looks beyond them to the seething crowds and finds in their inarticulate applause a groping acknowledgment of their Lord. He hears the happy shouts of the children and again thanks the Father that he has "hidden these things from the wise and prudent, and revealed them onto babes." Then as the sun beats down and glints upon the stones beneath him he finds all creation responding to its God. No; it's not true that Nature stares with indifference on the agonies of men. The stones shout aloud—the stones he would not turn into bread, the stones they picked up to throw at an adulterous woman, the stones that were built into that shining temple, the stones that are strewn in the valley where David killed Goliath, the stones that are the mute companions of mankind through good and evil—the stones will shout aloud as the Son of God is enthroned upon his cross.

This is the challenge of Palm Sunday—to find the light where the darkness is most absolute and to recognize in the Crucified our Savior and our God. Perhaps we, his disciples, have kept silence too often about the living center of our faith. We have had so much to do, so many things to talk about. And now, in unexpected places, the stones are crying out. Jesus is abroad again—in books, in paintings, in youth movements, in musicals, in scribbles on subway walls. Our task in the Church is not to stand with the Pharisees shocked and rebuking, but to tear away all the trimmings in which Jesus has been hidden, to disperse the fog of verbiage that seems to surround him, and to let him speak. A word like this one we have lived with this morning conveys Jesus' own witness to his claim upon our lives. Whoever, inside or outside the Church, wants to know more about him, wants to know who he is, and wants to know where a faith can rest in this baffling and threatening world, must hear him and watch him as he moves through the growing darkness of Holy Week to the Easter dawn.

Our salute to Jesus on this day cannot be that of the ignorant Palm Sunday crowd. We know what was about to happen. And so our acclamation must come from our vision of the Lord who died for us, and our conviction that in him God shines upon us the only light that can follow us through every possible darkness to the perfect day.

Maundy Thursday: "Room at the Inn"

EDITOR'S INTRODUCTION

THE GOSPEL LESSON THAT introduces this sermon demonstrates the vibrancy of the New English Bible translation. And the biblical story itself is so arresting that David Read can't help but re-tell it in his own words. In this way a small but searching light is focused on the Passover feast that Jesus shared with his disciples when they met in that upper room in Jerusalem on the eve of his arrest and crucifixion.

In Read's imaginative re-telling, the innkeeper listens in to the talk around the table. He hears Jesus speaking, "and it was as if he, and those at the table, were hearing the words of God himself. One word kept recurring again and again . . . "

That word was—but wait. Let the word come to us afresh as we hear David Read re-tell the story in his own imaginative way.

MAUNDY THURSDAY: "ROOM AT THE INN"

A Sermon preached by David H. C. Read at Madison Avenue
Presbyterian Church on Maundy Thursday, April 8, 1982

Text: *"He replied, 'As soon as you get foot in the city a man will meet you
carrying a jar of water. Follow him into the house that he enters and give
this message to the householder: "The Master says, 'Where is the room in
which I may eat the Passover with my disciples?'"* Luke 22:10, 11 (NEB)

Readings: Luke 22:7–20 (NEB)

"ROOM AT THE INN." Let me assure you right away that it is not my intention
to surprise you with a Christmas sermon on Maundy Thursday. The standard title at Christmas, on which thousands of sermons have been written,
is "No Room at the Inn." The innkeeper at Bethlehem is usually vilified as a
cruel, hardhearted creature who turned away the pregnant Mary from his
door and let the Son of God be born in a stable. I have come to doubt this
interpretation of the story. The man may have done the best possible in the
circumstances. In any case, if you look again at the story in the Gospels you
will find that he isn't even mentioned. We are simply told that there was no
room at the inn.

On the other hand the man I want to introduce you to tonight comes
into the story of that Thursday night in Holy Week—even if very briefly.
And my guess—although I've never seen it suggested anywhere—is that he
was an innkeeper. Let me remind you of what was going on in Jerusalem
that night.

It was the Passover season and hundreds of pilgrims had come to the
Holy City. Probably most of them, like Jesus and his companions, were biv-
ouacked outside the walls and entered the city only for ceremonies at the
Temple or to hold family-style Passover feasts in hired rooms. Jesus evidently wanted such a room but, in view of the uproar caused by his entrance
to the city on Palm Sunday, was anxious to keep secret the place where he
was to be with his disciples. So he made quiet inquiries as to where a suitable
room could be found. They found one. It could have been a private house
but my suggestion is that it was an inn—one of those establishments where
it is always possible, even today, to hire a private room for a group to have
a meal. He would come to terms with the innkeeper and then explain the
need for utter secrecy.

The innkeeper has a suggestion. He will send one of his servants, carrying a water jar, to a certain gate of the city. When the disciples arrived

they were casually to follow the man until he reached the inn. To make sure that the innkeeper was letting the right party in, a code was arranged. The disciples were to say: "The Master says, 'Where is the room in which I may eat the Passover with my disciples?'"

So it came about that, on that Thursday evening, the disciples slipped into the city, spotted the man with the water jug, followed him to the inn, and gave the password. A little later Jesus himself arrived and mounted the stairs to that upper room. It was big enough to hold them all comfortably as they reclined around the table where the food and wine were already prepared.

From the text of Luke's Gospel I have little doubt that something like this is what happened that night. Now let me do a little imagining.

I see that innkeeper as extremely curious about what was going on under his roof. Like most innkeepers he knew how to turn a blind eye to what happened in one of his private rooms. And I don't think he was the kind of man who would love to betray some religious or political group to the police. But if you had been in his shoes wouldn't you have been more than a little inquisitive about this group of twelve—and especially their mysterious leader whose face one couldn't forget. They had closed the door, but every experienced innkeeper surely has his peephole through which to observe his guests. And isn't this what we are doing tonight—finding a peephole of history through which to see and hear what happened in the upper room?

They were a highly nervous group, he noticed. Under the calm eyes of their leader they fidgeted uneasily and every now and then he caught a glint of a dagger under their cloaks. One of them, he noticed, sat near the door and kept edging towards it as if he would soon slip away. The Passover ritual began. He heard Jesus say something extraordinary about longing to have this meal with them before his death. The innkeeper must have wondered why. This was a young man in the prime of life. Then came the usual great prayers of thanksgiving and he thought he had never heard anyone speak these hallowed words with such power and simplicity. He prayed as if he was talking to his own father. Then, as the ritual with the cup and the bread was performed he overheard some astounding words. As Jesus broke the bread and passed it, he said: "This is my body." As he offered the wine, he said something about a new covenant "sealed in my blood." The innkeeper knew all about the old covenant of God with his chosen people, to be solemnly recalled at the Passover season, but what was this new covenant, and how could this strong and healthy man speak about his blood being shed? And what did he mean by saying: "I tell you, from this moment I shall drink from the fruit of the vine no more until the time when the kingdom of God comes."?

This was no ordinary Passover meal. This man in the center was different from all others he had seen presiding at such a service. As the restless figure near the door received the bread he rose and slipped out as if he were choking and had to get away. From then on the innkeeper could sense a holiness—a concentrated presence of God in that room that seemed to enclose him too. There was room at that table now for another one. As he looked at the men there he felt he was one of them. For these were not professionally pious people like the Pharisees, or scholars like the scribes, or mystics like those Essenes who lived apart and prayed for the coming Kingdom. They were like the typical working men who dropped in for a drink at the inn.

He listened. Jesus was speaking—and it was as if he, and those at the table, were hearing the words of God himself. One word kept recurring again and again. Love. He was speaking of God's love for him and his love for God. Then he spoke of God's love flowing through him to reach into their hearts. And what was this he was saying about love? "As the Father hath loved me, so have I loved you: continue ye in my love. If ye keep my commandments ye shall abide in my love; even as I have kept my Father's commandments, and abide in his love. These things I have spoken unto you, that my joy might remain in you, and that your joy might be full." Joy? What was this joy on the lips of a man who was expecting soon to die? Yet somehow this joy was being passed on to the group around the table. He was linking them together in a bond of love and joy such as the innkeeper had never known. And peace. Yes; to these frightened men, on the eve of some strange and terrifying event, he was speaking of peace. "Let not your heart be troubled, neither let it be afraid."

The room seemed bigger. It seemed to expand to enclose all who are yearning for a new way of love, and a joy and peace that could endure through all trials and terrors, and passed all human understanding. Then Jesus rose and lifted up his eyes and hands in prayer. He could hear the prayer, but like millions after him, he could not fully understand. Jesus was talking with his Father in heaven. He was praising him and yielding himself totally to his will. There was a fervent prayer from the little group around him: "Holy, Father, keep through thine own name those whom thou hast given me, that they may be one as we are . . . I pray not that thou shouldest take them out of the world, but that thou shouldest keep them from the evil . . . Sanctify them through thy truth; thy word is truth."

The innkeeper felt the power of words that soared beyond his understanding. Jesus was clearly binding this little group into a close fellowship of love, and preparing them for a special task in the world. What would they do? Would he ever hear of them again? And was there possibly room for another—even a rough innkeeper? Suddenly he heard another prayer—a prayer that seemed to reach through the walls of that little room and soar through time and space. "Neither pray I for these alone," said Jesus, "but for them also which shall believe in me through their word; that they all may be one; as thou, Father art in me, and I in thee, that they also may be one in us: that the world may believe that thou hast sent me."

I see the innkeeper leave his peephole and retire to his room. It came like a light from heaven. Jesus had prayed for him! He knew then that somehow he would meet these men again and that he would come to believe in their Lord. He had caught the vision of a world that was truly one—one in a love that was radiant and infectious, a love that flowed from God through this Jesus who was going to die but must surely live again and forever. Where would this vision lead him? Perhaps to the ends of the earth; perhaps just to keep his inn going— but with a new atmosphere as he would seek to do justly, to love mercy, and to walk humbly with the God he had seen in Jesus.

All this about the innkeeper is my imagining. What is not imagining is the fact that you and I are here, gathered around a table where the same Jesus is our host. "Do this in remembrance of me," he said, and such a remembrance is our peephole into the supper of that holy night. It is sheer fact, and not a fairy tale, that for two thousand years, and in almost every land, the Supper has been celebrated, and the words of Jesus repeated in a thousand different languages. And still the word goes out: There is room!

There is room for every kind of man and woman who feels the impact of Jesus and is willing to call him Lord. If you have looked through that peephole tonight and seen the frail and foolish and bewildered group around the table, you will have recognized yourself. No one can enter this room with an engraved ticket certifying our status as upright citizens who need no repentance. We come because we know our need. We come because we know that nowhere else can we find these needs so wonderfully met. The sign outside the inn that Jesus keeps on earth is "Come unto me, *all* ye that labor and are heaven laden, and I will refresh you" and inside it is written: "Whoever comes to me I will in no wise cast out."

Good Friday: "Today Shalt Thou Be with Me in Paradise"

EDITOR'S INTRODUCTION

WHILE ONE OF THE criminals who died alongside Jesus taunted him, the other criminal simply asked Jesus to remember him when he came into his glory. Jesus made it clear that he *would* remember him: "Today shalt thou be with me in paradise." In the language of theology, David Read notes, "this is just what we mean by justification by faith alone. The response of Jesus shows that the man was 'justified'—made straight, made right with God by this simple act of trust."

Read further notes that this simple act of trust is expressed in the Gospel stories in a variety of ways. And Jesus accepts them all, from "Zacchaeus offering to repay all whom he had cheated," to "a wise crack like that of the Canaanite woman who told him that even dogs could eat the crumbs from the master's table," to "a reaching out from the crowd to touch the hem of his garment by an ailing woman." What matters is not the theological preciseness of the phraseology but the heart's desire. "Lord, remember me," the thief on the cross says, and the assurance is given: "If I go and prepare a place for you, I will come again, and receive you unto myself; that where I am there you may be also."

GOOD FRIDAY: "TODAY SHALT THOU BE WITH ME IN PARADISE"

A Sermon preached by David H. C. Read at Madison Avenue Presbyterian Church on Good Friday, April 17, 1987

Text: *Today shalt thou be with me in paradise.* Luke 23: 43

LUKE ALONE OF THE Gospel writers tells us the story of the two others who were crucified with Jesus and shared his agony. All three had been condemned. In the middle hangs Jesus of Nazareth, judged totally innocent by Pontius Pilate, by one of the robbers beside him, and by the entire world ever since. It is conventional opinion that the other two were guilty—this one even confessed that he was—but which of us today would really be willing to say that, whatever they did, they *deserved* such a punishment that is surely to the highest degree "cruel and unusual"? The point is that, in contrast with Jesus, they were guilty, and they were dying, and they were scared. There was absolutely nothing at this point that they could do to atone for their sins. And that is where we are in the sight of God, unable to save ourselves. None of us is that Innocent One who was also dying.

One of the robbers takes the advice given by Job's wife in his extremity of suffering: "Curse God and die." He has been harshly judged for his impenitence and for his mocking cry to Jesus: "If thou be Christ, save thyself and us," but under such fearful torment can we be sure that we would feel no resentment against the God whom we had been taught to trust? The other robber, even in his agony, was moved by the presence of Jesus beside him. He knew something about him, not just that he was innocent but that he spoke of a kingdom where he would be king. Like many others he believed it would be the messianic kingdom to be established at the end of time. So he said: "Lord, remember me when thou comest into thy kingdom." And Jesus responded at once, promising far more than he had asked. "Verily I say unto thee, *today* shalt thou be with me in paradise."

There are two ways we can ponder this story. One is the way of the dogmatic believer who tries to extract from it information concerning our future destiny, making it fit into some rigid calendar of events. That way lies confusion and a rash of speculation. "If the penitent thief was to meet Jesus *that day* in heaven what about the burial and the resurrection? Would Jesus leave him again until he had finally "ascended into heaven." And how can we fit this story into a strictly orthodox chronology according to which the thief would be "asleep" until the general resurrection of the dead? Those whose minds work this way are unlikely to get far with this story—or with much else in the Bible.

The other way is to let the story speak to us as believing Christians who also believe that there is much we cannot know about such things as time and eternity, or conditions in that other world, and let these words make their own impression on us. Let me tell you what came through to me as I read again this brief and loaded dialogue that Luke reports.

"Lord, remember me when thou comest into thy kingdom." "Remember me"—that's all. I don't hear these words as a solemn, warning cry like that given to Hamlet by his father's ghost. It's much more like the quiet and sincere way in which we might say it to a friend at a moment of parting. And it's modest. There's no sense of self-importance or claim on the generosity of Jesus. It's a simple, perhaps *the* simplest, confession of faith. This would be an ignorant man in the matter of religion. I doubt if he had any profound ideas of who the Messiah was or the nature of his kingdom. He was like one of these rough characters we sometimes meet who don't even know what theology is but recognize a good man when they see one and find God in him without asking how.

He didn't offer to make amends for his sins. How could he? He didn't repeat the Shema (The Lord thy God is one God), far less the Nicene Creed. He didn't promise to be good. And he couldn't, literally, lift a finger to help Jesus from his cross. "Remember me." That's all. It seems so inadequate, so casual. Yet, in the language of theology, this is just what we mean by justification by faith alone. The response of Jesus shows that he was "justified"—made straight, made right with God by this simple act of trust.

You and I can learn from that. As you know, I have the utmost respect for theological study and the importance of the Christian doctrines. I think we need to use our minds on the things we profess to believe, and that there are treasures in the Bible to be mined by all who are serious about the Christian way. But I note in the Gospels that Jesus exacts no one single way in which we should respond to him. He accepted a gesture like that of Zacchaeus offering to repay all whom he had cheated, a wise crack like that of the Canaanite woman who told him that even dogs could eat the crumbs from the master's table, an act of faith like that of the centurion who courteously asked him to cure his servant from a distance "for I am not worthy that you shouldest enter under my roof," a reaching out from the crowd to touch the hem of his garment by an ailing woman, as well as the overwhelming confession wrung from Thomas, "My Lord and my God." It is good to know that, whether we are in desperation, in confusion, in doubt, or under a load of guilt, it is enough to say: "Lord, remember me."

Then I heard again with a new sense of astonishment the very simple answer of Jesus. Again we are not hearing religious language, or explanations of doctrine. He doesn't say anything about what some evangelists like to call "God's Plan of Salvation." Not does any ecclesiastical practice come into the picture. He doesn't say: "Sorry: we can't arrange for your baptism in the circumstances." No, it's just a very simple promise, prefaced with the word "Amen" which was his way of saying: "I really mean it: this is absolutely true." "Today you will be with me in Paradise."

In the vocabulary of the time there were various words that referred to life after death, and there was no exact definition for any of them—Sheol, Hades, heaven, eternal life, the new age. He chose the happiest one of them all—Paradise, a word borrowed from the Persians that originally referred to the beautiful garden of a prince and had been adopted by some Jews to mean a kind of resurrected Garden of Eden. Jesus just murmured: "You will be with me there this very day."

There is no place in the Gospels where Jesus describes what heaven is like. The nearest he came was when he said of the dead: "They are like angels", but we don't know what angels are like. The one assurance he gives—and it is enough for me—is "You will be with me." This is what he had said at the Last Supper: "If I go and prepare a place for you, I will come again, and receive you unto myself; *that where I am there you may be also*." Because I live, you shall live also."

This is still his response to each one of us who dares to whisper: "Lord, remember me."

The Season of Easter

Easter Day: Resurrection! Why I Believe

EDITOR'S INTRODUCTION

JESUS ROSE FROM THE dead and is alive forevermore. That's the Easter message in a nutshell. But why believe it? What gives this message credibility? David Read himself came to believe the message, he tells us in this confessional sermon, simply because the risen Christ encountered him one day. There came a time when, "without argument and without any emotional crisis," his adolescent agnosticism dropped away and "religion from being a duty and a bore exploded within as the living Christ came to take possession."

This Easter sermon was preached forty years after that watershed moment. Another thirty years slipped by before Read went to his grave still believing that Jesus was his one lasting hope in life and death, and in life beyond death.

"Subjectivity is truth," said Kierkegaard. So it is with the truth of the Resurrection. We believe it, if we believe it at all, because the subject of the Resurrection, the living Lord Jesus Christ, has spoken to our own inner self, summoning us to faith and hope and love. It's as simple and mysterious as that.

EASTER DAY: RESURRECTION! WHY I BELIEVE

A Sermon preached by David H. C. Read at Madison Avenue Presbyterian Church on Easter Day, March 30, 1975

" . . . *If Christ has not been raised from death, then we have nothing to preach, and you have nothing to believe.*" 1 Corinthians 15:14

Readings: 1 Corinthians 15:12–20; John 20:1–16

SINCE THIS IS THE twentieth Easter sermon I have preached from this pulpit, I looked for the strongest text I could find. Here it is. It goes straight to the point and hits both you and me in the spiritual solar plexus. "If Christ has not been raised from the dead, then *we* have nothing to preach, and *you* have nothing to believe."

If these words strike you as a wild exaggeration let me remind you that Paul is speaking within the Christian community. He's not saying that all religious speaking or writing by those who don't believe in the Resurrection are worthless, or that apart from this particular belief there's nothing worth believing. He's simply declaring that the Christian Church stands or falls by the truth of the Resurrection story. It is a matter of historical record that the Church came into being because a number of ordinary people were convinced that Jesus had risen from the dead, that it spread across the world by the dynamic of this belief, and that its strength and weakness in every generation, including our own has been in direct proportion to the vitality of the conviction that the crucified Jesus was seen alive again and is alive for evermore. Remove this item from the Christian creed and the whole structure collapses. We have nothing to preach, and you have nothing to believe—as Christians. Paul goes so far as to say that if we subtract this element of eternity, this supernatural dimension from the Christian story, and attempt to live by the memory of a Jesus who is dead and gone in the expectation that we too shall soon be dead and gone, then the Good News becomes Bad News. "If our hope in Christ is good for this life only, then we deserve more pity than anyone else in the world." In other words, it's better to be a pagan with two feet on the ground than a Christian hobbling on one leg.

If this sounds like saying that if you have difficulty in believing that Christ came alive from the dead, you should not be a member of the Church, hold on! Remember Paul was writing to members of the Church and was not about to throw anybody out. Does it surprise you to learn that some of these Corinthian Christians openly denied the Resurrection? At least they denied that there was going to be any resurrection for them. It might have happened to Christ, they said, but as for us there's no hope of anything beyond the grave. Funnily enough, we have reversed this way of thinking. Many today assume that there will be some kind of resurrection, some form of eternal life for them, but doubt that it could have happened to Jesus. One way or another there was as much doubt and confusion among the very first Christians as there is today. And nothing that I am going to say about my own belief must be interpreted as implying that unless you can say Amen you should say Goodbye. I am grateful for the fact that during my own period of doubt and rejection nobody suggested that I should withdraw from the family of the Church.

Let me add this too before I come to my own testimony. This one central belief has been held by an astonishing variety of people, brilliant and simple, sceptical and credulous, practical and mystical, and each one has understood it in his or her own way. Even among the clergy there is no uniformity about our beliefs as to what exactly happened on Easter morning even among those who are radiantly convinced that Jesus was seen alive again after his crucifixion. There have been only three regular preachers in this pulpit since the year 1905. Anyone senior enough to remember them all will agree that Dr. Coffin, Dr. Buttrick, and I did not come out of the same mould, that we had different backgrounds, experiences and temperaments. Yet, Easter by Easter, the word has sounded here across these years that Jesus Christ is risen from the dead and is alive and present with us now, and I feel totally at one with my predecessors in its proclamation. Hallelujah, Henry! Hallelujah, George!

Resurrection!—not Resurrection? This morning I say: Damn those question marks that have wriggled through too many sermons in recent years. I'm not raising a question but declaring what I believe to be a fact. And you have every right to ask: Why do you believe it?

Perhaps you have your own answer. It always astonishes me that many seem to think that I believe in a doctrine like the Resurrection because I am a minister. It's as though they think that a certain number of curious beliefs are tied around one's neck like a clerical collar, and that the collar itself was fitted on at birth. Every clergyman, you know, was once a layman—and if you have any complaints about the quality of the ministry, remember that we have only the laity to draw upon! No, I don't believe in the Resurrection because I am a minister. I became a minister because I came to believe in the Resurrection.

Why did I come to believe in the Resurrection? Again you may have an answer ready: "You believe in the Resurrection because you were raised in a Christian tradition." Right. I have no desire whatever to wash away the fact that I was baptized as an infant, nourished in a family that accepted the faith without being particularly "churchy," and exposed through childhood to the main tenets of Christianity. I've no use for the kind of Christian testimony that dismisses the influence of home and Church and claims that the great discovery was mine alone. Whatever you profess today from atheism to fundamentalism, your parents and others had a lot to do with it. The great theologian, Karl Barth, when asked by a professor of philosophy how he, with his broad culture and penetrating mind, could believe in Christian doctrines like the Resurrection, answered simply: "Because my mother told me." Sure, one of the reasons I believe is that my mother told me. And to this day a strong element in my belief in the resurrection is the number and the quality of the people who told me.

The apostles told me—people like Peter and John and Paul. I still find it an anchor of my faith whenever doubts creep in (and without doubts there is no true faith) that such very human characters not only wrote down their solemn conviction that the Jesus they had seen crucified was alive again, but were willing to die rather than deny it. I find it hard to conceive that men like that would risk their lives for a hoax or a delusion. Then there are the others who told me—what a cloud of witnesses they are—brilliant intellectuals, Augustine, Aquinas, Calvin, Pascal, Schweitzer; poets like Chaucer, Milton, Donne, Blake, Hopkins, T. S. Eliot; novelists from Bunyan to Updike; the artists and architects who have celebrated the Resurrection in paint and stone; and who can forget today the music of Bach. I think also of the wits and most of the really hilarious people I know today. Then there are those we call the saints, men or women whose sheer goodness left its mark upon the world. They all believed that Jesus rose from the grave—and they are not all dead.

After that orgy of name-dropping (as a prominent minister in Scotland was reported to have said the other day: "If there's one thing the Queen and I have in common, it's a dislike of name-dropping.") you may be tempted to say: "Granted the impressive roll call of those who believed in the Resurrection, I still want to know why *you* believe. Or is your faith really second hand?"

For answer I take you to a time when, in my late teens, I realized that Jesus is alive. Don't ask me to explain it, but it was like the difference between reading a manual on swimming and jumping into the deep end, between reading *about* World War I and being *in* World War II, between being a spectator at a play and being on the stage, between looking at Jesus through the different lenses I had been offered, by believers and unbelievers, and suddenly finding him looking at me. Without argument and without any emotional crisis, my adolescent agnosticism dropped away and religion from being a duty and a bore exploded from within as the living Christ came to take possession. I don't remember having any serious questions about what happened on Easter morning. After all, I had come to believe in the Resurrection in the same way as the first disciples did—by meeting the Risen Lord. The empty tomb didn't convince them. They ran away afraid but, we are told in Matthew's Gospel: "Jesus met them and said, 'Peace be with you.'" Jesus met them—and he had met me.

Yes, I know all that can be said about teenage religion and the fantasies of youth. Don't think that I haven't analyzed, criticized, and sometimes discarded things that I believed then. This vital experience of the living Christ has been bombarded by the doubts that arise from psychological insights and historical and literary investigation (a seminary sees to that!) and—much more severely—by trials and tragedies of which I never dreamed in my boyhood. Through them all, even when the clouds came down and seemed to blanket all faith and hope, I can only say that I was conscious of being held—held by a power of God which had the shape of Jesus Christ, crucified and risen. The fact that it was Jesus who rose from the dead came to mean more and more for I knew that the One who held me had been himself through the worst any of us can know. I learned what Christian experience teaches—that my faith is not in my faith but in him; or, as the old hymn has it: "Let me no more my comfort draw from my weak hold on thee; In this alone rejoice with awe—thy mighty hold on me."

Yet belief in the Resurrection has been for me much more than this rescuing power in times of distress. It has given the sparkle of eternity to the beauty, the joy, and the moments of exhilaration that come to us all. It's as if the Risen Christ throws his blessing into the radiance of love and friendship, the splendor of the universe, and the laughter of every day. He tells me that the sound of joy is echoed in the heart of God and that the end of the human journey is neither a bang nor a whimper but a Hallelujah chorus. When you share today, no matter how simply, in that song of the angels, how can you not believe that "on the third day he rose again from the dead?"

Today, more than ever, I believe in the Resurrection for, above all, it stands for the triumph of life. As a generation we are being swamped by the tidings of death, as if the suicidal impulse was taking possession of the human soul. The forces of negation are in the saddle—violence is embraced as a friend, life is an expendable commodity, anger and hate are celebrated as liberators, and despair is the god of the stage, the screen and the novel. In the middle of all this the Risen Christ calls again for the affirmation of life and hope. "Because he lives, we shall live also." That is not just a promise of heaven but of life, freshness, and vitality here and now. The touch of Jesus is the touch of life, and never was humanity in greater need of it.

Across the nation today a forest of TV antennae are tuned in to the news of death and destruction. This morning the towers and steeples of the Christian Church rise up to catch again the news of life and hope. For me this news is not just a whiff of optimism we try to look on the bright side. It is anchored in a piece of solid news, news of an event that happened when the dark side was all that could be seen—the coming alive of the One who had died and descended into our hell. He is for me today the Lord of all life-giving forces because I see in him the God who had conquered the brutal negations of sin and death, the one who answers our suicidal "I am not" with his tremendous I AM. That is the Bible name of God, and the Word of Jesus is "I am the resurrection and the life."

That's what puts the exclamation mark for me and not the query on the story of the Resurrection. Why do I believe? In the end, you know, it's not a matter of argument and weighing pros and cons. When I read again, after all these years, the Bible stories of Easter morning, my mind may be asking questions that were not there twenty or forty years ago. I hope I shall always go on having new questions until I can ask the Lord himself. But within me faith leaps in response with the unarguable certainty of one who falls in love. It is, if you like, something I cannot help. Some months ago there was one of those brighter moments in our city life when a young Frenchman, Philippe Petit, had a rope slung from one tower of the World Trade Center to the other and proceeded to walk across it. When they sent him for psychiatric examination he was found to be perfectly sane. And when they asked him why he did it, his answer was just: "Well, if I see three oranges, I have to juggle; and if I see two towers, I have to walk." Well, perhaps the only answer to my question this morning is: when I hear the story of the Resurrection I have to believe.

Forget the theories, the arguments, the rationalizations. This is very personal—as personal as the meeting in the morning mists between a woman and a stranger. In two words we hear the Resurrection faith. "Mary"—can you hear your name? Listen through the mists of our confusions. "Master," master of my life, master of all life, our Lord and our God. Say it—and you will know why I believe.

How to Hear the Easter Story

EDITOR'S INTRODUCTION

DAVID READ DID NOT dogmatically insist that every last miracle in the Bible must be affirmed by members of the Christian Church. He did, however, suggest that the miracle of the Resurrection is indispensable. And he found it interesting that in our day when agnostic intellectuals become Christians "they do not embrace some watered down version of the faith, said to be digestible by the modern mind, but the story of Jesus, the Son of God, crucified and truly risen from the dead."

Among such modern day converts who have embraced a robust resurrection faith, Read notes, are C. S. Lewis, John Updike, and Frederick Buechner. Parenthetically, we might recommend the following works by these resurrection-affirming writers: *Mere Christianity* and *The Lion, the Witch and the Wardrobe* (Lewis); *Pigeon Feathers* and *In the Beauty of the Lilies* (Updike); and *Wishful Thinking* and *Whistling in the Dark* (Buechner).

Read suggests in this sermon that we read the Resurrection narratives neither skeptically nor uncritically but with hearts and minds open to the risen Christ who can suddenly come to us through any manner of shut doors.

HOW TO HEAR THE EASTER STORY

A Sermon preached by David H. C. Read at Madison Avenue
Presbyterian Church on Easter Day, April 10, 1977

> Text: *"And after eight days again his disciples were within, and Thomas with
> them: then came Jesus, the doors being shut, and stood in the midst, and
> said Peace be unto you."* John 20:26
>
> Readings: 1 Corinthians 15; John 20:1–16

"THEN CAME JESUS, THE doors being shut"   the real Jesus, not a ghost or
a vision, but a Jesus so real they could see on his hands the marks of the
Calvary nails. And yet the doors were shut, locked and bolted like any New
Yorker's—and for the same reason: they were afraid. These were hunted
men, the friends of the executed agitator.

By the real Jesus I mean the man we read of in the Gospels, who ate and
drank, laughed and wept, and had his hopes and fears like any of the rest of
us; not a shadowy figure who flickers across the screen of history, a phantom
creation of the fevered imagination of some first-century religious fanatics.
Tonight millions will watch on their television screens "Jesus of Nazareth,"
and see a real Jesus—not *the* real Jesus for that is beyond the power of any
actor, but a Jesus real enough to convince the most skeptical that there was
such a person and that the events recorded in the Gospels belong to history
and not to fairyland. It is ironical that many who most fervently claim to be
the modern disciples of this Jesus were so incensed by the thought that he
could be shown as truly human that they deluged the network with protests
against a film they had never seen and scared a timid sponsor to withdraw.

It was the real Jesus who came into that room "the doors being shut."
And so we are confronted with the miracle of the Resurrection. It was the
same Jesus with whom they had sailed on the lake, slept under the stars on the
Galilean hills, feasted in disreputable homes, and come sweating up the dusty
roads to Jerusalem. But now they knew what they had sometimes sensed before—that there was another dimension to this man they loved. The Resurrection had released in him the divinity he had laid aside, and he was no longer
the captive, like us, of space and time. If you ask me what kind of body this
was that could carry the marks of his wounds yet pass through closed doors, I
have to reply: "I don't know." I'm not, I hope, arrogant enough to suppose that
I know all about the mysterious intermingling of body and spirit that we think
we have explained with the blessed word "psychosomatic," or crazy enough to
think that I can explain, or explain away, the one great miracle on which the

Christian faith depends. Let me just say that it's something like this I have in mind when I try to imagine what kind of people we may be in heaven, and repeat those debated words of the Apostles' Creed: "I believe in the resurrection of the body and the life everlasting."

The story of the Resurrection of Jesus is frankly the story of a miracle—if by miracle you mean, not some spectacular divine conjuring trick, but an event totally beyond our powers of explanation through which God speaks to us. If you say: "Do I have to believe in miracles to be a Christian?" my reply would be: "Not in any more than you have to—and among those in which I, for one, have to believe are the Incarnation and the Resurrection— Christmas and Easter." It is worth noting that in our day when agnostic intellectuals become Christians they do not embrace some watered down version of the faith, said to be digestible by the modern mind, but the story of Jesus, the Son of God, crucified and truly risen from the dead. C. S. Lewis, Dorothy Sayers, Lin Yutang, John Updike, Frederick Buechner—read what Updike is confessing in that poem printed in the bulletin. Listen to these words from Buechner talking to a group of students: "So what do I believe actually happened that morning on the third day after he died?" He goes on: "I can tell you this: that what I believe happened and what in faith and with great joy I proclaim to you here is that he somehow got up, with life in him again, and the glory upon him . . . I was not there to see it any more than I was awake to see the sun rise this morning, but I affirm it as surely as I do that by God's grace the sun did rise this morning because that is why the world is flooded with light." "He got up." As Updike says: "Make no mistake: if He rose at all it was as His body."

During the Sundays of Lent we have been listening in this church to some of what I call the strong stories of the Bible. This is the strongest story of them all—the story of Jesus who lived and died and rose again. It is incomparably the strongest story in the world. It created the Church that survived the sword of the persecutors, the scorn of the philosophers, the crimes of its leaders and the folly of its members, to spread into every corner of our world shouting that "Jesus is risen, and Jesus is Lord!" This story created the law, the art, the ethics, and the education that shaped the Western world for a thousand years—and has yet to be replaced by any other story in our world, although the Marxist one is having a good try. And—most important of all—this strong story is proving capable today, as in the past, of so gripping the mind and soul of people like you and me that their lives are transformed, and they can speak of their experience as of nothing less than being "born again." When *this* story becomes *your* story life begins anew.

But how do we hear it? We don't hear every story in the same way. A student doesn't hear the story he has to sweat over for an examination with the same delight and intensity as the story he reads in a letter from his fiancée. I don't hear the story that came to me the other day from a self-confessed agnostic, telling me how a radio sermon had reached him at six in the morning when he was alone up in the California mountains and set him thinking about Christ, in exactly the same mood as I hear the story sent in to me by the Internal Revenue Service. There are ways to hear—and there are the doors we slam to keep from hearing.

Millions in our day have slammed a door of solid skepticism. If they listen at all to the story of the Resurrection it is with total disbelief—the same disbelief, by the way, that we read of in the New Testament. The disciples at first rejected the story of the women who came running with the story of the empty tomb—"the apostles thought what the women said was nonsense, and they didn't believe them." When these apostles became convinced there was this odd man out—"Thomas was not with the rest when Jesus came. So the disciples told him: 'We have seen the Lord.' He said: 'Unless I see the mark of the nails in his hands, unless I put my fingers into the place where the nails were, and my hand into his side, I will not believe.' " Thomas—the patron saint of the logical positivists! And then there is the report of the Athenian egg heads to Paul's story of the Risen Christ: "When they heard of the resurrection of the dead, some mocked."

It's not so much mocking that closes the door today. It's just the bland assumption that, of course, this story can't be true. It's the pervasive, old fashioned dogmatism—miracles don't happen: this story about Jesus is as dead as he was and can't be resurrected. I read a few days ago a review of a new production of Beckett's fascinating play "Waiting for Godot." Not only did the critic pronounce this play the greatest of our era but went on to say that its message is the "ultimate statement" about our human life. This is how we are brainwashed today. A good writer can say, without causing a ripple of comment, that the philosophy of the absurd, enshrined in the story of those characters who wait for the God who never comes, is the "ultimate statement" thus dismissing the joyful affirmation of the Gospel that has proved itself, and is still proving itself, the strongest story in the world. Yet still Jesus comes, even that door being closed; and more and more of those who had ceased to give the Christian story a hearing are beginning to listen in a new way. Sure, it's a miracle—but there comes a moment when the most hard-bitten skeptic is ready to drop the dogma and listen again. And then the miracle is not explained or proved but happens again: Jesus comes right through that door.

But there are probably more today who are not so much sheer skeptics as nostalgic half-believers. They would like to accept the story as they hear it in the Bible. They rejoice in the signs of returning faith and are happy when the churches show signs of new vitality. But they find themselves swivelling between belief and unbelief. Browning's Bishop Blougram describes their attitude:

> "All we have gained then by our unbelief
> Is a life of doubt diversified by faith,
> For one of faith diversified by doubt:
> We call the chessboard white—we call it black."

So it is very tempting to settle for the symbolic resurrection story. Whatever happened at the tomb that morning surely we can say that Easter means that life will triumph over death, and that hope is the true posture of the human spirit. Not for a moment would I belittle this way of accepting the Easter story or attempt to rob the half-believer of the Easter joy. Some of the greatest spirits of our time have been men and women of intellectual integrity who could not profess what they do not believe, but want to throw their weight on what Disraeli once called "the side of the angels." If you are on that side, God bless you! I would only make two remarks. One is that, whatever sense it makes, the symbolic hearing of the Easter story was not the hearing of the apostles, was not the hearing of the first Christians, was not the faith that swept across the world, and is not normally the kind of hearing today that brings about that reorientation we are learning again to call "rebirth." And the other is a plea to realize how thin that door of half-belief really is and to be ready to find at any moment that the living Jesus walks right through it and says: "Reach your fingers here; see my hands. . . . Happy are they who never saw me and yet have found faith."

Then, of course, it is possible to hear the Easter story out of sheer habit. We church goers are so often locked in the narrow room of religious routine. The doors are closed, not by unbelief or half-belief, but by use and wont. Yes; yes; this is the way it goes:

> "Advent, Christmas, Lent, and Easter;
> There's always some old fast or feast or
> Other event in the Church's Year—
> World without end I begin to fear."

This could be the thickest door of all. Jesus believed in religious routine. We read that every Sabbath he attended the synagogue "as his custom was." But the people he found hardest to reach were not the skeptics, the half-believers, the scoffers, the down-and-outs, and the up-and-outs, but the believers who were so encrusted with inherited convictions that the Spirit of Life could find no entrance. It was to one of them, you remember, that he spoke of being "born again"—not to the scoffer and the rascal. And it was to one of them, Saul of Tarsus, that he suddenly appeared on the Damascus road, the door of his heart being shut. At any moment it can happen to any of us for whom the story lies dead and unexamined in the back of our minds.

How then do we hear? With minds alert to what is being reported by the eye witnesses. With minds open to the possibility that this was no ancient legend of someone being brought to life again, but the supreme miracle in which, as C. S. Lewis put it, God leaned against the fly-wheel of history and reversed its direction. With hearts ready to respond to the music of Easter, to let the risen Jesus come not only through the channels of our thoughts but through the glorious affirmation of believing song, believing organ, and the sound of trumpets. And with the realization that we are not alone, but surrounded by the Church Catholic in every land this morning, and by the great company of heaven who respond to our whisper of "He is risen" with the eternal chorus: "Hallelujah! He is risen indeed."

"Then Jesus came, the doors being shut." The real Jesus. It can happen to you right now.

Easter Belief: A Crutch or a Goad?

EDITOR'S INTRODUCTION

THIS WAS DAVID READ's last Easter sermon before retirement. His text is an odd one for Easter Day: "Saul, Saul, why do you persecute me? It is hard for you, this kicking against the goad." Trust Read, however, to unpack the text in a way that seems just right for the occasion.

A goad, the dictionary tells us, is something that pricks, urges, or stimulates somebody into action. This is exactly what happens in the Resurrection, Read suggests. The risen Christ prods, stimulates, *goads* us into action. And our resistance is a 'kicking against the goad.'

As the sermon draws to its conclusion, David Read becomes quietly personal: "I may well be kicking against the goad that prods me to spend more time in prayer, more money on the work of Christ's Church. Yes, the living Christ is the Way, the Truth, and the Life. I am reassured of that every time I am able, in a small way, to obey, so, like Paul, I am able to say, deep down, 'to me to live is Christ' and even to add 'and to die is gain.' But I need those prods."

Don't we all?

EASTER BELIEF: A CRUTCH OR A GOAD?

A Sermon preached by David H. C. Read at Madison Avenue Presbyterian Church on Easter Day, March 26, 1989

> Text: *"Saul, Saul, why do you persecute me? It is hard for you, this kicking against the goad."* Acts 26:14 (NEB)
>
> Readings: Acts 26:12–18 (NEB); Luke 23:55—24:11 (NEB)

BEFORE ANYONE BEGINS TO wonder what on earth—or in heaven—this text has to do with Easter, may I interject a personal note?

It would be absurd to pretend that it has never crossed my mind in preparing this Easter sermon that it will be the last one I preach as minister of this church. Since 1956 when I preached my first one, I have had the joy of proclaiming here the most important message the Church has to offer thirty-two different times. (If any mathematician wants to correct me and say thirty-three, let me remind you that in 1981 I was in Australia.) I am immensely grateful for the annual celebration which I have shared with this loyal congregation and other friends for so long and wish you all a Happy Easter for the years to come. With this great theme it is the message and not the messenger that matters, and this messenger hopes to go on proclaiming this message so long as his voice holds out. No more nostalgia. You will agree with me, I hope, that we are not met this morning to celebrate the retirement of David Read but the resurrection of Jesus Christ.

Sometimes a preacher is asked: "How can you possibly find new things to say, year after year, about such a familiar theme as Easter?" The answer should be "No problem." In the first place, the biblical preacher has the whole New Testament to wander through to find a text and a theme. For not a page of it would have been written if the apostolic writers had not believed that Jesus had risen from the dead. Some, like Peter, James, and John, had been eye witnesses of the event; others, like Paul and the author of the Revelation, found themselves confronted by a living Lord who knew their name: "Saul, Saul, why do you persecute me?" "When I saw him," we read in the Revelation, "I fell at his feet as dead. But he laid his right hand on me and said, 'Do not be afraid, I am the first and the last, and I am the living one; for I was dead and now I am alive for evermore.'"

Thus the living Christ shines through the writings of the New Testament backed by the Old without which we cannot fully understand. And we hear of the impact of the Gospel—for this is the Good News—on a vast variety of men and women and also on the different societies and varied cultures in which they lived. It isn't as if Christians have gone on commemorating the miracle of this man's rising from the dead as we commemorate in our time the heroes of the American or French revolutions. Believers who celebrate Easter are confronted by a living Lord who has something to say to us *this* year which may, especially as the pace of history accelerates, be different from what he said to us in 1988 or 1987 or, for some of us, 1920.

As I thought about the times we live in, a rather peculiar text kept ringing in my ear. It came from the story of the sudden transformation of Saul the persecutor of the Christians into Paul, the passionate disciple of Christ who launched the great Christian mission to the Gentiles of which we are the fruit. Paul told the story once on an occasion even more solemn and impressive than a Senate hearing for he was making his defense before King Herod Agrippa, his sister Bernice, and Felix the governor. It seems odd that this array of top brass would want to listen to Paul, but Luke tells us in his matter-of-fact way that "Felix came with his wife Drusilla, who was a Jewess, and sending for Paul he let him talk to him about Jesus Christ." So Paul boldly and with dignity told his story. "As I was on my way, your Majesty, I saw a light from the sky, more brilliant than the sun, shining all around me and my travelling companions. We all fell to the ground, and then I heard a voice saying to me in the Jewish language, 'Saul, Saul, why do you persecute me? It is hard for you this kicking against the goad.'"

This was no model conversion such as we are all supposed to have as we convert to Christ. Every encounter with the living Christ recounted in the New Testament is different, and highly individual, and today he speaks to *you*—in *your* language. But what struck me this time around as I listened again to Paul's account was one word: "Goad."

A goad, according to an up-to-date dictionary is "A stick with a pointed or electrically charged end, for driving cattle, oxen, etc.; a prod." I began to think how many of us today when picturing an encounter with the living Christ would ever use this image. A recent Gallop poll tells us that a surprising 66 percent of Americans when asked the direct question: "Would you say you have made a commitment to Jesus Christ or not?" answered yes. How many of these, do you think, would describe this commitment as experiencing the pricking of a goad, getting an unexpected electric charge, feeling some kind of prod? In our day wouldn't we be more likely to speak in terms of being attracted, won over, or being comforted, getting hold of a crutch to rely on in dangerous and confusing days?

We've all heard the accusation that religion is a crutch to lean on when we're in trouble, a comfort when we're depressed. And so it is, if it's the right kind of religion. George Buttrick, my predecessor, used to say here that the preacher's job was to comfort the afflicted. He also went on to say that it was also to afflict the comfortable—and that's where the goad comes in. But before I get to that, let me say that I believe that the Easter message most surely brings tremendous comfort to all who worry about what lies beyond death—Christ does; or whether light or darkness will be the end of the human story—there will be no night there; or whether sin or grace will triumph in the end—grace will. In the Anglican Prayerbook the words of Christ inviting us to the Table of Holy Communion are called the "comfortable words". Of course, "comfortable" in the King James Bible was a strong word, with the emphasis on the "fort", the fortress of faith. But the word is there. Listen to Paul again: "Blessed be God, even the Father of our Lord Jesus Christ, the Father of mercies, the God of all comfort, who comforteth us in all our tribulation, that we may be able to comfort them which are in any trouble, by the comfort by which we ourselves are comforted of God." Call this a crutch if you like, but the only real question is whether it is a reality or an illusion. On this issue we have to make up our minds, and I, for one, would prefer the company of Albert Schweitzer and Mother Theresa to that of Bertrand Russell and Sigmund Freud.

On this day when the joy of the Easter message overflows from the churches to the uncommitted and unconvinced, I don't grudge anybody the comfort they may find in the songs of Easter and the old familiar story. But I want us all to think again about the goad, and perhaps to feel the prod. What do we mean when we invite people to commit themselves to Christ? It is apt to sound today like an offer of a quick fix for all their troubles. But the encounters with Christ we read about in the New Testament are not like that. He does not appear as the smiling savior with all the answers. He certainly didn't to Paul. The voice he heard didn't say "Here you are; come my way: I have the secret of success." It said, "It is hard for you, this kicking against the goad." The Christ who met Paul on the Damascus Road didn't just appear out of the blue. He had been prodding him for months, and Paul had been resisting just as we do when we realize that a commitment to Christ is much more than an embrace from the Comforter, or the timely offer of a crutch. The blunt fact is that not all of us find the thought of such an encounter simple and attractive, and every one of us, however committed, have known moments when we would rather avoid the prod of the Risen Christ.

A letter I received recently from a believer startled me with this confession: "I know that part of me likes the absence (of God) because the idea of his presence is so terrifying. Jesus scared me no end, and I suspect that a 'close encounter' would be disastrous." This is an element in the encounter with Christ we don't hear much about today, but it's right there in the Gospel stories. There's that story of Peter when he was overcome by the mystery and majesty of Jesus one day on the Lake of Galilee and cried out: "Depart from me; for I am a sinful man, O Lord." Then there are these stories of the women and the men who first saw Jesus alive again after his crucifixion. They were terrified. Indeed the original ending of Mark's Gospel is "they were afraid." It was only then that they could hear the voice of the true Comforter: "Cheer up: I have overcome the world."

When I think back on my own encounters with the living Christ, especially in times of crises, I am grateful for the rescuing hand that led me through even as he had been through it and come through. And I think of Easter services when the risen Christ was so real and near I could have sung the Hallelujah Chorus for ever and ever. If this were not true how could I have gone on preaching it? But, looking back, I am equally grateful for the goad (with or without the electric shocks).

For instance, a close encounter with Christ always raises the question of the direction one's life is taking. The prod comes: Is the master motive of my life really to do God's will, loving him with heart and mind and strength and my neighbor as myself? Or has some other goal, some other motivation tried to take over? There are times when it is much more comfortable not to ask that question. It could upset my plans.

Then there is that really painful prod that comes when we listen again to the kind of life Jesus demands of us in, for instance, the Sermon on the Mount. That's not comfortable. We don't like having our peace disturbed too much by the needs of our neighbors, do we? Or by the suggestion that we might do more to fight the injustice and corruption of our society. Or by the kind of discipline that discipleship demands. I may well be kicking against the goad that prods me to spend more time in prayer, more money on the work of Christ's Church. Yes, the living Christ *is* the Way, the Truth, and the Life. I am reassured of that every time I am able, in a small way, to obey, so, like Paul, I am able to say deep down, "to me to live is Christ" and even to add "and to die is gain." But I need those prods.

Then the goad of the living Christ comes at me from another direction. For the disciple there is no retirement. Of course, there comes a time for all of us when we withdraw from our normal occupation. And that can be a temptation to sit back and let the world go by. That's when we should feel that goad. Because Christ is alive for us whether we are ten years old or a hundred, and here is the program for the Christian: "All I care for is to know Christ, to experience the power of his resurrection, and to share his sufferings, in growing conformity with his death, if only I may finally arrive at the resurrection from the dead. It is not to be thought that I have already achieved all this. I have not yet reached perfection, but I press on, hoping to take hold of that for which Christ once took hold of me. My friends, I do not reckon myself to have got hold of it yet. All I can say is this: forgetting what is behind me, and reaching out for that which lies ahead, I press towards the goal to win the prize which is God's call to the life above, in Christ Jesus."

Other People's Religion

EDITOR'S INTRODUCTION

THE TEXT FOR THIS sermon concerns Peter's post-Easter conversation with the risen Lord. Clearly there was a special relationship between these two which led Jesus to confide the pastoral care of his church to Peter: "Feed my lambs. Tend my sheep. Feed my sheep." Yet John would appear to have been the disciple closest to Jesus' heart. When Peter, showing signs of jealousy perhaps, asked Jesus concerning John, "What will happen to him?" the answer was blunt and to the point: "What is it to you? Follow me."

Since David Read preached this sermon the world has become increasingly secular in Europe and America, and increasingly Islamic in Africa and the Middle East. Christians the world over have accordingly found themselves taking more and more of a back seat to people of other religions and none. Thus the temptation today to join Peter in anxiously putting the question to Jesus: "Lord, what will happen to them?"

The Lord's answer surely remains the same: "What is it to you? Follow me." In other words, don't worry about what's happening to people of other religions and none. *Your* task is to follow Christ—and leave the rest to God.

OTHER PEOPLE'S RELIGION

A Sermon preached by David H. C. Read at Madison Avenue Presbyterian Church on April 21, 1985

Text: *"When he caught sight of him Peter asked, 'Lord what will happen to him?' Jesus said, 'If it should be my will that he wait until I come, what is it to you? Follow me.'"* John 21:21, 22 (NEB)

Readings: 1 Kings 17:8–24; Acts 4:7–12 (NEB); John 21:20–25 (NEB)

"WHAT WILL HAPPEN TO him?" "What is it to you? Follow me." At first sight we may well wonder what it was that earned Peter this royal brush-off from the risen Christ. For us it is a natural question. Peter has just had a very intimate conversation with the Lord in which his loyalty had been challenged and then strongly affirmed. Christ had then confided to him the pastoral care of the Church: "Feed my sheep," and warned that it would lead to his martyrdom. As Peter was reflecting on this he caught sight of John just behind them. John up to that point had seemed the closest to the Lord. This Gospel calls him "the disciple whom Jesus loved." Peter may well have thought of him as the special favorite—and was perhaps a little jealous? Anyway, it was natural enough for him to wonder why John had not been the one to get this solemn charge. "When he caught sight of him, Peter asked, 'Lord, what will happen to him?'"

Christ gives a cryptic reply and then brusquely adds: "What is it to you? Follow me." *You* follow me. The Greek is very rough and colloquial—three little words meaning "What's that to you?" or "Mind your own business." We could well be as shocked as Peter must have been. Isn't caring deeply for our neighbors at the heart of the Christian faith? Doesn't the Bible keep insisting that we have to be as concerned about their welfare as we are about our own? Think of the eloquent sermons that have been preached on the text: "Am I my brother's keeper?" Yet here is Cain's cynical evasion of responsibility almost literally on the lips of Christ: "Are you your brother's keeper?" Is this the same Christ who tells us to love our neighbor as we love ourselves? And didn't the great apostle Paul say explicitly: "Look to each other's interest and not merely to your own"? It has seemed to many Christians that the Gospel not only insists that we care about others but even gives us license to intrude into the inner sanctuary of their souls.

This sharp response of Jesus—"What is it to you?"—is upsetting to many of our ideas about our Christian duty, which is why I have chosen to think about it with you this morning. Peter's question about John—"Lord, what will happen to him?"—sounds perfectly natural to us. They had been companions through the ministry of Jesus. Peter had been told what was in store for him. Surely it was in order for him to point to John and ask: "Lord, what will happen to him?" We are all concerned about what is going to happen to us—next week, next year, or in forty years' time, and we have exactly the same concern about the future of those dearest to us. It is disturbing to think that Christ could say to us: "What's that to you? Mind your own business!"

Then think for a moment how this remark of Jesus could undermine our call to evangelize, to reach other people with the Gospel. If Christ really meant what he said when he commanded his disciples to "Go. . . . and make disciples" is he now revoking that command, telling us to let people alone on the grounds that their religion is not our business? Think for a moment of the intense desire we may have that an unbelieving friend, or it may be one of our own family, should find the peace and joy we know in Christ. Is it wrong for us to have this concern? Have we no right to pray: "Lord, make John, make Mary a Christian"?

Some will find it intolerable to think that Christ might reply: "Mind your own business." Of course, others may be relieved to shuck off all responsibility for sharing our faith with those we love.

One way or another, this incident is certainly puzzling and reminds us that the bumper sticker that reads "Christ is the Answer" might better read: "Christ Raises the Questions."

I found this incident, this remark of the Lord to Peter, leading me first to seek some simple solutions to the questions I have raised. Then it seemed not quite so simple, and I was led on to listen to the words of Christ as they apply to our dealings with other people, and especially other people's religion. "What is it to you? Follow me." It's a rough text, but sometimes it takes just that to make us listen.

I found that nearly all commentators interpret these words as a rebuke to what we call "idle curiosity." It is pointed out that Jesus was impatient with questions that had little to do with a life devoted to the Kingdom of God. He refused to take seriously the little story his critics dreamed up about the woman who married seven brothers in succession, after each one died with the trick question: "Whose wife will she be in heaven?" He had little time for people who wanted details about coming events, or satisfaction for queries about conditions in the after-life. So he was just telling Peter—and us—not to be nosey.

It may be that this is all that is meant by Christ's rebuke. We can all plead guilty to prying into questions that are not really our business. And there are many today who are entranced by speculations about what is going to happen to us in the years ahead. Hence the popularity in our day of horoscopes and fortune tellers of all kinds. The air waves resound to the sound of preachers delving into the books of Daniel and the Revelation, each coming up with his own exact predictions of the end of the world, Armageddon, the rapture of the Church, the fate of each one of us. I can hear our Lord saying: "Idle curiosity! What's that got to do with you; it's all in God's hands. You get on with the job of following me."

But I have difficulty in writing off Peter's questions as idle curiosity. He must have been truly concerned about his friend John. So I have to ask: Is there a point in our concern for other people beyond which we must not go? Think again of the ones for whom you pray pleading with God for them to come to faith in Christ. This is a natural prayer, a good prayer. But I think we are being warned here that it is possible to make such a prayer a little too much like: "Lord, make John, make Mary, more like me." We may think we know just what kind of believers they should be. We may forget that no one can be brow-beaten into the kingdom—even by our prayers. Our Lord always respects the freedom of each one of us. It is surely best to commit those for whom we pray to God, trusting him to care for them more than we ever can. There is also the possibility that we can be so anxious about the soul of our neighbor that we neglect our own, so anxious to win a new disciple that we forget the call to us. What the Lord is saying to us is what he said to Peter: "*You* follow me. I'll take care of your brother and sister." I am reminded of the story of the Hindu who was constantly being invited by a high pressure, obnoxious evangelist to accept Christ. One day he looked him in the eye and said: "What makes you think that Christ can do more for me than he's done for you?" In the end, it's our life as a disciple that counts for more than any of our arguments or prayers.

"What about this one?" Today that question is often raised in the field of comparative religion. I have seldom spoken to students about the claims of Christ without the question being raised: "What about the Muslims? What about the Buddhists, the Hindus?" "What about the billions who lived and died before Jesus was born?" We have to be modest and reserved in answering such questions. On the last one I like the answer given by John Donne in one of his sermons: "To me, to whom God hath revealed his Son, in a Gospel, by a Church, there can be no way of salvation but by applying that Son of God, by that Gospel, by that Church. Nor is there any foundation for any, nor any other name by which any man can be saved, but the name of Jesus. But how this foundation is presented, and how this name of Jesus is notified, to them amongst whom there is no Gospel preached, no Church established, I am not curious in inquiring. I know God can be as merciful as those tender Fathers present him to be; and I would be as charitable as they are. And therefore, humbly embracing that manifestation of his Son which he hath afforded me, I leave God to his unsearchable ways of working upon others, without further inquisition."

"Without further inquisition." Trust John Donne to find the right words. In these days of closer contact with adherents of other faiths, we are bound to think again about the Christian claim, and to answer questions with humility and respect, remembering that it is Christ we are representing, not our own religion we are trying to stuff down another's throat. But when this question is raised by those who have been raised in the Christian tradition, it can often be a smoke screen to obscure the claim to be a real disciple. There are many today who raise the question: "What about this one—this Muslim, this Buddhist, this primitive ancestor who died a million years ago?" who ought to be told: "What is it to you? *You* follow me." Anyone raised in a Christian tradition is challenged first to a decision about Jesus Christ. It is only if one can say: "Yes; I've examined again the story of Christ, the books of the New Testament: I've experienced Christian worship and seen Christian love in action, and I've come to the conclusion that the claims of Christ are false"—only then does the question of plunging into another religion become legitimate.

In all my experience as a minister I have heard all kinds of reasons for dropping out of the Church. "Somehow I gradually got out of the habit of church-going." "When I was in trouble nobody in the church seemed to care." "The worship seemed remote and said nothing to me." Or it may be some tale about an unfortunate incident that happened twenty years ago, or, more honestly, it could be the remark: "I just got bored with the whole business." The one reason for dropping out I have never heard is this: "I left because in another religion, another movement, I found a better Savior and a better Lord than Jesus Christ. "*You* follow me!" To be a follower of Jesus Christ is not to brush off all other faiths as totally false and deceptive, and commend our way of life as infinitely superior. It is to be grateful that we have heard his voice and humbly bear our witness to the One beside whom we can place no other.

The Fourth Gospel leaves us with this last glimpse of the risen Christ with his disciples. It seemed a curious story with which to end the book. Yet, as we let it come alive for us today, we can see how the Lord is equipping all future disciples for their mission in the world. We are not to be the kind of Christians who are so eager to intrude into the sanctuary of another soul that they forget the claims of their own discipleship, or the kind who enlist God in their efforts to make someone else's religion more like their own. (I once heard a story about my predecessor, Dr. Henry Sloane Coffin. Right in this chancel an angry parishioner who had a disagreement with him accosted him and suggested that they should immediately kneel down and pray about it. "No," said Dr. Coffin, "you're not going to bounce your case off God!") Then we are not to be the kind of Christian who keeps raising excuses for being a poor disciple by pointing to the lives of others: "What about this one, and that one? Surely I'm doing a better job than they." "Mind your own business," says Christ. "*You* follow me."

In the end discipleship is *our* response to the call to *us*. When I preached on Easter Day on the call of Jesus: "Behold, I stand at the door and knock," we were faced again with the fact that it is *our* door, your door, my door, and not our neighbor's where we hear the voice of Jesus. "It is you I am speaking to," he says. "No one else can open *your* door. *You* open it. *You* keep opening it. Never mind about my plans for others. *You* follow me."

Prayer: Give us grace, O God, truly to hear thy call through Jesus Christ to be his disciples and keep us from letting anything get in between; through Jesus Christ our Lord. Amen.

Is God a Bore?

EDITOR'S INTRODUCTION

SEVERAL YEARS AGO THE son of a prominent minister in our town was asked by his teacher at school if he planned to become a minister like his father when he grew up. "Oh, no," said Jimmy. "My father says it's a big bore." Needless to say, that remark shot through town provoking more than a few chuckles. We laugh but the question is a good one: *Is* the ministry, is the church, is God himself basically a bore?

Many people would seem to think so. Yet surely nothing could be further from the truth. Granted, ministers can be boring. Religion itself can be boring. Even *God* can appear to be boring. But let the good news of the Gospel engage us in all its startling freshness, and surely heads will not have cause to nod. The real bores, David Read claims in this sermon, are sinners. After all, "there are comparatively few ways in which we can mess up our lives and defy our God."

The Gospel, on the other hand, delivers us from a life of boredom and offers "communion with a God who has a purpose for his human family, however mysterious it may sometimes seem, and a design for the lives of such apparently insignificant creatures as you and me." Something has surely gone wrong with the presentation if the people in the pews are stifling yawns.

IS GOD A BORE?

A Sermon preached by David H. C. Read at Madison Avenue Presbyterian Church on April 25, 1982

Text: *"Praise be to the God and Father of our Lord Jesus Christ, who in his great mercy gave us new birth into a living hope by the resurrection of Jesus Christ from the dead!"* 1 Peter 1:3 (NEB)

WHEN THERE WERE ONLY a few Christians in the whole world, that's how they felt and that's how they spoke. Peter can't even begin his letter without breaking into a shout of praise expressing the joy and excitement of the Gospel of Jesus Christ—"great mercy," "new birth," "living hope."

For these men and women living in a merciless world, a drab and despairing world, the news of a living and loving God who had given his Son to share our human sorrows, let him be crucified, and then raised him from the dead, was so thrilling and transforming that it was like starting life all over again. They were born again.

Now that the Good News has been around for about two thousand years and there are estimated to be over one billion Christians in the world, we would have to admit that to a great extent the excitement has died down, the joy is muted, and the songs have lost their sparkle and their glow. You may say that loss of enthusiasm is inevitable as any movement moves from the excitements of the early days to become a familiar establishment. You don't find the zest and fervency of the Founding Fathers among the citizens of this Republic today. Nor is there any sign of the rapturous mood of the October Revolution in the average Communist country today, where the present generation seems as bored with Marxism as many on this side of the Curtain profess to be bored with Christianity. Wordsworth noted the same trend within a few decades of the tumultuous French Revolution. Looking back on its beginnings, he wrote: "Bliss was it in those days to be alive, but to be young was very heaven." When that Revolution, after massacres and wars, had settled into a new establishment, the bliss had gone and the fervor had vanished.

But Christianity, as we hear from the New Testament, was meant from the beginning to keep its note of freshness, vigor, and new birth. And, to a surprising extent, it has—but only where the New Testament Gospel is heard anew in the power of the Holy Spirit, only where God is experienced as alive and active, only where Jesus Christ is received as a contemporary Savior. In every corner of the world today, there are men and women who really know the mercy of God as the sure foundation of their lives from day-to-day, who rejoice in the living hope imparted to them by the resurrected Christ, and who find in him the kind of new birth that makes them welcome every new stage of their pilgrimage with lively expectation and contemplate the end with joy. But all of us have to fight our tendency to lose our spiritual zest and let the glowing words of the Gospel—love, mercy, hope, faith, resurrection—be swallowed up in the routine vocabulary of religion. The poet William Cowper knew this very well when he wrote the hymn beginning, "O for a closer walk with God." I often wonder if we should really sing the second verse where he confesses his lapse from grace: "Where is the blessedness I knew when I first saw the Lord?" Every time I sing it, I hope it's not true. There's no reason to be found in the New Testament to indicate that what began as sheer rapture should end as a bore. It is ironic that even the phrase "born again," which indicates the heart of any real Christian experience, has in recent years become something of a bore as it is applied by the media to a special segment of the religious community.

I chose the somewhat shocking title for this sermon, because it seems to me that one of the greatest obstacles to the evangelism of the Church today is the widespread feeling that the worship of the churches is boring, the activities of the churches are boring, religion in general is boring, and that therefore it would follow, though this is seldom expressed, that God is a bore. Since I obviously don't believe that God is a bore (although I did for a few years in adolescence), otherwise I would not have devoted my life to the service of his Church, I want to confront, head-on, this whole business of being bored by religion. For I am more and more persuaded that this is a major factor in countries like ours, which have had centuries of Christian tradition and where there is little element of risk in being known as a Christian. Any time I have gone, in recent years, to speak about the Gospel in colleges and universities, I have usually found little opposition. These are not times when a Christian speaker meets vociferous skeptics spoiling for an argument about the existence of God or the resurrection of Christ. He is much more likely to meet with the faithful while the great majority profess total indifference. They would probably say that, while the subject of religion has a certain intellectual interest, the life and worship of the Church is one big bore.

It's not just religion that is found boring by this generation. In recent years it has become almost the most pejorative adjective in the language. I'm sure I'm not the only parent who hears from day to day, that grammar is boring, or that a lecture was boring, or that a movie was boring, or that writing a letter or cleaning up a room is excessively boring. I suppose we always used the word, but it seems to have taken on a new life in these days when everything around us is programmed to provide as much titillation, rapid change, and spurious excitement as possible. TV directors are terrified they will lose our attention if the scene doesn't change every few minutes, and newscasters on the radio seem to think no one will listen unless the news is delivered in breathless haste, shouted at the top of their voice, or accompanied by the sound of clicking typewriters. Everywhere, we are invited to take the quick, the easy, the stimulating way of learning a skill, or acquiring a foreign language. Homiletics teachers warn seminarians that the attention span of a congregation is about ten minutes: beyond that they will be bored. (Some of us preachers can, of course, bore people in five.)

So, before I make the point that real religion should never be boring, let me suggest that, at times, by "boring" we just mean "demanding." Life is not arranged for us so that every minute of the day we are stimulated and entertained. Everything worth doing, every skill we acquire, every rich experience of literature, music, and the arts has an ingredient of the demanding, which means hard work, even dull and monotonous work. We can't enjoy a happy home unless someone does the boring work of sweeping and washing up. We can't enjoy playing some gorgeous music unless we have done lots of boring practice. The same goes for the tennis champion, or the golfer. In fact, it seems as though the highest delights and accomplishments require the greatest amount of dull and plodding preparation. Yet, we are constantly tempted to suppose that there are short cuts—instant ways to play a piano, acquire a language, become a good dancer, short cuts to the classics, and recipes for a quick, slick philosophy of life.

This last leads me to question the notion that religion must be always instantly gratifying, and that what we call "salvation" can be acquired by a quick emotional response to an electronic evangelist. Those who have found a vivid faith in God, those who know about the joys that Peter is talking about—the great mercy of God, the new birth, and the living hope—are people who, in a real sense, have worked at their religion. I mean by that, giving serious attention to things like prayer, reading the Scriptures, and the beliefs that we have inherited. Peter himself was raised in Judaism and must have learned the law of God, the prayers of the psalmists, and what demands are made on the believer. I'm sure that with his temperament, the boy Peter must have complained many times that his religious duties were boring—whatever the Aramaic word might be. Then, all the disciples spent the time after the risen Christ had returned to heaven in what you could only call plodding payer and searching of the Scriptures. It was to a group of men and women who knew the boring side of religion that the fire of the Spirit came on the day of Pentecost.

What all this means is that we have no right to expect that religion should be all sparkle and thrill, and that worship should be first-class entertainment. There's an element of demand in any worthwhile faith. The Gospel of grace is free. We don't have to prove ourselves before we can be accepted by God. No one knew that better than the apostle Paul, yet he is the one who tells us that we have "to work out our own salvation with fear and trembling." Let's watch how we use the word "boring." We may just mean that we are not willing to give the same serious attention to the Lord our God as we do to our work, our physical health, our homes, or even our hobbies.

Now, let me turn to the basic question: "Is God a bore?" and answer with a resounding NO! I would turn the tables and say that it is life without God, life without the presence of the Risen Christ, life without the dimension of prayer, life without the hope of heaven, that is narrow, cramped, dull, and ultimately despairing. If we have not demonstrated that in the churches it is our fault, our timid and faltering response to the Gospel of Christ.

"Praise be to the God and Father of our Lord Jesus Christ!" Think what this world would be without a song of gratitude to God, without the vision of his creative power and the profusion of his gifts. Imagine waking up on a bright Spring morning with no one to thank for its beauty and delight. I am grateful for all that science has taught us about the formation of the universe and the development of life, but all this knowledge can be dull and even boring unless there is something in us that responds to the psalmist's shout of joy:

"Praise the Lord from the earth, ye dragons, and all deeps; fire and hail, snow and vapors, stormy wind fulfilling his word; mountains and all hills; fruitful trees and all cedars; beasts and all cattle; creeping things, and flying fowl, kings of the earth, and all people . . . young men and maidens; old men and children; let them praise the name of the Lord: for his name alone is excellent; his glory is above the earth and heaven . . . praise ye the Lord!"

And what could be more stimulating and inspiring than what our text calls the "great mercies" of this God? Instead of watching life go by as "a tale told by an idiot, full of sound and fury, signifying nothing" (which is the essence of boredom), we are offered communion with a God who has a purpose for his human family, however mysterious it may sometimes seem, and a design for the lives of such apparently insignificant creatures as you and me. To a generation that has been tempted to view life as ultimately meaningless, with Jean Paul Sartre's "No exit" as the last word to be said, the Bible still offers the great mercy of a God who puts meaning and purpose back into the picture. Those who wrote these books were as aware as we are, of the shadows that hang over our mortal life. Yet, King David, who had his share of these shadows (not to mention a lot on his conscience) could say: "Thou art my lamp, O Lord; and the Lord will lighten my darkness. For by thee have I run through a troop: by my God have I leaped over a wall." You could hardly say that David found his God a bore!

Then comes the Gospel with its news that God's purpose has been brought to a vivid focus in the life, death and resurrection of Jesus Christ. This is his purpose—to bring us out of darkness into the light of Christ, to shape your life and mine in the image of his Son, to bring the whole human story to a triumphant end when, through the struggle and the agony in which we share his cross, the Risen Christ will usher in the Kingdom of his love. That is the living hope that came with the Resurrection of Jesus Christ from the dead.

Now that I have mentioned the hope that goes beyond the grave, let me admit that we have often made eternal life sound the most boring of all Christian beliefs. Hymns that talk of "resting for ever," books that suggest an endless existence of unrelieved religiosity, make me sympathize with the little English girl who said, "If I am very, very good in heaven, may I sometime have a little devil up to tea." Since I am convinced that there is no one less boring than God, I expect eternal life to be infinitely more thrilling than the best we know here. "As it is written, Eye hath not seen, nor ear heard, neither have entered into the heart of men, the things that God hath prepared for them that love him."

Can you imagine a more stimulating and infinitely varied program for your life than the adventure of growing into the likeness of Christ? I once thought that this might involve the depressing thought that we are all intended to be turned out in the end from one mould. Then I discovered that, on the contrary, God created us all very different, and he wants us to be even more different in our new life in Christ. When you come to think about it, there are far more ways of being good people than being bad. Shakespeare could have said of Christianity rather than of Cleopatra: "Age cannot wither, nor custom stale her infinite variety." On the other hand, what could be more boring than the resources of sin? There are comparatively few ways in which we can mess up our lives and defy our God. A friend of mine once expressed this thought in a little ditty he composed called: "I'm looking for an original sin." The vicious circle of narcotics, the dull routine of promiscuity, the dreary repetition of pornography, the comparatively few ways of savaging our neighbors—all this has been known for centuries. But what we do not know, what we can only glimpse, are the infinite possibilities of doing God's will and seeking to reflect the image of Christ. A discovery it takes time to make, is that, in the end, sinners are much greater bores than saints. And that goes for what is happening to us.

So, I invite you to join in the apostle's shout of joy and carry it with you as a refrain that can never be drowned, even on those days when the clouds are heavy and our spirits dimmed. "Praise be to the God and Father of our Lord Jesus Christ, who in his great mercy gave us new birth into a living hope by the resurrection of Jesus Christ from the dead!"

Mother's Day: Home-Made Religion

EDITOR'S INTRODUCTION

MOTHER'S DAY, AS WE all know, is flavored with sentiment. The question for the preacher is whether to ignore the sentiment, or connect it with the Gospel. David Read chooses to make the connection here, taking as his text Paul's words to Timothy in which the apostle commends the sincerity of Timothy's faith and the positive influence of Timothy's grandmother and mother.

Read goes on to acknowledge the influence that our mothers and grandmothers have generally had on our lives. Thanks to that influence most of us "first became aware of God, or at least of that dimension of the holy, the sacred, the mysterious Beyond to which every child is sensitive."

The sermon concludes with testimony from the Chinese philosopher and novelist Dr. Lin Yutang whose own conversion to the Christian faith, as described in his book *From Pagan to Christian*, took place in the very church where David Read was preaching. Lin Yutang had been taken to MAPC by his wife only to recognize that he had been "drifting," and had now "arrived." "The Sunday morning when I rejoined the Christian Church," he later wrote," was a homecoming."

MOTHER'S DAY: HOME-MADE RELIGION

A Sermon preached by David H. C. Read at Madison Avenue
Presbyterian Church on Mother's Day, May 12, 1985

Text: *"I am reminded of the sincerity of your faith, a faith which was alive in
Lois your grandmother and Eunice your mother before you, and which, I
am confident, lives in you also."* 11 Timothy 1:1–7 (NEB)

Readings: Proverbs 1:1–9; 2 Timothy 1:1–7 (NEB); Matthew 15:1–9 (NEB)

TIMOTHY WAS A FIRST-CENTURY convert to Christianity—and a good one.
"I am reminded of the sincerity of your faith," says the apostle. Sincerity,
the Greek word is literally "unhypocritical." He hadn't become a Christian
for the wrong reasons, but because he truly believed and wanted to be a
disciple. In any case, there wasn't much to be gained by becoming a church
member in those days. On the contrary you might be risking your life. The
spectacular growth of the Church in the first three centuries, which keeps
puzzling the historians of today, had a lot to do with this sincerity. These
early converts were, on the whole, neither saints nor scholars. They didn't
pretend to be without sin, nor did they swallow in one big gulp a mass of
complicated doctrines. Like those who are confirmed in this church, they
were ready to say sincerely: "Jesus Christ is my Lord and Savior."

From the stories in the New Testament we may have formed a rather
romantic and unreal picture of these early converts. We think of them as
men and women who experienced a sudden and shattering change as they
received Christ into their lives. It is described in startling metaphors, like
coming out of darkness into light, moving from the kingdom of Satan to
the kingdom of Christ, being turned around, being born again. We get the
impression that their conversion was a purely personal event in which their
religious background, their family and previous training played no part.
Like Paul on the road to Damascus, they were confronted by the living
Christ, and, in a flash, their lives were turned inside out. Baptism was thus
for them a vivid sign of a mature man or woman washing away their old life
and emerging from the water a new creation.

This picture, these stories, bother some Church members today who
have never had such a dramatic, once-for-all experience. They have been told
that once upon a time, when they were helpless infants, they were baptized.
They may have some recollections of training in Sunday School. The time
came when they were asked to make a profession of faith, and they did so
perfectly sincerely but with no overwhelming sense of beginning a new life in

Christ. The first time I heard a fiery youth evangelist, when I was a teenager, I was shocked by his assumption that the little group of us, all from solid Presbyterian homes with parents who were church members and had us baptized, were not Christians at all unless we had responded to the particular appeal he was making. Looking back, I would say he was right to startle us with the truth that faith is not something we acquire by sheer osmosis but requires a personal decision, but miserably wrong to imply that our baptism, the faith of our parents, our church experience, meant nothing at all.

Recently I have been struck by the fact that our picture of the first Christians as people who were snatched from paganism to Christianity in one dramatic moment is not the whole story by any means. In the first place, it is made clear that there was a spiritual background behind every conversion. The new and radiant experience of Christ was not the first influence of God upon the soul. We think of Paul turning his back on all that had gone before—"forgetting those things which are behind"—and "pressing toward the mark for the prize of the high calling of God in Christ Jesus," but did you notice what is said in this passage from the letter to Timothy? "I thank God," writes the apostle, "whom I, *like my forefathers*, worship with a pure intention. . . . " Does that sound like a man who has totally repudiated all that he had been taught at home and was now meeting his God for the first time? Then, in the second place, we must remember that most of these first Christians got married and had families. Is it assumed in the New Testament that these children had no experience of God at all until at some later point they experienced a sudden conversion?

This is where I want to introduce you to these two women whose names surprisingly occur at the beginning of this letter. I shouldn't say "surprisingly" since, as I have often indicated, the Bible is a great name-dropper. Unlike books of philosophy or religion, it doesn't dwell in the abstract but keeps telling us about people, real people with names. The Word of God comes to us through very human stories. Even those endless genealogies are a tribute to God's concern with people. So here are Eunice and Lois—Timothy's mother and grandmother. (They are both Greek names: "Eunice" means "beautiful victory"—a lovely thought as the young mother beholds her newborn child; and Lois means "more desirable." Had the mother been disappointed in a boy who came before?)

Why do these two come butting in when the apostle is trying to encourage his young friend Timothy to "be strong in the grace that is in Christ Jesus," and to "endure hardship as a good soldier of Jesus Christ?" If the apostle believed that nothing mattered but Timothy's own personal experience of conversion, he would have reminded him of it right away. But the first thing he has to say about Timothy's faith was that it was already "alive in

Lois your grandmother and Eunice your mother." We know virtually nothing about Lois and Eunice, but I doubt if any woman in the Bible has had a higher tribute paid to her. The apostle doesn't begin by saying "Do you remember that great moment when you gave your life to Christ?" He says: "I am reminded of the sincerity of your faith, a faith which was alive in Lois your grandmother and Eunice your mother before you, and which, I am confident, lives in you also."

This is what I mean by "Home-made Religion." I hope nobody thought I was going to offer some sort of "do-it-yourself" kit for cooking up a religion of your own. That's not too difficult, you know. People dream up new religions constantly and often market them with considerable success in these days of confusion and anxiety. What I am talking about is the exact opposite of this. We are thinking now of the religion that we first met in the home, religion communicated, deliberately or unconsciously, by mother and father—traditional religion, if you like, that which sustained our ancestors, that which runs right back to the days of the apostles.

I would guess that for the majority of us here home-made religion represents what rubbed off on us in infancy and childhood, chiefly from our mothers. (I sometimes feel that the rhetoric of Mother's Day in this country seems to be directed to the minority of us who have the privilege to be mothers, whereas the emphasis should be on the point that every single one of us had a mother.) And it was from her in the home environment that we probably first became aware of God, or at least of that dimension of the holy, the sacred, the mysterious Beyond to which every child is sensitive. A cousin of mine had a child who was born totally deaf, and therefore almost entirely unable to speak. She managed gradually to communicate with the child and indicate the names of familiar objects. To communicate what we call abstract ideas was much more difficult, and when it came time to giving her some religious instruction my cousin was baffled. To her astonishment she soon found that there was no difficulty at all. The child made it known that, of course, she knew about God and was aware of his presence. Today there are many who do not have any home-made religion to turn to in difficult times, but nearly all are aware that there is such a thing. Live religion is not only a question of sudden moments of illumination, such as can come to those who have no family religious tradition at all, but is deeply rooted in the home—for us, the Christian home.

For the last hundred years or so, there has been a succession of revolts against the ethos and the religion of the home, yet something always lingers. Robert Burns who was a mighty satirist of the Church and the tight and sometimes ugly morality of the Kirk had still fond memories of home-made religion. In "The Cotter's Saturday Night" he describes with genuine reverence the family gathered for prayer, with the father solemnly reading from the Bible, the mother smiling as the children gathered round. There's no trace of satire but a moving wistfulness in his recreation of the scene. "They never sought in vain that sought the Lord aright!"

In the 1920's and 30's there was a vigorous attack on what was called the old Victorian bourgeois morality and the ideal of the Christian home. Religion was thrown overboard by many in an attempt to reach a new kind of freedom in which traditional values, marriage vows, ancient traditions of all kinds gave way to a new morality—if the word could be used at all. I've been reading some of the literature of that time and realizing how pitifully these hopes were dashed. The belief that a brave new world of peace and prosperity for all could be constructed by eliminating any religious dimension was proved tragically false. Again in the 1960's and 70's there was a period when religion shared in the general trend towards a rejection of all past values. Not everything the youth of that time was reaching for was wrong. They were not always wrong in the targets they chose to attack. But recent years are giving evidence of second thoughts about the values that were rejected, particularly religion. I sense a new questioning of the proposition that the old home-made religion was phoney, and a longing for a faith that is sincere, unhypocritical, and with deeper roots than the latest philosophy. This could be a generation that has again the vision of the religion that has endured through the centuries, that can spring alive again today, and can be passed on to the generation now being born.

Let's go back to Lois and Eunice. The more I think about them the more extraordinary it seems that they should have found their way into the Bible at all. The apostle, paying tribute to young Timothy's sincere faith, might have talked about his youthful decision to follow Christ, about the solid instruction he had had in the faith, perhaps about some books or sermons that had given a boost to his beliefs. Instead he talks about his mother and grandmother, thinking, I am sure, of the kind of home they had created where he must have often visited. Perhaps he met Lois and Eunice at Timothy's baptism. One of the reasons we baptize infants is to dramatize the fact that our religious life does not begin with an adult decision but with the family in which we are raised. It is in home-made religion that we find the roots of our faith. In that extended family home where grandmother and mother lived and Christ was head of the household, the grace of God was with young Timothy.

I am aware that much has happened to the Christian family since then. We all know of the forces that have led to the breakdown of old family patterns, some deliberate and destructive, some avoidable. But the vision of a homemade religion is kept alive in a truly believing church. Increasingly, a church has to be a substitute for the old-style family, with Church School teachers playing the role of Lois and Eunice. It is not easy in a large metropolitan church to preserve this family feeling, but it can be done. The children received here in holy baptism are confided to their parents who promise to "teach them the truths and duties of the Christian faith and by prayer and example to bring them up in the life and worship of the Church," but they are also confided to us all in this family of Christ, and we receive them joyfully in this larger home, promising to pray for them, and rejoicing in that great line of children, you and I included, stretching back to the beginnings of the church.

I see each such child as an evangelist. They call silently to us to think again about our own baptism or our own sincerity of faith. I close with a testimony given some years ago by Dr. Lin Yutang, the Christian philosopher and novelist. He was one who had been given home-made religion by his Christian parents. Like many he sloughed it off in adolescence and spent many years as a genial, inventive, and successful pagan. Then, one day, his wife brought him to this church. Something happened which he describes in a book called: "From Pagan to Christian." Listen to the words with which he describes his return to the faith:

"Looking back on my life, I know that for thirty years I lived in this world like an orphan. I am an orphan no longer. Where I had been drifting, I have arrived. The Sunday morning when I rejoined the Christian Church was a homecoming."

Prayer: We are grateful, O God, for every holy influence upon us from the past, and we pray that we may again receive with joy the message that has come down the centuries from Jesus Christ, thy Son. Amen.

Ezra—The Preacher at the Watergate

EDITOR'S INTRODUCTION

BEFORE THIS BOOK WENT to press, I shared the manuscript with family and friends, and asked for critical feedback. Bruce McLeod in particular asked for more sermons reflecting David Read's oft-cited advice from Karl Barth on the need to link the Bible and the daily newspaper.

Bruce reminded me that the time frame of Read's pastorate in New York coincided with "the assassinations of JFK, RFK, MLK, the great racial upheaval, the Poverty Gap (Bill Webber's East Harlem Protestant Parish was just up the road from MAPC), the Biafra tragedy of the late 60s (1000 kids a day dying of starvation and LBJ saying get those kids off my TV set), the nuclear cloud terrifying the world since the Cuban Missile Crisis in 1962, the Berrigans and the Peace Movement, the Vietnam War, and LBJ's resignation, Watergate, the Berlin Wall, etc. etc." Couldn't there be a few more concrete indications that Read was addressing these critical issues as they were exploding all around us?

The question is a good one and prompted me to include this sermon which Read preached as the Watergate scandal was breaking upon Washington and the country in the spring of 1973.

EZRA—THE PREACHER AT THE WATERGATE

A Sermon preached by David H. C. Read at Madison Avenue
Presbyterian Church on May 13, 1973

Text: *"And all the people gathered as one man into the square before the
Watergate; and they told Ezra the scribe to bring the book of the law of
Moses which the Lord had given to Israel."* Nehemiah 8:1

THE FIRST THING I must say this morning is that this sermon was not produced by the expedient of looking up the word "Watergate" in a concordance,
discovering that the word does indeed occur in the Bible—and jumping off
from there. This text is emphatically not a mere pretext on which to hang
some thoughts about the current uproar and confusion.

What happened was this. Like all of you I have been shocked and worried by the revelations that have already been made and deeply concerned
about what is still to come. We are, as a nation, going through a traumatic
experience from which will come not only more pain and grief but also the
possibility of a cleansing and a healing. It is a situation that no preacher of
the Word of God can ignore. So my thoughts travelled over the contents of
the Bible and finally settled in the territory of the prophets of Israel. They
were the people who knew how to declare the Word of God to a nation
in the throes of moral, religious, and political crisis. I looked at Amos, at
Micah, at Isaiah, and then I remembered those two characters from a different period and of a different style whose words and actions are preserved
for us in the twin-book of Ezra-Nehemiah. At that point I began to think of
the dramatic incident of the reading of the Law of God at a critical moment
in the nation's history—and when the word "Watergate" flashed into my
mind as the place where it happened, this sermon was born. Let's forget the
coincidence and stay with the story.

"And all the people gathered as one man into the square before the
Watergate." (If anyone thinks that the expression "as one man" indicates the
traditional exclusion of women from such an assembly, notice that verse
two specifies "*both* men and women.") Who were these people? They were
the Jews who had either survived the massacres and deportations when
Jerusalem was sacked or had come trickling back from exile. We are at a
comparatively late date in Old Testament history. The old conquerors, As-
syrian and Babylonian, had in their turn bitten the dust, and the new world
empire was Persia. And the Persian monarch, Artaxerxes, had allowed the
emigration of Jews back to their homeland under the leadership of Ezra

and Nehemiah. The story of the reconstruction of Jerusalem at this time is thrillingly described in these books, but the emphasis falls on the moral and religious reconstruction—and that's what concerns us now. This was a confused people, exposed to all kinds of ideas and practices that were totally foreign to the faith of their fathers. They were living through all kinds of revolutions and were exposed to violence, corruption, and the insecurities of an age of rapid change. Yet somewhere in their souls they remembered a covenant with their God, a moral law by which their fathers lived, and groped for a renewal of the great simplicities and assurance that come from faith in that God and obedience to that law. In short, they were a bewildered people with both a bad conscience and a hungry hope.

"All the people." The note of solidarity begins to speak to us. At our Watergate we have to realize that we are in this together. Every question raised by this squalid affair makes ripples that reach out into every corner of the land and every section of the population. For too long we have sought scapegoats for our troubles. The blame for lawlessness, violence, and all kinds of immortality was laid on certain groups according to taste—the shaggy generation of protesters, the inhabitants of the ghettoes, the Mafia, the media, the permissive intellectuals. Now that we have found criminality and lying in the heart of the establishment itself we are forced to recognize that immorality and lawlessness knows no frontiers of class or race or culture. There is no section of the nation so immune in its respectability and lip service to law and order, morality and religion that it cannot be touched by temptation. I am reminded of a remark of James Agate the drama critic: "Every age gets what it wants, including the things it does not un-want hard enough to prevent them." And the Word of God confronts us all.

This is what these people of Jerusalem did in their time of crisis. They reached back to the roots of their faith and morals as one man. "They told Ezra the scribe to bring the book of the law of Moses which the Lord had given to Israel." And that is what Ezra began to read from his high pulpit at the Watergate. It was probably the Book of Deuteronomy. "Know therefore this day and consider it in thine heart, that the Lord he is God in heaven above, and upon the earth beneath: there is none else. Thou shalt keep therefore his statutes and his commandments." "Beware that thou forget not the Lord thy God. . . . Lest when thou hast eaten and art full, and hast built goodly houses, and dwelt therein; and when thy herds and thy flocks multiply, and thy silver and thy gold is multiplied, and all that thou hast is multiplied; then thine heart be lifted up, and thou forget the Lord thy God." That's the sort of thing we need to hear today right up to the highest levels of government. In terms of our society we need to hear this Word of God: we need to reach back to our soundest roots. From the sophistication that despises the piety of the Puritan, from the cynicism that brushes off the current scandal as just "politics as usual," and from religion that is merely decorative and benign, we have to turn to the Word that cuts "like a two-edged sword."

This is not a call to look backwards to some mythical time when America was inhabited by a race of saints who honored their God and lived by the precepts of the Bible. There never was such a time; and living religion is never a matter of backtracking to some Garden of Eden. Yet there is a liberating word that was planted in this nation, a genuine piety that nourished our beginnings and we should be grateful that its continuing echo has made possible the dragging of these plots and subterfuges into the light of day.

What would be the elements of a new Puritanism as our response to the Word of God today? I suggest that they are outlined for us already in this story.

"And Ezra opened the book in the sight of all the people . . . and when he opened it all the people stood. And Ezra blessed the Lord, the great God: and all the people answered, 'Amen, Amen,' lifting up their hands; and they bowed their heads and worshipped the Lord with their faces to the ground." All right: so it is a vignette from the ancient East and we are not given to worshipping like this in twentieth century U.S.A. That's what we used to say, but now we're not so sure. One of the signs of the Spirit right now is the recovery of this kind of lively participation in worship, and the loosening up of our formalities and restraint. Anyway what really matters is the note of *reverence* that comes ringing through this story. These were people suddenly brought face to face with the reality of the God they had nearly forgotten.

Reverence is not a matter of external formalities—like having invocations at public events, stamping "In God We Trust" on our coins, or saluting the clergy with the title "Reverend." (I have no objection to any of these things, except when someone calls me "Rev. Read"!) Reverence is an inner attitude of heart and mind. It is a sense of holding one's life as a trust from God. It is keeping oneself accountable to his law, and being grateful for his mercies. It is honoring what we know to be right and true. It is respecting all human life and treating all our neighbors as members of God's family. It is accepting the animal kingdom and the natural world as a solemn trust, not to be wantonly ravaged or destroyed. Reverence means a recovery of the sense of the holy, a sense that is nourished in the sanctuary and expressed in every aspect of our life as individuals or in society.

A new Puritanism will seek again this active, strengthening, purifying recognition of the holy. We shall learn what it means to begin our prayers with the words: "Our Father who art in heaven, hallowed be thy name." How do we go about recreating this sense of reverence in ourselves and in the generations that follow? I believe that it begins in the home, and that the first lesson in reverence comes to us from our parents. In the course of my ministry I have seen again and again how even the most casual and secularized of parents show true signs of reverence when their first child is born. If that can be strengthened so that when the child is growing he is conscious that his parents are not free agents but are also under an obligation, that they too have a heavenly parent to whom they owe obedience and love, the sense of reverence will be instilled and never totally forgotten.

I cannot help remembering today the mother who nearly reached her hundredth birthday on the 4th of May. Without question my first sense of the presence of God, my first inkling of what the "holy" means, came from her. It was not that she spoke much about it. With true Scottish reticence she said little about religion, but in dozens of little ways she conveyed to me something of the awe, the mystery, the obligation, and the love that give meaning to the name of God. It is the Church's task to be such a mother to the whole human family, and I see a primary task for every congregation to be the nurturing of such an attitude in the home, in business, and in social and public life.

The next note I hear in this passage is that of *repentance*. Confronted by the Word of God this people wept. There is no indication that Ezra was accusing them of any specific sins. We have a way of thinking of repentance as some dramatic exercise in breast-beating indulged in by religious people—usually long ago. And we associate it with the denunciation of some particular vices and follies. Jesus noted that religious leaders are fond of such denunciations. He must have heard many tirades in the synagogue against the sins of the common people of his day. What happened then, and what happens now, is that repentance becomes a way of confessing other peoples' sins. Within the Church in recent days we have heard the establishment confessing the sins of the rebels, and the rebels confessing the sins of the establishment. This kind of vicarious confession is a trick of the Devil: it obscures what the Bible means by repentance.

"Mea culpa; mea maxima culpa!" is the true cry of the penitent. When the Word of God springs to life it is not our neighbor who is accused but you and me. The Puritanism of Jesus consisted in his insistence that we face up to our own sins. We are not to catalogue the sins of others like the Pharisee in the Temple who thanked God he wasn't like other men. We are to be like the publican who simply cried: "Lord, be merciful unto me, a sinner."

The new Puritanism must act as a solvent for all the rationalization and complications with which we have surrounded the call for honesty, purity, humility, justice, and love. To repent is to admit our personal failure to speak and act in our daily life with the divine simplicity and the directness of Jesus. It is to confess our share in the erosion of reverence, in the tampering with eternal values, in the moral apathy, in the pursuit of the easy way, in the worship of success—all those things which, when they erupt in a national scandal, make us deeply ashamed.

Reverence, repentance. . . . yes, but just as the Gospel of Jesus Christ has something more to say, so this story of Ezra ends on a different note. If anyone thinks that what we call Old Testament religion is just a matter of the proclamation of the law of God and the condemnation of those who break it, you have not heard the song of the Bible. For the great prophets and poets constantly sang of the law as a source of happiness and joy. "Blessed is the man whose delight is in the law of the Lord." "Thy statutes have been my songs in the house of my pilgrimage." "Thy law is my delight." "Great peace have those who love thy law; nothing can make them stumble." It was with this kind of celebration in his mind that Ezra made his unexpected response to the penitence of his people. "This day is holy to the Lord your God: do not mourn or weep." Then he said to them, "Go your way, eat the fat and drink sweet wine and send portions to whom nothing is prepared; for this day is holy to our Lord; and do not be grieved, for the joy of the Lord is your strength."

Reverence, repentance—and rejoicing. That's the whole story of the people at Jerusalem's Watergate. I speak of a new Puritanism, for the old Puritanism, with all its virtues, was deficient in this spirit of celebration of the gifts of God. We admire the simplicity and integrity they imparted to this nation, but somehow we cannot quite hear them bidding the people to "eat the fat and drink the wine" in a glorious festival of praise in which the needs of the poor were not forgotten. ("Send portions to him for whom nothing is prepared.") What is needed now is a positive Puritanism, a return to the simplicities and clarities of the law of God that is suffused by the joy of those who really live by his grace.

This is why I cannot but believe that even from the shame and shock that we are experiencing, a greater good may come. That is the Gospel. God will work in all things for good with them that love him. It is good for us all, like the Prodigal, to come to ourselves—to realize that we have been sliding towards a society without reverence, and without repentance, and that we were becoming calloused and cynical in the presence of corruption. It is good to be awakened to the re-creative power of the Gospel, and to experience the true atmosphere of the Father's home where "they began to be merry."

This is the word that comes from Ezra to us, from Jerusalem to Washington. Reverence—the renewal of our nation's deepest faith; repentance—confessing our own, not other peoples' sins, and turning towards a new simplicity and honesty of word and deed; and rejoicing in the glad acceptance of the grace of God that can make a new Puritan both humble and infectiously happy. "The joy of the Lord is your strength."

The Season of Pentecost

Pentecost Sunday: Alive Inside

EDITOR'S INTRODUCTION

PENTECOST CELEBRATES "THE INNER power that makes Christmas more than a sentimental symbol, Good Friday more than a memory of a distant sacrifice, and Easter more than a straining to re-capture a miracle of long ago." So states David Read in this Pentecost sermon that rejoices in God's presence and action in bringing Christ alive inside us through the power of the Holy Spirit.

It happened when the miracle of Pentecost first broke upon the early Christian community, and it happens afresh as the miracle of Christ's presence breaks upon us today.

Read, meanwhile, cautions us about two forces that resist the in-breaking power of the Spirit: (1) "Our lower nature," which is to say those sins of the spirit and flesh that rule out God and neighbor from the equation of daily living. And (2) "a rigid adherence to a conventional code of behavior and a legalistic religion."

Pentecost, Read concludes, is here to provide "the touch of life at the very center of our being," thereby enabling us to "come alive each day in the certainty that we are loved."

PENTECOST SUNDAY: ALIVE INSIDE

A Sermon preached by David H. C. Read at Madison Avenue
Presbyterian Church on Pentecost Sunday, May 21, 1972

> *"Moreover, if the Spirit of him who raised Jesus from the dead
> dwells within you, then the God who raised Christ Jesus from
> the dead will also give new life to your mortal bodies through his
> indwelling Spirit. It follows, my friends, that our lower nature has
> no claim upon us; we are not obliged to live on that level. If you do
> so, you must die. But if by the Spirit you put to death all the base
> pursuits of the body, then you will live. For all who are moved by
> the Spirit of God are sons and daughters of God. The Spirit you
> have received is not a spirit of slavery leading you back into a life
> of fear, but a Spirit that makes us sons and daughters, enabling us
> to cry 'Abba! Father!'"* Romans 8:11–15 (NEB)

DID ANYONE GIVE YOU a present this morning and wish you a Happy Pentecost? Are the television screens spangled with happy choirs singing about
the Holy Spirit? Is there a Pentecost program on the stage at Radio City?
And did you come to church this morning with the sense of elation you feel
at Christmas or Easter?

I know there are reasons why this has become the forgotten festival of
the modern Church. The popular imagination has nothing so vivid and appealing to latch on to as the Child of Bethlehem and the Victor over death.
Who can picture the Holy Spirit? Somehow the story of what happened to
the disciples on the day of Pentecost is less resonant and evocative for us
than the narratives of the Nativity and of the Resurrection. Even in this
psychedelic age most people are out of their depth with "rushing mighty
wind," "tongues of fire," and the language miracle called "glossolalia." Yet,
probably the real reason for our neglect of this festival is our lack of a vital
experience of what the Bible calls "the Spirit of life." Our religion has been so
much a matter of rules and routine, or of bustling activity that it is only occasionally that we know that spiritual power by which it comes alive inside.
When it does then we shall want to celebrate Pentecost as the climax of the
Christian Year.

For that is what it is. We open with Advent and Christmas; we mark
the way of the Cross through Lent and holy Week; and we announce the
triumph of Easter—but none of these celebrations are more than clock-
work observances, a remembering of past events, unless they come alive
inside. Real faith, real worship, real Christian activity spring from an inner

coming-to-life of familiar doctrines and accepted duties. The disciples had been through that first Christian Year with Jesus himself. They had glimpsed the truth of the Incarnation; they had walked with him through his Lent and Passion; they had seen him die; they had even seen him alive again. Yet here they were on the Day of Pentecost, limp, confused, dispirited, with no idea of what might happen next. What happened was the touch of Life. The Spirit came and all that they had known and lived through was suddenly alive inside them. This is why the Church made Pentecost the climactic festival of the Christian Year. For it speaks of the inner power that makes Christmas more than a sentimental symbol, Good Friday more than a memory of a distant sacrifice and Easter more than a straining to re-capture a miracle of long ago. Pentecost says: "All this is real for you *now*. God did not bow out of his world once he had raised Jesus from the dead. He did not fade away when the last page of the New Testament was written. His Spirit is his presence and his power here and now." And Pentecost says: "All this can be real for *you* now. His Spirit is the intimate, personal, inward assurance of that love he demonstrated in Christ. Your faith is then not an effort to believe some distant miracle: it is a joyful response to an inward presence. The Spirit is not a vague, recondite concept of the theologians. The Spirit is what is at work when you simply say: 'Father.' And to say that—and mean it—is to come alive inside."

"If the Spirit of him who raised Jesus from the dead dwells within you, then the God who raised Jesus from the dead will also give new life to your mortal bodies through his indwelling Spirit." Did you hear that? The very same divine power that brought Jesus back to life is at work now to give new life to these mortal bodies of ours. What kind of life? Obviously not just the physical life that keeps us going, but an inward renewal and liberation, a spiritual life that gives meaning and direction, and which can expand while the body decays. As Paul put it elsewhere: "Though our inward humanity is in decay, yet day by day we are inwardly renewed."

Throughout this passage the word I keep hearing is "life." The Holy Spirit is, as the Nicene Creed magnificently says, "the Lord and Giver of life." To receive the Spirit is to be alive inside.

We all know the difference between being alive outwardly and alive inwardly. Have you ever had somebody say: "You're looking great!" when inwardly at that moment you felt low, flat, depressed and half dead? Don't you know people who are enormously fit and energetic yet curiously empty inside? When you try to get beneath the surface and discover what really makes them tick there seems to be nothing there. And isn't it fatally possible for a nation to be alive and kicking in all directions with a rising Gross National Product and great economic and military muscle in world affairs—and yet to be dead inside? So it is with the Church, which should be helping to keep a nation alive inside. It can be prosperous and influential, a bulwark of the establishment—yet dead inside. It can equally be radical and revolutionary—yet dead inside.

My vision for this Church of ours is that we should match the liveliness of our activities and our increasing response to the needs of our city with a corresponding upswing in the spiritual awareness and sensitivity of all our members. Your greatest need and mine is for the experience of the Spirit by which we come alive inside. This is why we are letting this Scripture speak this morning, for here we touch the living center of the Gospel, a truth so simple—and yet so powerful—that it can reach every single one of us and make all that we profess here to believe come alive inside.

Paul presents the Christian life to us here in the simplest possible terms. "All who are moved by the Spirit of God are sons of God." In spite of all that has been said about Paul's dogmatism, his complicated theology, his intolerance, we must confess that this is a gloriously comprehensive definition of the Church. The family of God, his adopted sons and daughters (Paul loves to use this image—Jesus, the eternal Son of God, and us as his adopted children, chosen and nurtured by his love. The King James' translation is: "Ye have received the Spirit of adoption, whereby we cry, Abba, Father") consists of those who "are moved by the Spirit of God." To be alive inside is to live in response to this indwelling Spirit. There is therefore no rigid pattern for the Christian life. It cannot be captured and pinned down like a dead butterfly. The Spirit will move us in all kinds of directions, giving a freshness and variety to any true Christian community. Yet that same Spirit will enable us to accept and value one another as members of the same family, disciples of the same Lord.

What are the forces that work against this way of living, this joyful response to the Spirit within? They are the same today as when Paul wrote.

(1) "Our lower nature," we read, "has no claim upon us." The first obstacle to our spiritual life and health is this "lower nature." The new translators wisely use this expression instead of the traditional "flesh." For when we read about the struggle between the flesh and the spirit we are apt to think that the Christian life consists in suppressing the desires of the body in favor of the impulses of the soul. That is a doctrine of Greek philosophy. It is not the Gospel. The lower nature, according to the Bible, is not to be identified with physical desire. It includes unbridled lusts of the body but also much more—envy, anger, idolatry, pride, greed and all those sins of the spirit against which Jesus directed his fiercest condemnation.

To live by our lower nature simply means giving way to every impulse without regard for God or our neighbor. In a sense it is taking the line of least resistance. In nearly every generation someone comes along to persuade us that human nature is so fundamentally good and trustworthy that, if all restrictions, all traditional moral rules, all so-called inhibitions of religion are swept away, we shall enter a paradise of freedom, creativity and joy. Today this theory goes by the sophisticated name of "permissiveness." There are, of course, degrees of license indicated by this term; but in its extreme form it means being permitted, and permitting oneself, to do whatever our instinct or passing whim dictates. Not too long ago this was being commended as the way of life, under the slogan: "Away with the taboos: express yourself: live it up."

At the moment it looks as though the younger generation in particular is seeing through this deception, is discovering that complete permissiveness means anarchy and anarchy means slavery and slavery means death. We are painfully learning that human nature, set free from all restraint, is not to be trusted—in other words that the Bible story of sin is more realistic than many, even within the Church, had thought, to live by yielding to every passing desire, to obey the impulses of this "lower nature" means that we are enslaved to passions we despise and contribute to the dissolution of the society by which we live. But, says the apostle, "we are not obliged to live on that level. If you do so you must die." Then he presents the alternative: "If by the Spirit you put to death all the base pursuits of the body, then you will live." He offers the power of the Spirit—that same power that raised Jesus from the dead—as the means to raise us from subjection to our lower nature. To come alive inside is to yield to this power—in other words to let the Spirit of Christ within us take over the controls.

(2) The other obstacle to this life in the Spirit is quite different in kind and effect. Just as at the present time the proponents of permissiveness are often opposed by equally violent upholders of a "law and order" that has ugly overtones of moral dictatorship and oppression, so the Christian is often tempted to subdue the passions of his lower nature by rigid adherence to a conventional code of behavior and a legalistic religion. There has been a perversion in the Church from the beginning whereby the image of the Christian has become that of a grim, censorious, anxious, conscience-ridden character rigidly attached to morals and rituals of a past generation. More than a whiff of this still seems to attach to the name "Presbyterian" in some quarters. (I read in a novel: "Pop used to say about Presbyterians, it don't prevent them committing all the sins there are, but it keeps them from getting any fun out of it.")

We don't smash that image by bending over backwards to show how little we care for traditional morality, decency and order. There is a trend in some quarters of the church today to despise and deride anything our fathers and mothers held sacred, a cult of what I like to call "Unholier-than-thou." The answer lies in the rediscovery of the true freedom of those who "are moved by the Spirit of God." They may be young or old, conservative or radical, traditionalists or innovators, mystical or practical—they have discovered the secret of living by the Spirit, and being alive inside.

If our religion is just a matter of observing certain rules, professing correct beliefs and upholding the conventions we may be outwardly respectable but dead within. The way of the Spirit that Scripture reveals to us is not a *via media* between the permissive and the moralistic, or between the activist and the pietist. It is a highway above them all.

What Pentecost stands for is the touch of life at the very center of our being. It is what we need more than anything else—the release from our lower nature, from our dull conformities, from our pride—and, above all, from our fears. "The Spirit you have received is not a spirit of slavery leading you back to a life of fear, but a Spirit that makes us sons"—the Spirit of adoption—"enabling us to cry 'Abba! Father.'"

When Jesus was a child "Abba" was his word for "Daddy." It is one of the few Aramaic words that have survived in the New Testament—because the disciples must have been so astonished that he could tell them to use such a word to talk to God. Now here is Paul, who could build a theology that scholarship has not yet exhausted, telling us that the root of the whole matter is being able to say "Father." Really to do that—to be here in the middle of this dangerous, complicated and baffling modern world and utter the word that expresses our confidence that he is alive around us and within us, is to open that window to the Spirit that makes us alive inside. A dead religion, a formal faith can leap into life as we realize that we truly belong, not to an institution or a cause but to a family, and that the secret of coming alive each day is the certainty that we are loved.

God of the Galaxies:
God of the Sparrow

EDITOR'S INTRODUCTION

THE IMAGERY IN THIS sermon calls to mind Jaroslav Vajda's vivid hymn of praise:

> God of the sparrow
> God of the whale
> God of the swirling stars
> How does the creature say Awe
> How does the creature say Praise

The sermon also puts one in mind of John Updike's story "Pigeon Feathers" which portrays a young boy's quest for faith amidst panic over mortality. The despairing teenager is finally reassured by a mystical encounter with some dead birds whose feathers speak to him, however quietly, of the One who says: "Are not sparrows two a penny? Yet without your Father's leave not one of them can fall to the ground. As for you, even the hairs of your head have all been counted. So have no fear: you are worth more than any number of sparrows" (Matthew 10:29, 31).

Like Updike, like Vajda, like Jesus himself, David Read finds both the unimaginably large and the infinitely small, both the vastness of space and the tininess of creaturely existence, held together in the reassuring center of God's love.

GOD OF THE GALAXIES: GOD OF THE SPARROW

A Sermon preached by David H. C. Read at Madison Avenue
Presbyterian Church on May 28, 1978

Text: *"He healeth the broken in heart, and bindest up their wounds . . . He
telleth the number of the stars; he calleth them all by their names."* Psalm
147:3, 4

Readings: Psalm 147; Colossians 1:13–20; Matthew 10:24–31 (NEB)

"HE HEALETH THE BROKEN in heart . . . he telleth the number of the stars."
When the psalmist, writing about 2500 years ago, chooses these two areas
in which to celebrate his God—healing and the stars—you might say that
he was setting up a road block between his way of thinking and ours. In our
day for most people the healing of the broken in heart is the province of
psychiatry, and the question of the stars lies with astrophysics. Neither psychiatry nor astrophysics had been dreamed of when the psalmist wrote: he
could hardly have chosen two topics more calculated to give us a sense of the
immense advance of human knowledge, particularly in this century when
so many astounding discoveries have been made both about the working of
the individual psyche and the nature of the universe.

So the superficial reader today, finding a Gideon Bible in his motel
room lying open at this psalm, might say to himself: "Quaint old fellow this
writer: he thinks of his God as being interested in treating his neuroses and
at the same time peering around the skies to count the number of the stars
and think up a name for each. I suppose some people still get a bang out of
this kind of religion but how they reconcile it with modern psychology and
modern astronomy beats me." I'm assuming that this reader is not only one
for whom the word "God" has little meaning except as an expletive, but also
that poetry of any kind is for him a closed book.

There may not be many, at least in this country, who are totally convinced that modern science has relegated all religious ideas to the dust
bin of history, but I am sure that there are millions outside and inside the
churches, who are vaguely disturbed by the fact that believers rely for their
inspiration on books that were written when the universe seemed an infinitely smaller and cosier place than it does today, and no one had ever
heard of the super-ego and the id. They may even be tempted to think that
the notion of God used to supply an explanation for mysteries of the soul
and of the cosmos which we no longer need. I find this sort of old fashioned
agnosticism still common among the older generation, but there are many

signs that it has lost its grip upon the young—among whom, as we all know, religious movements are bursting out all over.

They are shrewd enough to note that the stunning advances of science and technology are simply tools put into our hands, neutral instruments that cannot by themselves lead to a better life for the human race. The real questions concern meaning and purpose and so they are looking for answers, not in technology, but in art, in ethics, and in religion. And when we do that it soon becomes apparent that there is no parallel whatever between the progress of scientific knowledge and the illumination that comes to us from the artists, the prophets, and the saints. Who would claim that we have advanced far beyond the works of Michaelangelo, of Shakespeare, of Mozart, or are infinitely brighter than Socrates or Isaiah, or have reached plateaus of holiness beyond the reach of Paul or Francis of Assisi? That's why another generation is now opening that Gideon Bible and is ready to believe that a man who never heard of Freud or Einstein might have something still enormously important to say to us about God.

Within one week recently I encountered two people who symbolized for me the gap between the old dogmatic atheism based on the assumption that science has eliminated God and the new mood of openness to truth how ever it may come. I met them both under the glare of television lights. The first was Dr. Madelyn Murray O'Hair who explained cheerfully that she had been raised a Presbyterian but that when she read the Bible for herself she discovered it was all nonsense and embraced a scientific philosophy of life. She declared roundly that she held all believers in "intellectual contempt" and when I asked if that went, for instance, for Augustine, Pascal, and Albert Schweitzer she dismissed them all with a few ill-chosen epithets. A few days later on my "Pulpit and People" program I had as a guest Dr. Robert Jastrow, founder and director of NASA's Goddard Space Studies, Professor of Earth Sciences at Dartmouth, and Professor of Astronomy and Geology at Columbia University. He told me that he believed it had now been finally proved that the universe began with one sudden explosion about twenty billion years ago. When I asked what caused the explosion, he smiled and said while many scientists hate the idea of an unexplained event, he was perfectly open to the thought that it could have been God—although he was himself genuinely agnostic. I mention this, not to play the futile game of trying to enlist modern science on the side of religion and prove that God exists, but simply to celebrate the spirit of openness to truth and humility of mind that marks the more thoughtful of our contemporaries.

So perhaps we can listen again with fresh ears to the psalmist as he talks of the God "who telleth the number of stars; and "calleth them all by their names." In a flash of Hebrew poetry he rouses in us the sense of awe and wonder that comes when we contemplate the stars. He had the advantage of being often out in the desert with no flashing signs or neon lights to distract him from the panorama of the skies, or of reclining on the flat rooftop of his home on a brilliant star-filled night. But even we modern city dwellers have our moments when we are entranced by the canopy of the heavens. I remember once on a ship from Australia reclining by the stern as we slipped silently through the waters of the South Pacific. Above us the Southern Cross blazed in glory, and the sky was a sparkling dome of beauty and of mystery. From the remarks of fellow passengers I knew that I was not the only one who was thinking of his God. If the verse had occurred to me (which it didn't) "He telleth the number of the stars; he calleth them all by their names" the last thing that would have occurred to me would have been to contrast my astronomical knowledge with that of the psalmist. I might have remembered from my Old Testament studies that "telling the number" is a way of expressing the omniscience of God and that "calling by name" was a Hebrew image of creation. But I would have been satisfied to join in the adoration of the psalmist and rejoice in the wonder of his universe. The astonishing discoveries of astronomy in no way diminish our amazement at the mysterious cosmos in which we float. Rather does the vision of countless galaxies each composed of trillions of stars like our own receding at the speed of light expand my amazement at the works of God and my sense of his glory.

It is this sense of wonder that transcends mere fact and unites the souls of the sensitive in every age. "You'll never enjoy the world aright," wrote Thomas Traherne, "till the sea itself floweth in your veins, till you are clothed with the heavens, and crowned with the stars: and perceive yourself to be the sole heir of the whole world, and more than so, because men are in it who are every one sole heirs as well as you. Till you can sing and rejoice and delight in God, as misers do in gold, the kings in sceptres, you never enjoy the world aright." To enjoy the world aright in 1978 we still need this Bible word of the God of the galaxies.

It is not the Bible but our own narrowness of mind and limited imagination that lead us to think of God as exclusively concerned with this little corner of the universe and the human family that clings precariously to this tiny planet. Therefore I am not disturbed but exhilarated by the immensities revealed by modern astronomy and by the possible discovery of other intelligent creatures elsewhere in space. The "Father almighty, maker of heaven and earth, and of all things visible and invisible" may have other families made in his image and beyond our imagining.

(Incidentally, Dr. Jastrow warns us against conceiving such creatures as the kind of mechanized blobs of nothingness that potter on the science-fiction movie screens. He says that since our galaxy is a comparative newcomer any visitors from outer space would probably be as far beyond us as we are from the worm—physically, mentally, and spiritually. That's a sobering but entrancing thought!)

So here is the God of the galaxies: "He telleth the number of the stars; he calleth them all by their names." To worship "in spirit and in truth" is to be, at least sometimes, just overwhelmed by the mystery and majesty of God. But let me be quite realistic. How many today come to a service of Christian worship chiefly for this reason? Would it not be more true to say that, in these times of tension and in the pragmatic and unpoetic atmosphere in which we live, most people come to church seeking some kind of stabilizing faith by which to live, some healing for the spirit? I'm not trying to divide a congregation into an elite that revels in the adoration of the transcendent and the majority who simply want, as I have heard it said, to "have their batteries charged." After all, there is enormous therapeutic power in seeing our daily problems in the perspective of the God of the galaxies and resting our lives and our minds on his infinitude. And there is no sure healing for our souls in anyone less than "God the almighty." The glory of the Gospel to which we are responding is that it offers us a God who is *both* the creator Spirit who "telleth the number of the stars" *and* the One who draws infinitely close and "healeth the broken in heart, and bindeth up their wounds."

I find that quite a lot of people today are baffled by what seems like two rival views of God. "Either," they say, "God is this vast mysterious force that rules the galaxies and sustains the universe—in which case he couldn't possibly be any more bothered about me than I am over the minute insects I step on as I walk through the woods; or else he is the divine Friend, the heavenly Pal, the Man Upstairs, the heavenly Bellhop attending to my needs—as some religious people seem to think of him." Yet if there is one clear teaching from beginning to end of the Bible it is that God is *both* Lord of the universe *and* "our refuge and strength, a very present help in time of trouble"—though never just a convenience at our disposal. When you stop to think about it there is no contradiction whatever in the thought of a being who is great enough to control the universe *and* great enough to be concerned with everything and everybody within it. Even in our human experience we don't judge greatness simply by the vastness of the organization a man or woman controls. A great leader is not judged simply by the millions of followers but by the concern shown for individuals. A great librarian is not the one who controls the largest number of books but the one who knows, within reason, what is in them. An infinitely great God must be one who is great enough to perform the miracle of knowing all about you and me.

And that is exactly what Jesus constantly taught. His Father was one who ruled the universe but was intensely concerned with each human life on the planet. Once when he was thrilled by the response of his disciples whom he had sent out to teach and heal he broke into a sudden prayer: "I thank thee, O Father, Lord of heaven and earth, that thou hast hid these things from the wise and the prudent, and hast revealed them unto babes." For him the "Lord of heaven and earth" was concerned about these "babes." Then it was Jesus who dealt with the fears of his disciples by reminding them that they were of infinite value to God and, almost incidentally, let slip the astonishing remark: "Are not sparrows two a penny? Yet without your Father's leave not one of them can fall to the ground." For him the God of the galaxies *is* the God of the sparrow. Nothing in the wide universe of his creation is too minute, too unimportant, to slip beyond his care.

So, for the psalmist, the one who "telleth the number of the stars," the one whose breath sustains the universe, is also the one who draws infinitely near to each of his human family to "heal the broken in heart, and bind up their wounds." As often in our Christian experience what looks like an impossible paradox turns out to be the most powerful and sustaining truth that can grip the soul. We meet here a God so great that, even as we meet in this sanctuary dedicated to his worship, we echo the prayer of Solomon at the dedication of the temple in Jerusalem: "Behold, the heaven and the heaven of heavens cannot contain thee; how much less this house which I have built," and at the same time we meet a God so great that he knows us each by name, knows us through and through, knows our hopes and joys, our fears and our worries, and can heal every broken heart. Like two great arcs of light these two truths converge and we find ourselves looking at the face of Christ. He is the image of the God of glory. "The whole universe," says Paul "has been created through him and for him. And he exists before everything, and all things are held together in him." And he is the image of the God of grace. He is still the same Jesus who gives himself to one man, woman, or child as if there were no one and nothing else to care for. As we meet him we know that the God of glory *is* the God of grace; and the God of grace *is* the God of glory.

So the poetry of the ancient psalms joins with the hymns of today in celebrating the God of the galaxies and the God of the sparrow.

> "Lord of all being, throned afar,
> Thy glory flames from sun and star;
> Center and soul of every sphere,
> Yet to each loving heart how near."

The Lord of the stars is here to heal our broken hearts. The cosmic Christ still says to each of us that we are of infinite value and adds: "So have no fear."

A Big Enough God

EDITOR'S INTRODUCTION

How many sermons are preached on the Trinity on Trinity Sunday? Both liberals and conservatives tend to shy away from the subject. But not David Read! In this sermon Read approaches the mystery of God's triune nature by speaking about the divine Self that is conscious of the divine "I" even as the Self-conscious Deity encounters us in all the mysterious oneness of God's inner being.

If that doesn't make much sense, you try speaking about the Trinity. Read at least tackled the subject whenever Trinity Sunday came around, speaking, however haltingly, about the heavenly Father who discloses his inner Self to us through the Son of God in the mysterious power of God's Spirit.

At Christmas the Church celebrates the miracle of the Incarnation; at Easter the miracle of the Resurrection; and at Pentecost the miracle of the Holy Spirit. Give David Read credit for attempting at least to understand and celebrate, on Trinity Sunday, the miracle of God's inner, eternal life.

A BIG ENOUGH GOD

A Sermon preached by David H. C. Read at Madison Avenue
Presbyterian Church on Trinity Sunday, June 6, 1982

> Text: *"For the Spirit explores everything, even the depths of God's own na-*
> *ture. Among men, who knows what a man is but the man's own spirit*
> *within him? In the same way, only the Spirit of God knows what God is."*
> 1 Corinthians 2:10 (NEB)
>
> Readings: 1 Corinthians 2:11–16 (NEB); Matthew 11:25–30

ARE YOU A SELF-CONSCIOUS person? Your answer might well be: "I hope
not;" for we normally associate being self-conscious with being obses-
sively concerned with ourselves and the impression we are making on other
people. That can have the effect of making us extremely shy in company
or, on the contrary, self-assertive and domineering. When we say that an
actress, or a politician, or a preacher is self-conscious, we don't mean it as a
compliment. It's our way of saying that they are too conscious of the impression they are making and not really absorbed in what they are supposed to
be doing. One definition of "self-conscious" in a dictionary is: "Excessively
conscious of oneself as an object of observation to others."

But, there is another, and I would say primary, definition, and that is:
"conscious of oneself, or one's own thoughts, well-being, etc." In that sense,
we are all self-conscious. Unless we were, we wouldn't be human. It is part of
the mystery of being a person that we are aware of ourselves, the "I" that nobody else really knows. A tree is content to be a tree and, as far as we know,
never wonders: "What kind of tree am I meant to be?" A cow, chewing the
cud, is said to be ruminating, but surely not in the sense that she is pondering her own specific place in the great scheme of things. I know that dog
lovers will rise up to protest that they have a self-conscious pet who knows
his own name, but I will risk the opinion that, when I shout "Patches" to
our own little dog, she is not aware of her own self-hood, but merely thinks:
"There's that sound again, that means he wants something."

Anyway, we can be sure that you and I are self-conscious. I know what
it is to be me, and you know what it is to be you. Did you ever, as a child,
take a flashlight to bed with you, and then make a little tent with the bed-
clothes where you could just be you—with no one else around? We can do
something like that at any time—and all of us do. There is an "I" then, that
nobody really knows except us. The way Paul puts it is: "Who knows what a
man is but the man's own spirit?" This strange self-consciousness is possible,

because we have a spirit within us. Our spirit is not just a part of our body, or even of our minds. It is what you might call the inner self, that enables us to be real persons, and can control both our body and our mind.

We know how difficult it is ever to penetrate deeply into the real being of anyone else. No matter how closely two human beings may be related in love and friendship, one can never totally understand the other. So Paul can say: "Who knows what a man is but the man's own spirit"—and then he goes on to say: "Only the Spirit of God knows what God is."

That's a mind-boggling thought, isn't it? Just as there is a self that only my own spirit can know, so God has a self that only his Spirit can know. Spell that with a capital "S", and you have an insight into the meaning of the Holy Spirit about whom the Bible speaks. "Only the Spirit of God knows what God is." Just as no other human being can ultimately and totally know the real you, so no human being can claim to know ultimately and totally who, or what, God is.

Why tell me that? you might want to ask. Surely it's obvious. Did you invite me to church simply to send me away with a negative thought like that? All I can say is: Stay tuned: this is only the beginning of what the Bible has to reveal about the God who wants us to know and love him, the God whom we worship as Father, Son, and Holy Spirit.

We begin here, because this text reminds us that none of us should dare to speak of God as if we knew all about him. If there is a mysterious you, whom only your own spirit knows, so the God we worship must be at least as mysterious in his inmost being. In days when there is a lot of easy chatter about God, as if we knew all about him, it is good to listen to the sobering words of the great Anglican 17th century divine, Richard Hooker. He wrote: "Dangerous were it for the feeble brain of man to wade far into the doings of the most high, whom although to know be life, and joy to make mention of his name: yet our soundest knowledge is to know that we know him not as indeed he is, neither can know him; and our safest eloquence concerning him is our silence, when we confess, without confession, that his glory is unexplainable, his greatness above our capacity and reach. He is above and we upon earth; therefore, it behooveth our words to be wary and few." So, let me proceed warily and I'll try to let my words be few.

"Only the Spirit of God knows who God is." To have big enough thoughts of God, we must allow for that mystery of his own self-consciousness, that which he is in himself, which is totally beyond our understanding. It is not only the unthinking brand of popular religion that claims to know too much about God. There are many very serious thinkers who are searching for a God who is totally acceptable to the human mind, and can be fully understood. I am thinking, for instance, of those who reject a traditional doctrine like that of the Trinity, in favor of a simpler, more easily under-standable way of thinking about God. Away with all this stuff about three persons in one God, they say, and let's just worship one Supreme power whom Jesus called his "Father in heaven." Others would simplify still more and say: Let's just acknowledge something greater than ourselves without the complications of thinking of any kind of supernatural person.

But a God who is big enough really to be God must surely be at least as mysterious in his own being as we are, and must have at least those personal qualities which we know as will and love and creative power. The doctrine of the Trinity was not dreamed up by theologians in some incense-filled room and imposed upon the members of the Church. "One God in three Persons" was not a mathematical conundrum or a wonder drug "to be taken only as directed." It was just the best that the theologians could do to express the new and joyful revelation of God that came with the Gospel of Christ. It was an attempt to reflect the experience of the company of believers in every age, and to enrich their worship. To this day we are closest to the God we worship, not when we try to unravel with our minds the mystery of the Trinity but when we lift up our hearts and sing: "Glory be to the Father, and to the Son, and to the Holy Spirit, as it was in the beginning, is now, and ever shall be, world without end."

A God who has, like us, an inner life of his own which we cannot penetrate and a purpose that ranges through a vast universe of which we know a tiny fraction, is surely a big enough God. It is only his Spirit who knows the mystery of his being, for, as Paul writes here: "The Spirit explores everything, even the depths of God's own nature." It was a big enough God that Emile Bronte celebrated when she wrote:

> "Though earth and man were gone,
> And suns and universes ceased to be,
> And Thou wert left alone,
> Every existence would exist in thee."

Now comes a still more wonderful thought. This Spirit of God is not remote from us in the mystery of God's own being. Paul writes, "This is the Spirit we have received from God." He is the Spirit of Jesus Christ the Son, who comes so close to us that Paul could write: "We possess the mind of Christ." It is in Christ, this Jesus who is one of us, that we are enabled to learn who the eternal Father, maker of the heaven and earth, really is. He is the reflection of the divine glory. He is the Word that speaks to us from the silence. He is the presence with us that assures us of the Father's love.

You and I are self-conscious beings. Yes; but we also express ourselves to other people. We can't stay under that blanket forever. We reveal ourselves. We give ourselves away. That's what I am doing now. And that's what God did when he sent his Son to live our life, share our joys and sorrows, undergo our death, and rise to the life immortal.

Some find it hard to understand how the sovereign God, Lord of all that is, could possibly be concerned with this little corner of creation, and be interested in tiny creatures like you and me. Surely, we think, God must be too big to care about me. But this is just where we have to revise our ideas about a big enough God. We are surely not thinking solely in terms of size. Think of some great man or woman you have admired, one of the strong personalities of history, or of your experience today. The bigness of such persons is not measured simply by the power and influence they wield. What impresses me in such towering figures is their capacity to care for, and know individuals. When I think of the present Pope as a "big man" on the world stage today, I am not just thinking of the historic dignity of the office (there have been small men, weak men, even wicked men in that office). I find that I am seeing a picture of him bending over to speak to a child, or stopping to bless a woman doubled up in pain.

The God we worship is big enough to reach out to what Jesus called "the least of these my brethren." He is big enough to care about your needs and mine. He is big enough to come in Jesus Christ to share every joy and agony we can know on earth. He is big enough to let his Son be killed. "Greater love hath no man than this, that a man should lay down his life for his friends," said Jesus. But the divine love went farther. He laid down his life for his enemies. That is the love "so amazing, so divine," that "demands my soul, my life, my all." The God who is big enough to satisfy the thirst of my soul for the infinite and eternal, is also big enough to draw near to each of us and so fill us with his Spirit that we can say: "I have the mind of Christ." The God who is eternal love and joy and beauty is big enough to come into our hearts in the guise of a fragment of bread and a sip of wine.

As we have been thinking of the mystery of our own selves—the inner self that only our spirit can know, and the self we express to others, we know that we are still one person. And so the Church believes that the God we worship has his own inner self, known only to his Spirit, and that he has also expressed himself in creation and supremely in the Word who is his Son. And all the time he remains One God, the Father almighty. This is the God who is big enough to be adored, and big enough to satisfy the need of each one of us for a divine forgiving and refreshing love that is our only security in life and in death. Jesus speaks to us from the heart of the Holy Trinity and utters his invitation: "Come unto me." And, as we respond, we are enveloped in the grace of our Lord Jesus Christ, and the love of God, and the communion of the Holy Spirit. And if, as sometimes happens we are slow to respond, and resistant to his call, we can make John Donne's prayer our own:

> "Batter my heart, three person'd God: for you
> As yet but knock, breathe, shine, and seek to mend.
> Take me to you, imprison me, for I
> Except you enthrall me, never shall be free,
> Nor ever chaste, except you ravish me."

1940—2020:
God in Our Past and Future

EDITOR'S INTRODUCTION

Here is a suggestion: Consider developing David Read's sermon topic in today's time frame. For example, in 2017 the sermon could reach back 40 years to 1977, and reach ahead to 2057.

You might then speak about how the first woman Episcopal priest was ordained in 1977; how President Carter began pardoning Vietnam war draft evaders in 1977; how 15 countries, including the US and the USSR, signed a nuclear proliferation pact in 1977. Now jump ahead and think about what the world may look like forty years from today. What will our carbon-challenged climate be like? How will the proliferation of nuclear weaponry have affected the nations? What will the relations between Christians and people of other religions be like?

However the details play out, the message of the Gospel, Read suggests, remains the same. The God of the past, the God who created the universe and rescued his people in the crossing of the Red Sea and the raising of Jesus from the grave, the God who was with us in 1977 will still be with us in 2057, offering the world the promise of the Gospel and the reassurance of his love.

1940—2020: GOD IN OUR PAST AND FUTURE

A Sermon preached by David H. C. Read at Madison Avenue
Presbyterian Church on June 8, 1980

Text: *"I, I myself, am he that comforts you.*
Why then fear man, man who must die,
man frail as grass?
Why have you forgotten the Lord
your maker,
Who stretched out the skies and
founded the earth?
Why are you continually afraid,
all the day long,
Why dread the fury of oppressors
ready to destroy you?
Where is that fury?"
Isaiah 51:12, 13 (NEB)

Readings: Isaiah 51:9–16 (NEB); 1 Peter 5:6–11; Luke 21:25–33

THERE ARE TIMES—AND THIS may be one of them—when those who believe in God begin to wonder what on earth he is doing. I mean, literally
"on earth." In heaven, or some other sphere of existence, he may be active
and obvious, but what do we see of his so-called rule in human affairs? The
prophet wrote in such a time. His people, called in a special sense "the people
of God," were exiled in Babylonia. Jerusalem had been smashed: the Temple
was no more: the songs of Zion froze on their lips—"How can we sing the
Lord's song in a strange land?" Everywhere the armies of the conquerors
were in control. Nowhere was there any sign of an active, intervening God.
They could see nothing but "the fury of the oppressors."

I was reminded last week that, exactly forty years ago, there was such
a time. Hitler had unleashed the most devastating military force the world
had ever seen, and by June, 1940, Europe was at his mercy from the Russian
frontier to the Pyrenees. For five long years the great nations that lie at the
heart of European civilization were to know "the fury of the oppressors."
Any here today who were alive, and conscious, at that time—no matter how
far from the European cockpit—will remember the sense of powerlessness
and despair that gripped so many sensitive souls at that time. In spite of

prayers for peace the fearful war had erupted; in spite of prayers for deliverance the aggressors marched from triumph to triumph; in spite of pockets of resistance and superb acts of courage, the fury of the oppressors raged unchecked. And there were some who asked what God was doing.

On a radiantly beautiful summer day, the 12th of June, 1940, I stood on a clifftop above the little village of St. Valery on the Normandy coast. The gleaming waters of the Channel stretched out before me, and it was easy to imagine the coast of England not so very far away. Down below the village was a smoking ruin while around me was a sea of prisoners—almost an entire corps of the French army, including the British Highland Division to which I had been assigned in early May. A week before the last of the original Expeditionary Force had been evacuated from Dunkirk, and our task was to hold the line of the Somme for the defense of Paris. Then came the second wave of the German advance, and the line was soon pierced by the apparently invincible panzers. Our orders were then to fall back on Le Havre, but, unfortunately a certain General Rommel got there first. So the village of St. Valery became the mini-Dunkirk that failed. Almost none escaped, and the way to Paris was open.

If you're wondering what I was doing gazing over the Channel like a tourist at such a time, let me explain that one of Rommel's troops had discovered that I spoke German so I was summoned to an informal interrogation on the grassy edge of that great white cliff. First question: "You declared war on us, didn't you?" "Yes." "You didn't know we were so strong?" I shrugged my shoulders. Then came the key question, obviously designed for their amusement: "How long is this war going to last?" So, either inspired by a prophetic spirit or more likely remembering my father's tales of World War I, I answered: "Years and years and years." This was greeted by a roar of laughter, and a chorus of: "Vierzehn Tage (fourteen days) England Kaput." When I pointed to the expanse of sea in front of us and inquired how they proposed to get across, the reply was equally emphatic: "Airplanes, thousands of airplanes: England will be razed to the ground."

There was nothing cruel, or even unpleasant about these young men— one of them, down on the beach, had invited me to help myself to cans of tobacco he had spotted being washed up on the shore. They were naturally cock-a-hoop and felt they were just stating the obvious. And it seemed obvious to millions at that hour. There were many in this country who saw no possibility of ever checking the Nazi advance, or reversing their takeover of Europe. It was the supreme moment of triumph for the New Order that Hitler intended to impose upon the world—an order that rejected the God of the Hebrew prophets, the God and Father of Jesus Christ. A few days later on the line of march, a tank crew headed in the opposite direction stopped and, spotting my clerical collar, took a few moments to explain that the day of Christianity was over, the churches were finished, and a new world had come.

1940—forty years ago. It's a good Biblical number meaning, roughly, a generation. So, having looked back, I couldn't help projecting forty years ahead. A.D. 2020. Well, a lot of you will be around if there is a world to be around in. What do you think it will be like? It's never easy to see forty years ahead, but there has never so far been a time when guesses are more likely to be wrong. The train of human history that chugged along for centuries through every kind of landscape sometimes went through dark tunnels but always seemed to emerge again into the sunlight. For a couple of hundred years it seemed to accelerate so that many times the passengers have been scared, and now the acceleration is so tremendous, and almost uncontrolled, that hardly anyone dares to peer along the track for another forty years. Indeed the track seems no longer there. The coaches behind us seem to have been uncoupled, and this generation to have been switched onto a roller coaster that ends in space.

Our oppressors are not just the new Hitlers, but the machines we have created, the anonymous forces that seem to determine the way we go, the wave of cynicism and despair that threatens to engulf us, the renewed awareness of the powers of evil that can possess the human race. With all the information that pours in upon us from the media, we should be a balanced and instructed generation, but instead we are left floundering, unable to make sense out of the stories that pour in from every quarter of the globe. In comparison there seems to have been a kind of simplicity about world affairs forty years ago. Sure, we can reduce the present crisis to the rivalry of two superpowers armed beyond the wildest dreams of 1940, but then we watch them thwarted by an Iran or an Afghanistan, and a strange new factor has intruded in the shape of what we call the Third World, and a new China more inscrutable than ever. And, as for the beliefs that move the nations, we find that just when Marxism seems to be losing its appeal the Western democracies have drifted from the Christian tradition into a shallow secularism, a crude materialism, or a nihilism that finds no hope in either God or the human race. As we watch this strange kaleidoscope of events, and seem to hear no prophetic voice—except perhaps the muffled cry of an exiled Solzhenitsyn, and look in vain for a towering figure like Lincoln, Churchill, or de Gaulle, it is no wonder that there is a paralysis of the mind and soul, and few would dare to look ahead to the year 2000, let alone 2020.

Yet are we really in such a totally different situation from our ancestors? Human life has always been a precarious business, and one of the benefits of the backward look is to give us perspective from which to view the apparent chaos of our world. In spite of all the tragedies of the human story, and in spite of the "fury of the oppressors," there have always been, and are still, men and women who believe in a sovereign and a caring God, and therefore keep the flame of hope alive.

As we look forty years back and forty years on what is it that a Christian believes and what nourishes this hope?

First, we hear and accept the news that behind and within and beyond this human story there is this sovereign and caring God, who was in the beginning, is now, and ever shall be. "A thousand years in thy sight is but as yesterday when it is past, and as a watch in the night." That is where we find our perspective. And it is those who believe in God who walk with confidence and trust, who are not overwhelmed by the rush of events, or daunted by the fury of the oppressors. Forty years ago it was the men and women who had this faith who refused to believe that we had inevitably to pass into a Nazi world and treated Hitler's boast of a thousand year "Reich" with a holy contempt. And it is men and women with this faith who can look forty years ahead in the confidence that the goodness, justice, and love we long for are securely rooted in the heart of a sovereign God who "works for good in everything with those who love him." They know that neither "things present nor things to come can separate us from the love of God which is in Christ Jesus."

To the despondent Jewish exiles in Babylon the prophet brought the Word of this God. To many of them, and to all the Babylonians, it must have sounded utterly crazy, but here it is preserved for us to hear today when that Babylonian Empire is extinct and its glories swallowed in the desert sand.

"I, myself, am he that comforts you. Why then fear man, man who must die, man frail as grass?" Then we are reminded that this God is none other than the creator and sustainer of the universe. "Why have you forgotten the Lord your maker, who stretched out the skies and founded the earth?" In comparison with him what are these human powers before whom we cower? "Why are you continually afraid all the day long, why dread the fury of the oppressors ready to destroy you? Where is that fury?"

Forty years ago the Nazi fury raged over Europe. Where is that fury? Buried in the Russian steppes, the sands of North Africa, and in a solitary bunker in Berlin. Can we not believe that in God's sight the furies that oppress us today—the violent forces that lurk in every land, the anonymous terror, the evil passions that can plunge nations into war—are ultimately powerless compared with the goodness he has implanted in those who love him? What else do we mean when we pray: "Thy Kingdom come."?

Now the question comes: am I just talking about a final winding-up of history whenever it comes—tomorrow, in 2020 or ten thousand years from now? Are believers like those amateur actors who assure themselves that "it will be all right on the night?" You want to know: what about the interim? Is there nothing we can do? Can we expect no intervention of this sovereign God?

If we mean by "intervention" the notion that God normally lets his human family mess up his world, allows the wicked to seize power, and terrible things to happen—and then *occasionally* steps in to set things right, I must confess I cannot think that way. Rather I believe that God is *always* there, responsive to the cry of his people, but does not always intervene in the way we want. Forty years ago saw not only the Nazi triumph in Europe but Hitler's fatal mistake when he allowed the bulk of the British Expeditionary Force to escape from Dunkirk. At the moment an argument goes on in Britain about what some call the "miracle of Dunkirk." The survival of that force, which enabled the British to defy the Nazis alone for another year, changed the history of the world. Was it a miracle? Was that extraordinary tale of the rescuing ships of all shapes and sizes that straggled out of every port to bring the army home, of Hitler's restraining order to his armored divisions, of the mists that often shrouded the beaches from the Luftwaffe— was it an example of divine intervention, a miraculous answer to prayer?

The question could be argued forever. I would not base my faith in the sovereign God in any one example of a dramatic turn in human affairs. But I do believe that there is a divine power at work throughout history, a mysterious element in human affairs that defies the explanation of the historian. And I believe that it has to do with the response that we are ready to make to the command to remember the Lord our God and to the grace he offers us in Christ. What we call "morale" has a lot to do with how nations stand up to the moments of crisis and danger, and that morale depends on the faith within. I lived through the thirties in Britain and the continent of Europe. It was not a time of courage, confidence, and profound religious faith. On the contrary the same cynicism, selfishness, and apathy that afflict us today were rampant. If that had been the whole story there would have been no Dunkirk, no resistance to the demand for surrender, no elimination of the Nazi scourge. All the promises of the sovereign God are conditional—except the last. There *will* be a time, says the prophet, when the Lord's people shall come back, set free, and enter Zion with shouts of triumph, crowned with everlasting joy: joy and gladness shall overtake them as they come. The Christian Church has seen in that vision the promise of the ultimate fulfilment of God's Kingdom. Meantime we are given the condition that was given to the children of Israel. "*If* thou shalt hearken diligently unto the voice of the Lord thy God, to observe and do all his commandments . . . " the condition that was given by Jesus to his disciples: "*If* you keep my commandments. . . . *If* you seek first the kingdom of God and his righteousness . . . "

We therefore look back to the God who created the universe, to the God who has indeed rescued his people—"I cleft the sea and the waves roared"—the Hebrews never forgot the crossing of the Red Sea, and Christians have never forgotten the rising of their Lord from the engulfing seas of Calvary's horror—and we give thanks. And we look forward to 2020 or whatever year God grants us to see, confident that this same God goes with us—no, that he is there already. The most steadying force in any country and in any heart is the conviction that the God we see in Christ is in full control, yet waits, often apparently inactive for his family to respond to his commandments and his love. Often like the prophet we want to shout to him: "Awake, awake, put on your strength, O arm of the Lord," but still he tells us: "I neither slumber nor sleep: it is you who need to awaken to my voice. It is your arm of faith that needs to put on strength." What this amazing Book tells us is that God would rather have us yelling at him to wake up, than drifting along without giving him a thought. "You are my people," says our text, "I have put my words in your mouth, and kept you safe under the shelter of my hand." Forty years back; forty years on: four thousand years back; four thousand years on. The God of our past is the God of our future. Do you believe that?

Prayer: Enable us, O God, to walk forward day by day in the sure knowledge that thou art in control and enable us as a people to renew our strength inwardly as we look unto thee, through Jesus Christ our Lord. Amen.

Independence—Under God

EDITOR'S INTRODUCTION

THIS INDEPENDENCE DAY SERMON finds David Read maintaining that human liberties flow from the rescuing grace of the divine Creator and Ruler "in whose service alone is to be found . . . perfect freedom." The Declaration of *Independence* thus flows from the Declaration of *Dependence* that we celebrate on Thanksgiving Day.

This by no means suggests that one has to be an orthodox believing Christian in order to champion individual and national liberties. That clearly is absurd. Even so, Read claims that human freedom flows ultimately from "the divine Creator and Ruler in whose service alone is to be found that perfect freedom to which we are called."

Read preached this sermon, interestingly enough, in the same church in which President Trump's parents were married in 1938. Mr. Trump's parents would not appear to have been active in the congregation. Yet had they remained with MAPC, they might well have heard this gospel-rooted message according to which "the health of a nation, the health of the world, depends on the up-building of . . . groups of ordinary men and women who realize that their independence, their true freedom, depends on a humble profession of dependence on the grace of God." Without that humility the door is open for a most unhealthy, all too self-centred understanding of national independence.

INDEPENDENCE—UNDER GOD

A Sermon preached by David H. C. Read at Madison Avenue
Presbyterian Church on Independence Day, July 4, 1971

Text: *"And ye shall know the truth, and the truth shall make you free."*
John 8:32

THIS COUNTRY IS BLESSED with two national festivals that express in a
unique way the secret of a strong and healthy human family. One we celebrate today as we recall the determination of the small and scattered group
of settlers in this land to be free from outside control, free to make their own
laws, free to choose their own government, free to raise their own taxes, free
to go their own way in the traffic of the nations, old and new. This was the
Declaration of Independence, the birth certificate of a new and sovereign
people dedicated in a unique way to the pursuit of liberty and treasuring the
ideal of extending the frontiers of human happiness and peace.

The other national festival falls in November when we remember
with gratitude and family celebration the profound faith of the settlers and
founders of this nation as they gave thanks to God for his guidance and his
gifts. This was the Declaration of Dependence, the assertion that an individual or a nation can find liberty, happiness and peace only in recognition
of the sovereign God to whom we owe our ultimate allegiance and from
whom all blessings flow.

These two declarations—of independence from all kinds of human
tyranny and oppression and of dependence upon a divine source of guidance, hope and spiritual strength—may seem contradictory to those who
today interpret human independence to mean that man has now become
his own God and exult in his freedom from the sanctions of traditional
religion and morality. In fact, there is the strongest possible correlation between them. Not only in this land but throughout the world in every age
the struggle for human liberties has been waged by men and women in the
grip of a profound religious conviction of their utter dependence on God.
Whether it is Moses with his granite belief in the Lord who had called him
to lead his people out of slavery; or Socrates with his passion for the liberation of the human mind and spirit; or Paul fighting for the right of access
for all people to the liberating grace of God; or Calvin inspiring the battle
against all forms of state control over the Christian Church; or Lincoln with
his liberating vision of human rights in a free and united nation; or the men
and women of our own time who have risked their lives for the cause of

spiritual and political liberty in the struggle against totalitarian power or fought for human rights against ingrained prejudice and oppression—you will find a remarkable record of motivating religious conviction and humble dependence on God.

I am not saying that every fighter for national independence, or for individual liberties has been an orthodox believing Christian. Nor am I denying that in some cases these religious convictions were themselves the source of still farther oppression. What I do claim is that there is every evidence that the enlargement of human freedom has by and large been the achievement of those who acknowledged their dependence on a divine Creator and Ruler in whose service alone is to be found that perfect freedom to which man is called. Where revolutions in the name of freedom and independence have been carried through by those who wished also to throw off all religious allegiance and to deny the claim of the living God, they have usually resulted in the creation of a new slavery and new forms of subjection to tyrannical powers. What Moses knew, what Socrates in his own way perceived and what the greatest of our Founding Fathers understood was that real human liberty is not something to be realized in abstraction from the disciplines of the mind and spirit that seek to know the truth about our human life. Liberty and independence are empty words unless we have some conception of what human beings are meant to be, unless there is some inner vision of a life designed by some greater power than ours. It is this that Jesus is reported as saying in his dialogue with the leaders of his people: "Ye shall know the truth and the truth shall make you free."

At this point in our nation's history we might well think again about the great declarations of independence from the tyrannies of men and dependence upon the mighty truth of God's sovereign power and grace. Recent travels have given me an opportunity to look at the present upheavals of our country from a more distant perspective, and I have been struck by the fact that thoughtful people in Europe and elsewhere are anxiously watching the process of self-examination and self-incrimination that is going on here, and they are wondering whether the United States is going to find the necessary inner strength and nerve to surmount the domestic crises and to play a sober and decisive part in the development of a world order within which the frontier of justice, liberty and peace can be protected and extended. Every sign that America really stands by her ideals of independence and individual liberty and really is motivated by a faith in something higher than national self-interest or material prosperity is welcomed by the friends of freedom in every land. And every sign of cynicism and withdrawal from the struggle, every sign of tired acceptance of the easy way, every sign of weakening faith in the over-arching divine purpose and moral values is correspondingly deplored.

With this in mind we see the urgent task of the Church, amid all the necessary upheavals and re-adjustments of a changing world, to be the proclamation and embodiment of both freedom from all that oppresses the human spirit and a renewed dependence on the grace of God. It is unashamedly a theological witness we are bound to give. The Bible understanding of man is still the truth to which we are committed. We find it consistently from the opening pages of Genesis—man, set in a fascinating world of infinite variety and opportunity and given his independence beyond anything granted to plant or animal, yet subject to the will of his Creator. We see the path of man through the centuries in the light of this independence and dependence. Where he is close to the Father-God, he grows in freedom and rejoices in the exploration of the world around him: where he rejects the divine call and seeks to be his own God, he lapses into the slavery of his own baser passions and sets in motion the forces of hatred, violence and war.

It was this that Jesus was talking about when he raised the question of freedom with his own Jewish contemporaries. Then, as now, his people were passionately devoted to their independence and deeply resented being subject to any foreign power. "We be Abraham's seed, and were never in bondage to any man," they said. Not strictly true when you consider the record of consecutive enslavements to the imperial powers of the Middle East, yet true enough when you think of the constant renewal of the flame of freedom and independence in the Jewish soul. But Jesus' answer goes to the root of the matter. "Verily, verily, I say unto you, Whosoever committeth sin is the servant of sin."

Here is part of the liberating truth that brings real freedom. We cannot possibly be free and independent so long as we have no master beyond our own passions and desires. We cannot be free if we are subject to our uncontrolled and unimpeded self-gratification. Every child learns that real freedom comes in a personal acceptance of the rules of love, and that a playground full of unrestricted egos is soon a little hell where no one is really free anymore. Every wise adult knows that it is when he or she accepts the need for some kind of discipleship, an inner acknowledgement of dependence on the grace of God, that the shackles break and real freedom becomes possible.

So perhaps then we are ready to listen when a divine voice speaks to us in our prayers and in our worship, saying: "If the Son therefore shall make you free, ye shall be free indeed." To be dependent on this Christ is to be truly independent of all the tyrannies of men, or the enslavement of our lower nature.

There is no limit to this liberating power of Christ. This is why Paul could write: "Stand fast therefore in the liberty wherewith Christ hath made us free, and be not entangled again with the yoke of bondage." Last Sunday I heard these words read in a little church in the south of France and heard the local priest preach a moving sermon on the nature of true discipleship. The service moved into the Holy Communion, celebrated with words almost exactly the same as these we shall use this morning. At the close I thanked him for the service and said that I had been strongly moved to take communion with his people. "Why didn't you?" he asked. I murmured something about the rules of his Church, and he answered: "Rules? Didn't our Lord say that the rules are made for men, not men for the rules. It's one thing to break rules just for the sake of breaking them; it's another to break them for the love of God." It seemed to me that centuries of misunderstanding and enslavement to our prejudices fell away as he spoke, and I knew how true it was that "If the Son shall make you free, ye shall be free indeed."

In the Old Testament there was one great feast of liberation—the Passover when the people celebrated their deliverance from slavery by the overwhelming grace of God. In the New Testament there is one great feast of liberation, where the Lord Jesus says: "This is my body which is for you . . . this cup is the new covenant in my blood." If there is one place in the modern world where we are truly in touch with the liberating grace of God, it is here. If there is one place in the modern world where we are closest to the truth about ourselves and our neighbors and our nation, it is here. He comes to us with the bread and wine, saying: "Ye shall know the truth, and the truth shall make you free."

The health of a nation, the health of the world, depends on the up-building of such groups of ordinary men and women who realize that their independence, their true freedom, depends on a humble profession of dependence on this grace of God. This is our greatest contribution to our nation on this day of joyful remembrance.

"You're Not Lost—You're Here"

EDITOR'S INTRODUCTION

MOST OF US WOULD agree that a good illustration is a godsend in a sermon, right up there almost with one of Jesus' parables. The trouble with illustrations, however, is that they tend to draw more attention to themselves than to the actual theme or message of the biblical passage that they are illumining. Fortunately, in this sermon, David Read comes up with an arresting illustration that does in fact make the necessary connection with the text.

The illustrative line "You're not lost—You're here" was first spoken by a gas attendant on Long Island in response to Read's plea for help. "We're lost," said Read, pulling into the station after missing a road on a trip to Connecticut. "You're not lost—you're here" said the attendant, and Read saw at once how right the man was.

It then dawned on the preacher that he was listening "not just to a wisecrack from a kindly garage owner but quite simply to the voice of God." For this is exactly what Jesus had to say when he looked up one day and saw a Galilean misfit in a sycamore tree, a perfect illustration of one of the "lost" whom Jesus had come to "to seek and to save." When Jesus called the man to come down from the tree so that he could have supper with him, he was in effect saying to Zacchaeus: "You're not lost—you're here." And now through this sermon, he is saying it to us.

"YOU'RE NOT LOST—YOU'RE HERE"

A Sermon preached by David H. C. Read at Madison Avenue Presbyterian Church on August 1, 1982

Text: *"For the Son of Man is come to see and to save that which was lost."*
Luke 19:10

Readings: Ezekial 34:11–16; Luke 19:1–10

IN LUKE'S GOSPEL THIS powerful statement about the purpose of Christ's coming is attached to the charming and dramatic story of his encounter with Zacchaeus. This is one of the "lost" he had come to "to seek and to save."

The word "lost" in a preacher's vocabulary has acquired some sinister overtones. In some quarters to speak of the lost is to speak of the damned—those who are fallen away from God, guilty sinners. But the word is used in the New Testament in its ordinary, everyday sense, as when we say: "I've lost my passport," "I've lost my way," "My dog is lost," "She seems to have lost her faith." One of the earliest recollections most of us have is of being momentarily lost in a store or on the street. It's the feeling of being abandoned, not knowing where we are or where to go.

Zacchaeus has been a favorite target of the preacher's imagination for centuries. We know absolutely nothing about him except for what we are told in these few verses. So the temptation is to weave all kinds of fantasies about him. But the Gospel-writer surely means us to see him as one of the lost. As a Jew who had accepted the job of tax collector for the Romans he had lost contact with his own people. He was one of the despised and rejected. When he heard of the arrival in Jericho of the controversial young preacher from Galilee he couldn't rely on any friends to help him through the crowds so that, in spite of his short stature, he could get a glimpse of Jesus. So he climbed that tree. And up in the tree, with thousands swirling around, he must have felt lost. Many years ago on a visit to this country from Scotland I made my way to Times Square on New Year's Eve. There were about a million people there, but at that time I didn't know a soul in New York and felt terribly alone—lost, if you like, though I did know my way back to the hotel. Zacchaeus not only felt lost because of his isolation from his own people: he was lost inside. He had lost his sense of right and wrong, his sense of the presence of God. I think that's a fair deduction from his promise to Jesus, who had suddenly invited himself to stay the night with him: "If I have taken anything from any man by false accusation, I restore him fourfold." Inside he was drifting, with no clear sense of values, not really knowing where he was going, or what he really wanted—except to make money. And nobody seemed to care. He was lost.

A couple of weeks ago I was travelling with our son Rory from Long Island to Connecticut. We had taken the Orient Point car ferry, and when we disembarked at New London we almost immediately missed the road we were supposed to take. After a few miles we had not the slightest idea of how to get back to it, so we drew into a small garage. A genial old gentleman with a twinkle in his eyes appeared, and I said right away: "We're lost." He looked at us and shook his head. "You're not lost," he said, "you're here." I saw at once how right he was. "Here" for him was the most familiar place in the world—and that's where we were. So how could we be lost. In a few moments, brushing aside our maps, he told us how to go from here to there—the road we wanted, and I got him to fill the tank, and we drove off. But as we went his remark kept running round in my mind. "You're not lost—you're here." And it began to dawn on me that I was not listening just to a wisecrack from a kindly garage owner. Quite simply I was hearing the voice of God. He was saying to me, and now through me to you: "You're not lost—you're here."

"The Son of man is come to seek and to save that which *was* lost. What Jesus said to Zacchaeus, and to everyone he met as he travelled through the towns and villages and countryside, and to millions ever since, was simply: "You're not lost—you're here, and I'm here, your God is here, waiting for you to recognize him." That was the Gospel, the Good News. This is what makes the Gospel different from what is normally thought to be religion. In Jesus' day and in ours religion tends to be primarily a search for God. Through rites and ceremonies, through philosophies and theologies, the search goes on, like our search for that road in Connecticut. Even the religion that bears Christ's name often becomes just another groping after God—and some-times a very complicated one at that. There is, of course, a search involved in our desire for ultimate truth and meaning in the riddle of life, and the true disciple of Christ is always seeking more light. (I am reminded of the dying words of Goethe: Mehr Licht!), but the starting point for the Christian is that he has already been found. Jesus told story after story to drive home this Good News. The coin lost by the housewife was found. It had rolled away into the dust, as we say, accidentally, but it wasn't really lost. It was there. God knew where it was, even before the broom had disclosed its hiding place. The sheep had wandered away, not accidentally but carelessly, but on the mountainside God knew where it was, and soon the shepherd found it. The boy who left his father's house deliberately seemed lost in an alien land. But he didn't know it until "he came to himself" in the pigsty—and the moment he realized he was lost, he knew he was found. For the thought of home swept in on him and he said: "I will arise and go to my father." Already the Father's voice has reached him: You're not lost—you're here, here in my heart forever.

It can happen at any time and "here" can be any place. One Sunday last month, instead of being in church, I was 12,000 feet up in the Ecuadorean Andes with the sun straight overhead, a strong clean wind rushing past like the purifying Spirit of God. Below me lay an enormous ancient crater now filled with rippling blue water lapping round an island of slender trees. It was a place where, without the company of others, without that waiting bus, one could feel lost. And yet it was, and could always be, a place to know that one was found—to say "I'm here," as I did, to throw arms up to the skies and say: "I believe in God the Father Almighty, maker of heaven and earth, and of all things visible and invisible."

There are other times when feeling lost has nothing to do with the vast emptiness of sky or sea, or the threat of unknown paths among the mountains. Right here in the city there are hundreds who know exactly how to reach their homes by day or night, who are surrounded by clocks and maps and newspapers, who are enfolded nightly by the intimate world of television and the hum of the traffic outside—and yet feel almost totally lost. They don't know which way to turn for meaning, for strength of soul, for someone who really cares about them. Probably each one of us has known moments when, in spite of what we call our blessings, and in spite of the faith we profess, we suddenly feel lost, with familiar landmarks suddenly fading and no sustaining presence to tell us who we are and light the way ahead. At such moments, and for such people, I believe the inner word can come, the word that is heard, clearly or dimly, saying: "You're not lost: You're here. At this very moment I am here and you are mine." It is the voice of the Father about whom Jesus was so confident and gave us this Good News.

Sometimes this reassuring voice of God comes to us through another, through a friend or a stranger, or through that family of God we call his Church. It is, in fact, part of any church's business to be the "here" where the lost are found. Anyone drifting into a Christian church with that lost feeling inside ought to find the warmth of friendship and the reality of a worship that says: "You're not lost—you're here, here in the Father's family." If that never happens there's something wrong with our Christian communion, something wrong with our worship, something wrong with the way we are hearing the Bible. The poet Coleridge once said that he believed in the Bible for the simple reason that, as he said, "It finds me." A story, like that of Zacchaeus, can be just a fascinating tale from the Gospels, or a launching pad for some pulpit reflections: or it can be a Word of God that finds you and me, up there in the tree with that tax collector, feeling lost but hearing the incredible news that Jesus wants to come and share a meal with us.

That is exactly what he does when we are invited to the Table of Holy Communion. We come *together*—different ages, different jobs, different experiences, different moods, different feelings, and he binds us to him by the bread and wine of his Presence, so that none may feel lost. We come also one by one, for he knows our needs are different, and he brings us into communion with himself. "You're not lost," he tells each one, "you're here"—here at my table, here with my family, here for this precious moment when the Gospel speaks and you know that, with all your imperfections you are accepted, with all your sins you are forgiven, with all your doubts you are offered this immortal food and drink: "Take, eat, this is my Body; let everybody drink of the water of life freely." We can all do it. We can all know this place where we are found.

Sometimes we scarcely know it. We think we have still to work out all our queries, still to reach a point of certainty about the God we seek. Blaise Pascal, the brilliant 17th century French scientist and philosopher, struggled for years to reassure himself about the reality of God. In a fury of doubt one day as he sought to argue his way into a living faith, feeling lost in a maze of his own speculations, he heard a voice that said: "Comfort yourself, you would not be seeking me if you had not found me." At such a moment you and I know what it is to be found by God. It is God saying to us through all our cares, our worries, our doubts, our fears: "You're not lost—you're here." He is saying it to us now.

Epilogue

A Selection of David H. C. Read's Books

(Contact *www.abebooks.com* to order copies)

The Christian Faith, Abingdon 1956.

I Am Persuaded, T. and T. Clark, Edinburgh 1961.

Sons of Anak: The Gospel and the Modern Giants, Charles Scribner's Sons 1964.

The Pattern of Christ, Charles Scriber's Sons 1967.

Holy Common Sense, Abingdon 1968.

Virginia Wolf Meets Charlie Brown, Eerdmans 1968.

Christian Ethics, J.P. Lippincott Company 1968.

Religion Without Wrappings, Eerdmans 1970.

Overheard, Abingdon 1971.

An Expanding Faith, Eerdmans 1973.

Curious Christians, Abingdon 1973.

Sent from God: The Enduring Power and Mystery of Preaching, Abingdon 1974.

Good News in Letters of Paul, William Collins: Fontana Books 1977.

Go & Make Disciples: The Why and How of Evangelism, Abingdon 1978.

Unfinished Easter: Sermons on the Ministry, Harper & Row 1978.

The Faith Is Still There, Abingdon 1981.

This Grace Given, Eerdmans 1984.

Grace Thus Far, Eerdmans 1986.

Preaching About the Needs of Real People, Westminster Press 1988.

Selected Reviews

THIS GRACE GIVEN

Eerdmans, 1984

This Grace Given is the first installment of David Read's attempt to trace the hand of God in the shaping of his life's experiences. The Scottish born and bred preacher reflects on his ancestry, his childhood and adolescent religious experiences, his passion for travel, his well-rounded education at schools both in Britain and on the Continent, and not least his wartime experiences as a chaplain held prisoner for five years by the Germans.

As the jacket commendation notes, Read recounts his spiritual development in all its complexities with "extraordinary recall of detail and eloquence of language . . . From the day when his Irish Methodist grandmother stopped him from whittling a toy boat from a piece of wood on the Sabbath, to Good Friday, 1945, the day he was liberated as a POW of the Germans."

After the war, Read returned to Scotland with many of his "religious beliefs and practices . . . hasty judgments and prejudices" shaken up and winnowed in the sieve of prison life. Nevertheless he still wished to live by grace, and concludes this first installment of his autobiography with the promise of another to come.

GRACE THUS FAR

Eerdmans, 1986

This Grace Given bore an epigraph from Paul's letter to the Ephesians: "Unto me, who am less than the least of all saints, is this grace given, that I should preach among the Gentiles, the unsearchable riches of Christ." The second installment of Read's life story, *Grace Thus Far*, takes its title from one of the stanzas of the beloved old hymn:

> *Through many dangers, toils and snares,*
> *I have already come.*
> *'Tis grace has brought me safe thus far,*
> *And grace will lead me home.*

Grace Thus Far begins with Read's recollections of his first few days of freedom after five years as a prisoner. His "inglorious military career" finally behind him, he now became a pastor in a suburban church in Edinburgh, and then a chaplain at Edinburgh University. Then in 1956, Read accepted a call to become the minister of New York's Madison Avenue Presbyterian Church. These autobiographical reflections take him up to 1986, and find the "imported Scotch," as Read sometimes called himself, still displaying the desire "to see in both large and small events the presence and guidance of God."

    N.B. This Grace Given *and* Grace Thus Far *are available together in the full autobiography of David H. C. Read published under the title* God Was in the Laughter *(cf. p. 9).*

SENT FROM GOD: THE ENDURING POWER AND MYSTERY OF PREACHING

Abingdon, 1974

This book gives us David Read's Lyman Beecher lectures that he delivered at Yale University in 1973. Topics include: "The Survival of the Sermon in an Age of Distraction," "The Theological Backbone of the Preacher," "How to Listen to a Sermon," "Evangelism in an Electronic Age," and "How Long, O Lord, How Long? . . . And Other Questions Concerning the Conception, Production, and Delivery of the Sermon."

    Read lays down no hard and fast rules other than to say that every sermon should move from the world of the Bible to our world today, or from our world today to the world of the Bible. Method is arbitrary. But the connection between the two worlds needs to be made clear. The one world introduces us to God's self-disclosure in Jesus Christ while the other world is the one in which we live and move and have our being.

Noting with relief that the day of 'the prince of the pulpit' is over, Read maintains that the sermon should always be an integral part of the worship service and never an exercise in homiletical stardom. The preacher is simply a man or woman sent from God to live with God's people, talk with them, listen to them, feel what they feel . . . and share with them the glad tidings of the Gospel.

THE FAITH IS STILL THERE

Abingdon, 1981

This short but thoughtful book on basic Christian convictions is addressed to "that great company who still, with greater or less conviction, adhere to churches where the historic gospel is proclaimed in Word and Sacrament." Eschewing simplistic ideologies on both the left and the right, Read examines the vitality and confusion of contemporary American religion.

He pleads in particular for what he calls "a reasoned religion," that is to say, a religion where we use our heads and not just our hearts in seeking to understand the good news of Jesus Christ. To enhance this understanding Read considers afresh the significance of the historic creeds and the legacy of Christian humanism, offers advice on how (and how not) to read the Bible, and how (and how not) to reform patterns of worship.

"The faith is still there," Read concludes, and by the historic Christian faith he means "the gospel as attested in the Scriptures, articulated in the creeds of the early Church, reaffirmed by the Reformers, and kept alive in the worship of the denominations that belong to the mainstream of the Christian tradition." There is nothing flakey here, but also nothing fanatical: just good solid advice from one who knows well the enduring center of the Christian faith.

UNFINISHED EASTER: SERMONS ON THE MINISTRY

Harper & Row Publishers, 1978

Most of the sermons in this book were delivered on the National Radio Pulpit. This means that David Read was speaking to anyone in America tuning into the air waves of the day and not just churchgoers. The tone is accordingly more apologetic and personal. This is not to say that Read was ever pompous or overly formal in the pulpit. But there is obviously a difference between a formal public address and an intimate chat with a friend over a cup of coffee. These sermons are more like those chats.

It is clear throughout the book that Read enjoys discussing religion with "the agnostic, the curious, and the uninterested who tune in by mistake" as well as with regular churchgoers. While not overly assertive, he is certainly not timid or insecure. Read is simply himself in speaking from the heart about a gospel that he knows well and wishes to share with others.

Some of the titles in these talks include: "My Adventures and Misadventures With the Bible," "Thoughts When I Conduct a Funeral," "Through Hell With Jesus," "The Motherhood of God," "I'm Praying for You—So What?" and "O Church, With All Thy Faults, I Love Thee Still." That last title, incidentally, offers an illuminating twist on a line by the eighteenth-century English poet, William Cowper, who wrote in a moment of passionate patriotism: "England, with all thy faults, I love thee still . . . "

VIRGINIA WOOLF MEETS CHARLIE BROWN

Eerdmans, 1968

David Read was in his 50s when he preached the sermons that are collected in this book, and thus at the energetic peak of his career. Meanwhile, the equally energetic shock waves of the 60s were registering in America and beyond. Perhaps this accounts for the specially animated flavor of these sermons. Not that Read's preaching was ever listless. But the Sixties was certainly an explosive decade and Read, as the liveliness of these sermons suggests, rose to the occasion.

The sermon that gives this book its title is reprinted in the final chapter of this book, so we won't say anything more about *Virginia Woolf Meets Charlie Brown* other than to note the arresting way it holds together the biblical witness to God's grace in Jesus Christ and two culturally iconic theatrical productions that were taking place at the time on the doorstep of Read's parish.

Is God Over Thirty? is the title of another especially thought-provoking sermon in this collection. It is based on the Lukan text: "When Jesus began his work he was about thirty years old." Thus we are encouraged to re-think our image of God in the light of One who lived out the radical ethic of love in the life, ministry, death and resurrection of a young man who "was about thirty years old." We tend to think of God as infinitely old. This sermon reminds us that "to be ageless is also to be infinitely young."

OVERHEARD

Abingdon, 1971

Here is another collection of David Read's talks that were first presented on NBC's National Radio Pulpit. Read takes up questions that he has overheard, not in a literal clerical eavesdropping kind of way but simply by tuning in as best he can to the thoughts and opinions about religion circulating in the world at the time.

Thus he addresses such questions as "I Don't Know What You Mean by God," "Frankly, I'm Bored by the Bible," "Christianity Seems So Complicated," "They're Always Talking About Sin," "Religion Is for the Weak: I Don't Need a Savior," "I've Tried Prayer and It Doesn't Work," and "I Live a Pretty Decent Life: What More Do I Need?"

Read is not preaching here so much as he is speaking to us as a friend engaged in an intimate discussion about the things that lie deep. The message is the same as what one might hear at a formal worship service, but the tone is certainly more intimate and personal.

GO . . . AND MAKE DISCIPLES: THE WHY AND HOW OF EVANGELISM

Abingdon, 1978

Liberals in the ecclesiastical world tend to be more work-oriented, conservatives more faith-oriented. But the distinction itself is surely an unhealthy one. We should all be passionate about matters of social concern. And we should all be glad to share the beauty and joy of the Gospel in response to our Lord's call, "Go, and make disciples."

The call to evangelize is what David Read especially emphasizes in this book. The call to faith goes out to everyone: the blind, the lame, the deaf, the poor, the religious, the irreligious. This doesn't mean ramming the Gospel down anybody's unwilling throat. Or failing to hold in the greatest respect religious traditions other than one's own. But it does mean inviting others to join the Gospel parade. In Jesus' clear and challenging words: "Go forth and make all nations my disciples."

Again, this doesn't mean going around telling people that they need to be saved or they're on their way to hell in a handbasket. The Gospel doesn't seek to make people anything other than who they already are. Prodigals in the far country: that's who we are regardless of the religious or non-religious label we happen to be wearing. And the prodigal, Read reminds us in this book, "is a son away from home. He is no one else, he is nothing less."

HOLY COMMON SENSE: THE LORD'S PRAYER FOR TODAY

Abingdon Press, 1968

"Lord, teach us to pray," one of the disciples asked Jesus. And the Lord's response—"When you pray, say . . . " still offers the best counsel on the subject. In this book David Read takes us step by step through the model prayer. "Our Father" expresses the conviction that in prayer we are addressing the God of the entire human family. ("Our Mother and Father" we might say today by way of making the conviction here crystal clear.) That God dwells in "heaven" reminds us that, however much we squint and strain, God remains a mystery.

A mystery, yes, but One whose enigmatic presence is made real and near in the Lord who came amongst us, "who lived like us through storm and sunshine, who was hurt by what hurts us, who was crushed by the kingdom of evil, delivered to the powers of this world, and overwhelmed by the demonic glory of hell unleashed."

"He died." This was the moment, Read reminds us, "when all prayers ceased, when the world was darkness and all life absurd. And on the third day God brought him back to life, and life has never been the same." It was not a myth. It was Jesus, the same Jesus who encouraged his disciples to pray, and teaches us even now to pray, beginning with the familiar words: "Our Father, who art in heaven."

RELIGION WITHOUT WRAPPINGS

Eerdmans, 1970

Here is another collection of sermons that David Read preached during the explosive, questioning 60s. Even many of the titles of these sermons take the form of a question: "Who Plays God?" "Who Needs Horoscopes?" "Is God

Unfair?" "Too Much Talk?" "Soul Transplant Next?" "How Can We Believe in a God of Love?" "Who Needs God?"

The titles of some of the other sermons in this volume also signal the unsettled atmosphere of the time: "Uneasy Sanctuaries," "Doing Your Thing: Variety Without Anarchy," "Charisma is a Christian Word," and "Cool Christianity."

Finally, there's a sermon here titled "Pro-Existence" which finds Read urging Protestants and Catholics alike to give better expression to their overall unity in Christ. We all need to remember that "the common beliefs, the common values, the common burdens and the common experience of God's grace are infinitely more important than the matters that divide us."

The collection as a whole is dedicated to Read's son *Rory on his first birthday.* The following year David Read dedicated his book *Curious Christians . . . For my Mother in her hundredth year.* How many writers have been allowed to see the generations held together in their family from such a wide span of years!

CURIOUS CHRISTIANS

Abingdon Press, 1973

As the secular Sixties gave way to the religious curiosity of the Seventies, there was an explosion of interest in everything from theological works by writers ranging from Kierkegaard to Kahlil Gibran, exotic cults from Krishna Consciousness to the Jesus Movement, and theatrical productions from *Godspell* to *Jesus Christ Superstar.*

David Read for his part seized the occasion to join his Christian compatriots and anyone else who might be interested in exploring the fathomless depths and exotic heights of faith. Hence this book which reprints some of the addresses that he presented on the National Radio Pulpit program in the early Seventies. Almost all of these addresses reflect Read's own grounded yet adventurous mind and inquisitive spirit. Sample titles include "Curious Christians," "Unfreezing Your Image of God," "The Fascination of Jesus," "Beyond Death—Are You Curious?" "The Most Curious Book in the World," "Bethlehem—Let's Keep the Mystery," and one of Read's magical Christmas Tales: "The Inquisitive Angel: A Christmas Reflection."

"Only the musclebound atheist or the bigoted believer," Read notes in the preface, "is impervious to any invitation to explore the unseen world." True enough. But it helps when the guide is as theologically nutritious and stylistically engaging as David Read!

GOOD NEWS IN LETTERS OF PAUL

Ephesians, Philippians, Colossians, 1 & 2 Thessalonians and Philemon in Today's English Version

Introduced by David H. C. Read

Martin E. Marty edited this series of Good News Commentaries. He also supplied the general introduction, noting that the commentators are "people who are very much at home with the scholarly literature but who, in most cases, are not professional academic students of the Bible." People in other words like David Read who grasp "both the spiritual and the intellectual concerns of most Bible readers," but who are also able "to transmit what is most important from the world of the commentators, and to do what they can to help the *Good News* speak to a new generation."

Read's introduction to Paul's letters to the Ephesians, Philippians, Colossians, Thessalonians, and Philemon includes chapters on "The Man and his Audience," "Paul's Version of Christ," "The Key Words of his Gospel," "Understanding his Controversies," "Paul's Ethics and Doctrine of the Church," and "His Teaching about Human Destiny and Life Eternal."

Here is an opportunity for us to experience the kind of lucid theological scholarship that David Read might have given the church had he taken a theological post in Scotland in 1956 and not set sail for the great parish adventure that awaited him in America.

One Last Sermon

Virginia Woolf Meets Charlie Brown

EDITOR'S INTRODUCTION

"WRITING IS EASY," SAID the legendary sports writer Red Smith. "You just open a vein and bleed." That's what David Read does here. He opens a vein and out gushes the blood of wisdom in the form of a sermon based on two theatrical productions that were the talk of Broadway at the time: Edward Albee's searing drama *Who's Afraid of Virginia Woolf?* and the delightful musical based on the popular comic strip *You're a Good Man, Charlie Brown*.

Read resists the temptation to use these plays as simple illustrations of a black-and-white conflict between the good and the bad. On the contrary, he brings out the dark side in the "nice" Charlie Brown musical, and the encouraging side in the "nasty" Virginia Woolf play. Still, there is no question which play illustrates the gospel of grace and which one dramatizes the message of sin.

There is also no question that we are in the presence of a preacher who knows what it means to stand in the pulpit with the Bible in one hand and the daily newspaper in the other, an opened vein allowing the blood of God's love to gush forth.

VIRGINIA WOOLF MEETS CHARLIE BROWN

This sermon was originally preached by David H. C. Read in Madison Avenue Presbyterian Church on April 16, 1967, and later published in Virginia Woolf Meets Charlie Brown (Eerdmans, 1968). Grateful acknowledgment is made to Eerdmans for permission to re-print the sermon here.

> *"Make no mistake about this: if there is anyone among you who fancies himself wise—wise, I mean, by the standards of this passing age—he must become a fool to gain true wisdom. For the wisdom of this world is folly in God's sight. Scripture says, 'He traps the wise in their own cunning.'"* 1 Corinthians 3:18–19 (NEB)

WE ARE AT WORSHIP. That is a Christian activity. There is nothing else like it. When a church becomes alert to its worship all kinds of things begin to happen. Some of these things I have spoken of a few weeks ago. Alert worship means a real sense of God's presence, a confession of real sin and a receiving of real pardon. It means real sacraments and a real hearing of God's Word. But renewal of worship doesn't begin and end in church. It's simply a richer experience every Sunday morning. For true worship spills over into the life of home and business, city and nation. It raises the question of how we're going to live in this complicated world. If we mean what we say and do in the sanctuary, if we really hear the Word of God, then our daily life, our activities, our opinions, our use of time and money will have a different flavor. That's why we are now raising some disturbing questions of our times. Worship is not a hideaway where these things can be forgotten; it is a burning flame where we seek light and fire for the living of this hour.

In that flame we don't find all the answers to the questions that afflict us. There is no quick, clear "Christian answer" to all the controversies and dilemmas we find ourselves involved in. But there is such a thing as a "Christian style of life," a Christian approach, a Christian mood and temper. If there is not, then the New Testament is a most misleading book. For there it is most clearly stated that the Christian is called to a distinctive way of life. In fact, in the early days, Christianity was simply known as "the way." What bothers many of us today is the extent to which this "way," this "style of living" is recognizable in those who are called Christians in our modern world. Would it not be true to say that, while we are willing to make space for the worship and teaching of the church, a great deal of our behavior, our habits of thought, our opinions, at home, at business, and in our social life, are really determined by something else—by what the apostle called "the standards of this passing age"? These standards are often anonymous and undefined, but they press in on us with enormous power. Since we live in the aftermath of two thousand years of Christendom these standards are not obviously pagan, flagrantly unchristian, as they were in St. Paul's time. That's what makes it so easy for us to be unaware that our style of life is often being molded by that which is not Christ. And since most of us want to be considered wise, sensible, sophisticated citizens of goodwill we settle for this secret schizophrenia—being Christians by conviction but letting "the standards of this passing age" determine our views, our daily decisions, and our style of living.

That's why I want to bring before you St. Paul's biting contrast between the wisdom of this world and the foolishness of the Christian. "Make no mistake about this: if there is anyone among you who fancies himself wise—wise, I mean, by the standards of this passing age—he must become a fool to gain true wisdom. For the wisdom of this world is folly in God's sight. Scripture says, 'He traps the wise in their own cunning.'" It's not easy to grasp right away what is being said to us. We're accustomed to hearing from the Bible the praises of wisdom. "Wisdom is the principal thing; therefore get wisdom"; or even more vigorously, "Go to the ant, thou sluggard; consider her ways, and be wise." Yet here we are told that the secret of the Christian life is foolishness. In fact two levels of wisdom are being set before us—the wisdom of this world and the true wisdom, God's wisdom, and the path from the one to the other is what he calls foolishness. We're not being offered a passing paradox that occurs to the apostle on his way to more important matters. Everything he has to say to the Corinthians and to us flows from this understanding of the Christian way. "Make no mistake about this," he says, "if there is anyone among you who fancies himself wise. . . . He must become a fool to gain true wisdom." I suspect that it is right here—in our grasp of what it means to become a fool—that we are going to learn the secret of the Christian style of living. And it's here that Virginia Woolf meets Charlie Brown.

By a strange twist of literary history Virginia Woolf has come to mean for today's public, not the brilliant novelist, but Edward Albee's play, and the movie that shares the title, *Who's Afraid of Virginia Woolf?* That's what I'm talking about—the world of Martha and George, Honey and Nick, the four inebriated intellectuals who hold the stage for three acts of savage self-revelation. And by Charlie Brown, I hardly need to tell you I mean the world inhabited by the hero of Charles Schulz's comic strip "Peanuts" and the somewhat different quartet of Lucy, Linus, Sally, and Schroeder—not to mention the ubiquitous Snoopy.

If you had the stamina you could enter both worlds in the course of one evening, taking in an early performance of *You're a Good Man, Charlie Brown*, then sitting through three hours of *Who's Afraid of Virginia Woolf?* I don't think I'd recommend such a doubleheader—especially on a Saturday night, as I doubt if you would have recovered by eleven a.m. next morning. But I would certainly recommend the experience of both productions. They are, in their own very different ways, reflections of the world we live in, and in content and performance true works of art.

It's not my intention to attempt what you might call a Christian evaluation of either play. Still less, you will notice, am I going to tell you to go and see *Charlie Brown* because it's nice, and stay away from *Virginia Woolf* because it's nasty. Nice and nasty are not words that belong in the vocabulary of Christian criticism anyway. (There's a lot of rubbish that is perfectly nice. And a lot of the Bible that is extremely nasty.) I simply want to let these two plays speak about two worlds that we inhabit, one ruled by what the apostle calls our wisdom—"the standards of this passing world"—and the other by what he calls the "foolishness of God." It's the Virginia Woolf of our cynicism and sophistication that I want to meet the Charlie Brown of our naïve bewilderment and crazy hopes.

We meet Martha and George as they arrive home late from a party and proceed to prolong their befuddlement from the bottle. "In vino veritas"— and soon their mutual hates and resentments come savagely at us through the cut and thrust of their devouring dialogue. This is a middle-aged couple in a college community, and soon they are joined by a younger pair—Honey and Nick—against whose relative innocence but equal cynicism the relentless battle is played out. The conversation lays bare with a devastating ferocity the hell into which men and women of intelligence, culture, wit, and worldly wisdom can gradually descend. This is a world of cleverness without compassion, of wit without humor, of passion without values, of fantasy unredeemed by faith. We are exposed to the sophisticated cruelty of the games people play. We are watching civilized human beings indulging in spiritual cannibalism. These are people who know all the answers provided by the wisdom of this world, and with them they are descending into hell—the hell of alienation, lovelessness, hopelessness, and total loss of meaning. Somewhere in the darkness we sense that Martha and George are crying out for each other. Behind the cynicism there is an occasional surge towards the compassion that could redeem them, but in the end their only bond that seems to be left is a mutual fear. "Who's afraid of Virginia Woolf?" says George with his hand on Martha's shoulder. And the answer is, "I am . . . George . . . I am."

We say this is not our world; it is an extreme case of estrangement, and spiritual brutality. So it is; but the fact that it has been written, that it captivates a modern audience, tells us something about the wisdom of our world that we can sense behind the surface calm and rationality. When we come away from such a play saying, "Terrible; disgusting that people should behave like that," are we not a little like the Victorian lady who said to her husband after the curtain had come down on the corpse-strewn stage of the last act of Hamlet, "How unlike the home life of our dear Queen!" We know that the world of cynicism, of smooth egoism, of the euphoria of the three-martini lunch, conceals passions and hatreds that can tear men and women apart. And Virginia Woolf forces us to ask what saving word there is for us who "fancy ourselves wise . . . by the standards of this passing age."

Well, here comes Charlie Brown. And when I say that, I am not suggesting that all we have to do is to forget the world of alienation and lurking violence and indulge in the happy dream-world of the comic strip. As Robert Short has shown in his book *The Gospel According to Peanuts* this particular strip at least is dealing in its own way with just these problems of our age. Both *Virginia Woolf* and *Charlie Brown* are ultimately theological. The difference is that the one exposes original sin with appalling force and hardly a whisper of redemption, while the other, equally aware of our frailties, is lit by the spark of grace. For Charlie Brown—bewildered, unsure, inquiring, hopeful, put upon, yet courageous—is in many ways the fool that St. Paul is talking about. He is the fool we have to become in order to reach the higher wisdom.

There is a divine simplicity in Charlie Brown, the child of this age. It is not the lazy simplicity of those who dodge the challenge of the modern world, for he is entangled with it from morning to night. He has to deal with the complexities of human relations, the wiles of women, the obstinacy of things, the frustrations of a world of machines (why can't he fly that kite?), and the huge metaphysical problems and the ethical dilemmas of our day. When Sally asks him to forge a letter saying that she must be excused from school as she is needed at home, he launches into an indignant essay on moral theology: "I can't write that! Don't you realize that this is what is wrong with society? This is evasion of responsibility! This is what is eroding our society," only to be met with the smooth rejoinder: "I don't know what you're talking about . . . I'm too young and innocent." So poor Charlie, the truly innocent, learns the hard way how the world will take advantage of his virtues.

Thank God there is a Charlie Brown around in a sophisticated society. We may laugh at him, but perhaps more often we are laughing with him. And the laughter that rises from the audience at the play has a very different quality from that evoked by the cracks in Virginia Woolf. It is the laughter that belongs to what I might call the "Christian comedy of life." For when we accept the foolishness of the gospel, when we know something of what it means to receive the kingdom as a little child, when we let the ultimate simplicities come to the surface, something happens to the dark dilemmas, the world of alienation and despair. It's not that we shrug it off with a careless optimism. The Christian fool knows the horror of human sin and suffering. Didn't the Lord Christ take the fool's road to the cross when he could have lived and died as the sage of Galilee? But the Christian fool knows that the final word is resurrection and he sees through the darkness with the eyes of the risen Christ.

Did you see the clown in the film called *The Parable?* Here again is the Christian fool. He does nothing from mere self-interest, but gets himself involved in every trouble and misery he sees around him. He is willing to be taken advantage of, to be laughed at, to do the odd and eccentric thing—for all the time he is moved by the simplicity of love. That love takes him in the end to a supreme suffering through which new life and hope flows into a world of cruelty and despair.

Isn't our task as Christians today much less a matter of trying to adapt our beliefs to the wisdom of this passing age, much less a matter of adjusting our ethics to the norms around us, than of learning what it means to be fools for Christ's sake? The gospel begins with the foolishness of baptism. What is more absurd than to take a little child of the twenty-first century (for that's when they'll be at maturity) and sprinkle water on him in the name of a Jewish teacher of the first century? And how foolish it must seem for a sophisticated man or woman to dedicate their lives to the service of one whom the wisdom of this world hanged on a cross to die? And how foolish to talk of his being still alive. And how foolish, above all, to take the way of love when self-interest is at stake, to forgive when the instincts cry out for revenge, to be chaste when the world says, "Go ahead: enjoy yourself," to be charitable when we can so delightfully give vent to our prejudices, to be compassionate when it is so much more comfortable not to be involved. Yet all this is part of the way to which we are committed; it is the style of Christian living.

This is the folly that is so needed in the world of Virginia Woolf. For in God's eyes it is this empty, ugly, futile wisdom of the world that is the real folly. "Scripture says, 'He traps the wise in their own cunning.'" Isn't that what is happening to George and Martha, Honey and Nick? When Charlie Brown walks in we glimpse something of that Christian foolishness that is the road to real wisdom.

Is there something you and I can do this coming week that will inject the foolishness of Christ into some area in which we move? There may be a word of forgiveness and understanding to be said, a surprising word of hope where nothing was expected, a gesture of crazy generosity to be made, a new courage to take an unpopular stand. It might be a new experience of prayer, that foolishness the world—and even our own minds—cannot understand. It might simply be the discovery that our own faith is too subtle and complicated, and that it is still possible for us to recover the basic trust in Christ that underlies all our creeds and confessions. For behind all the turmoils and complexities of our daily existence and the agonies of a world that often seems out of control there's a voice that says, "Blessed are the meek: blessed are the merciful: blessed are the pure in heart: blessed are the peacemakers." We don't care who's afraid of Virginia Woolf, if we can hear him say, "You're a good man, Charlie Brown."

Acknowledgments

I WISH TO ACKNOWLEDGE my indebtedness to Madison Avenue Presbyterian Church for permission to reproduce these sermons by David H. C. Read. I particularly thank Business Manager, J. Richard Frey; Interim Minister, the Rev. Eric O. Springsted; and Pastor Emeritus, the Rev. Dr. Fred R. Anderson. Heartfelt thanks also to Bruce McLeod, Bryan Buchan, Robert Attfield, Todd McTavish, and Marion McTavish for stylistic suggestions; Ian McTavish, Sandra McTavish, and Susan Salt Taylor for computer advice; and Jana Wipf and the highly professional staff at Wipf and Stock for their careful editorial attention.